The Study of
Social Problems

EARL RUBINGTON and
MARTIN S. WEINBERG

The Study of Social Problems

Five Perspectives

Second Edition

New York   1977

OXFORD UNIVERSITY PRESS

PREFACE

When we conceptualized the first edition of this book, we thought many sociologists felt the need for a book that would provide a general format for teaching social problems courses. Moreover, we believed that instructors were looking for a framework of sociological theory rather than simply a description of various social problems. With this in mind, we studied the history of sociology and delineated five major theoretical perspectives on social problems: Social Pathology, Social Disorganization, Value Conflict, Deviant Behavior, and Labeling. In the first edition, for each perspective we provided an introductory essay dealing with the people and the works that fashioned it, the circumstances and the stage of American sociology in which it arose, and the characteristics that typified it. Following each introductory essay, we reprinted readings exemplifying the perspective, concluding with one that presented a critique of it. Finally, we provided questions for discussion and an annotated bibliography for further exploration of the perspective. Thus, we hoped that the book would provide a brief but comprehensive survey of social problems theory and lay a sturdy foundation on which the instructor could build his or her own approach to social problems.

To judge by conventional criteria, the first edition of *The Study of Social Problems* seems to have served its purpose. At the same time, however, instructors and students indicated that our introductory essays and certain articles were too obscure. In this edition, we think we have improved on our selections, and we have provided clearer and more readable introductions. In this regard, we are very grateful to Sue Kiefer Hammersmith for her major role in editing the introductions from the first edition so that this edition would be more palatable to the undergraduate reader. We hope the second edition will be viewed as an improvement, and that it will prove to be of even greater assistance to the instructor.

CONTENTS

I. the problem

1. Social Problems and Sociology

The morning paper reports a variety of social problems: war, pollution, traffic jams, and crimes. It also reports a downturn in the stock market, a decrease in automobile sales, rising prices, drug use in high school, an increase in cigarette smoking, and so on. After reading the news, readers find themselves upset about some of these reports and wanting to do something about them, they have mixed feelings about other news stories, and they are neutral or indifferent to many of the stories. On occasion, readers even experience secret or open delight at the misfortunes of others. The variety and inconsistency of these responses point to the complexities that surround the idea of social problems.

In addition, those who analyze social problems often differ among themselves. Some analysts say that modern society produces more social problems than do simpler societies; others disagree. Some say that modern society produces more problems than solutions, but others argue that the real difficulty lies in the overproduction of so-called solutions.

Trying to make sense of all this can easily result in confusion. Yet people continue to study social problems in an effort to understand how they occur and how they can be controlled. And more often than not the people studying social problems have been sociologists.

Sociologists have dominated the study of social problems for two reasons. First, sociology developed about seventy-five years ago, just when industrialization and urbanization seemed to be shaking the foundations of traditional society. At that time, there was a special interest in the problems people saw resulting from industrialization and urbanization, and sociologists, sharing this interest, took up the study of social problems as a relevant and challenging topic.

Second, sociology as a discipline lends itself especially well to the study of social problems. Sociology deals with social relations, those situations in which two or more people adapt their conduct to each other's. Most social problems arise in the course of, or as a result of, social relations. Few other disciplines in the late nineteenth century dealt with matters of this kind. Thus, partly by choice and partly by default, sociology arose to deal simultaneously with social problems and with social relations.

In this book, we look at how American sociologists have organized the study of social problems. We focus on the ideas and assumptions that have guided, and continue to guide, that study, and we examine the different perspectives on social problems that sociologists have developed. First, however, we examine just what sociologists mean by the term "social problem," how they came to study social problems, and how sociologists have differed in their treatment of social problems from time to time.

The Definition of a Social Problem

Some of the conditions we consider to be social problems were not so considered in earlier times. And some of the things our grandparents saw as social problems are accepted without question today. Some of the conditions we now ignore will undoubtedly come to be seen as social problems in the future. And there are probably some things that, regardless of their troublesome nature, never have been and never will be considered to be social problems.

What, then, makes a social problem? Sociologists usually consider a social problem to be *an alleged situation that is incompatible with the values of a significant number of people who agree that action is needed to alter the situation.* Let us consider this definition more closely.

An alleged situation. This means that the situation is said to exist. People talk about it, and it may receive coverage on radio, TV, and in the press. The allegation, however, need not actually be true. For example, a fear commonly expressed by white homeowners has been that desegregation of their neighborhoods would decrease the property values of their homes. Yet often the opposite is actually the case. There has been substantial demand for middle-class housing among blacks, and blacks have systematically been overcharged for such housing. As a result, after an initial period of panic selling by white homeowners, the same homes often sell for more after desegregation than before.[1]

Incompatible with values.[2] A situation is defined by people as a social problem in terms of certain values they hold. For example, pollution is considered to be a problem in light of the values people place on health and on preserving the natural environment. Traffic jams are considered to be a social problem in light of the value people place on their time. Communism is considered to be a social problem in light of the values people place on a capitalist economy and on certain types of personal freedom.

People are diverse and complex, however. Different people hold different values; and the same person may hold conflicting values. For these reasons, different people consider different things to be social problems. For example, while the environmentalist focuses on the problem of pollution, the auto manufacturer may be focusing on matters of profit and the economy. Thus, the auto manufacturer may see the government's requiring pollution control devices on cars as the real problem. Likewise, the driver who lives in a rural area where pollution is not apparent may value clean air, but he or she may also value good gas mileage. This driver, then, might agree with the auto manufacturer that the government's requiring pollution control devices, which cut gas mileage, is the problem.

Thus, what comes to be considered a social problem and in terms of what values is a complex matter. This is one of the most controversial aspects of the study of social problems, and it will be dealt with in more detail throughout this book.

[1] See, for example, the description of blockbusting in Leonard Downie, Jr., *Mortgage on America* (New York: Praeger Publishers, 1974), pp. 14–22.
[2] Note that many sociologists now emphasize "interests" rather than values. We recognize these types of considerations and consider "interests" to be subsumed under the term "values."

A significant number of people. How many people are "a significant number"? This question has no clearcut answer. And, of
course, some people are more "significant" than others. The
President of the United States, for example, is more powerful
than an ordinary citizen in determining whether or not a particular situation is defined as a social problem. Likewise, adults
are more "significant" than children are in defining social
problems, and middle-class people are more "significant" than
are lower-class people.

Sociologists would agree that in general the more "significant" people for defining social problems are those who are
more organized, are in positions of leadership, and/or are
more powerful in economic, social, or political affairs. So it is
not just a matter of numbers. The important point for the
study of social problems, however, is this: when sociologists
study social problems, they usually look at what other people
in the society consider to be social problems. Thus, in studying
social problems sociologists usually deal only with socially troublesome or deleterious situations that are recognized as problems by the public.[3]

Action is needed. Hand in hand with the definition of a situation
as a social problem is the call for action to remedy the situation. People say among themselves that something must be
done. They may write letters to the editor, circulate petitions,
or hold rallies. Laws or ordinances may be passed and regulations enacted. And organizations may be formed to deal with
the situation. Thus, sociologists generally regard social problems as situations that are not just troublesome but that, in
addition, people want corrected and/or are trying to correct.

---

[3] It should be noted, however, that an increasing number of sociologists
seem to object to the practice of studying only what the public recognizes as
social problems. Such an approach, it has been argued, leads sociologists to
neglect problems that are serious but unrecognized. Moreover, this approach is said to contain an implicit class bias in that troublesome conditions
are more likely to be regarded as social problems when upper-class people
label them as such. See, for example, Jerome G. Manis, "Assessing the
Seriousness of Social Problems," *Social Problems* 22 (October 1974), pp. 1–15;
Alex Thio, "Class Bias in the Sociology of Deviance," *The American Sociologist*
8 (February 1973), pp. 1–12; Alexander Liazos, "The Poverty of the Sociology of Deviance: Nuts, Sluts, and Preverts [sic]," *Social Problems* 20 (Summer
1972), pp. 103–20; and Kenneth Westhues, "Social Problems as Systematic
Costs," *Social Problems* 20 (Spring 1973), pp. 419–31. An excerpt of Westhues' article is included in Chapter 4 of this book.

If there is no call for action, then, most sociologists would not conceptualize the situation as a social problem even though it may be troublesome to a large number of people. For example, the sociologist may see the doctor's waiting room as one of the more aggravating situations in our society. Patients often have to sit for hours in a small room with nothing to do. Many patients would rather be home in bed, and some dislike being exposed to the infections of other patients in the waiting room. Yet we hear no call for action. Complaints are numerous, but no demand is made that the situation be changed. Thus, the sociologist is not likely to consider the doctor's waiting room as one of our social problems.

The Development of American Sociology

The study of social problems has been inextricably intertwined with the field of sociology as a whole. Changes in the study of social problems have been closely related to more general developments in the field of sociology, and the different perspectives on social problems reflect different perspectives on society in general. Before turning to the different perspectives, then, let us take a more general look at the field of sociology.

For centuries, people have thought about and studied their life in society. But it remained for Auguste Comte in 1838 to give that activity a name. He coined the term "sociology," which means the scientific study of society.[4] Comte's interests, like those of Saint-Simon, Marx, Tocqueville, Spencer, and other early European sociologists, arose from the crises of industrialism. Accordingly, the big questions for these early European sociologists involved issues of social order and integration, on the one hand, and social development and change, on the other. The first question asks: What holds a society together and makes it work? The second asks: Where is the society going and how is it going there?

In the same way, the post-Civil War upheaval and the rise of industrialism in the United States spawned an interest in studying this society. In the two decades after the Civil War, books had begun to appear on this subject. By the middle of

[4] Auguste Comte, *Positive Philosophy*, trans. Harriet Martineau (London: George Bell & Sons, 1896).

the 1890s, sociology courses were being taught in a number of American colleges. The first Ph.D. in sociology was granted in 1895, and the American Sociological Society was formed in 1905.

In the years that followed, American sociology continued to develop as an academic discipline, and it continued to deal with social problems. The ways in which sociologists dealt with social problems, however, changed from time to time. These changes reflect a succession of traditions in the development of sociology.

A "tradition" refers to beliefs, values, and customs. As new ideas are developed and as conditions change, these beliefs, values, and customs also change. In order to understand the study of social problems, and how it has changed over time, we must understand the changing traditions in the development of sociology.

The various traditions in the development of American sociology can be arbitrarily grouped into four stages: establishing a base (1905 to 1918); forming a scientific policy (1918 to 1935); integrating theory, research, and application (1935 to 1954); and cultivating specialties (1954 on).[5] The changing perspectives on social problems outlined in this book reflect these basic changes in the development of sociology.

1. Establishing a base (1905 to 1918). During the years between 1905 and 1918, a hardy band of pioneers established sociology in a number of American colleges. At that time, most of the leading American sociologists were ministers' sons who had moved from small towns to the rapidly growing cities and who had witnessed the changes resulting from America's recent conversion from a farm to a factory economy. Their primary emphasis was on the problems of society, and they saw urbanism as the main source of social problems.

These early American sociologists were guided in their thinking by the philosophy of moral progress—i.e., by the notion that in the long run societies improve in quality. Thus, they were more or less convinced that progress and moral uplift would occur. At the same time, they wanted to take a

[5] This discussion uses all the dates for the first three stages, some but not all the arguments, and none of the titles that appear in Roscoe C. Hinkle, Jr., and Gisela J. Hinkle, *The Development of Modern Sociology: Its Nature and Growth in the United States* (New York: Doubleday & Co., 1954).

hand in solving some of the problems they saw around them in their rapidly changing society. These early American sociologists tried very hard to eliminate these problems. Their conservative way of thinking, however, led them to advocate social reform rather than revolution.

2. *Forming a scientific policy (1918 to 1935)*. During this period, World War I dampened the optimism that had characterized the first period of American sociology. Increasingly, sociologists began to realize that if they were ever going to guide social action, they first had to develop a body of sociological knowledge. And the scientific method, rather than the values of small-town society, seemed more likely to produce such knowledge. Accordingly, during this period attention turned from solving the problems of society to developing sociology as a scientific discipline. The conviction grew among sociologists that science should be value-free, and working to solve social problems came to be regarded as somehow "unscientific."

3. *Integrating theory, research, and application (1935 to 1954)*. If the first period might be called an era of preaching, and the second period an era of retreat, then this period could be called an era of scientific contribution. During this period, sociologists became more professionalized, and they began to see theory, research, and application as integrally related. As they did so, they began again to accept social reform as part of the sociological endeavor. Basic research and applied sociology came to be seen as two sides of the same coin, and the predominant attitude was that a scientific approach would both solve social problems and develop sociology as a science.

4. *Cultivating specialties (1954 on)*. Since 1954, sociology has come of age. Both the number of sociologists and the number of sociology courses have multiplied. For example, from 1926 to 1946, a total of 1,094 Ph.D.s in sociology were granted in the United States (an average of 55 per year); in the ten-year period from 1954 to 1964, 1,729 were granted (an average of 173 per year); and in 1973 and 1974, an average of 330 Ph.D.s were conferred each year. At the same time, the sophistication of sociological work has increased tremendously.

Sociology has become specialized, and within the various specialties sociologists have begun to develop bodies of theory and findings.

After 1954, however, rumblings began to be heard. Many sociologists began to feel that, in their race to answer basic theoretical questions, they had ignored the problems of society. These sociologists began to feel that sociology had neglected its social responsibility and become an instrument of the status quo. This attack was echoed by the next generation of college students. Thus, the recurrent tension between social problems and sociological problems became relevant to the students of sociology as well as to sociologists.

Sociological Perspectives on Social Problems

A perspective, generally speaking, is a way of looking at things. A sociological perspective includes a basic orienting idea from which one's conceptualization and analysis follow, and it reflects a particular set of ideas and assumptions regarding the nature of people and society. There are, of course, different ways of looking at social problems, and in sociology five different perspectives have been popular. In large part, these perspectives reflect the tension that has existed since sociology first developed—the tension between concentrating on the problems of society, on the one hand, and on the development of sociology as a scientific discipline, on the other. As sociologists emphasized first one and then the other of these goals, they developed the five perspectives dealt with in this book. These perspectives resolved for their proponents the questions of what should be studied, how it should be studied, and how the study would contribute to reforming society and to basic sociological knowledge.

The five perspectives are: "social pathology," "social disorganization," "value conflict," "deviant behavior," and "labeling." Each perspective contains its own notion as to the definition, causes, conditions, consequences, and solutions of social problems. In order to understand better these alternative ways of looking at social problems, in the chapters that follow we will analyze each perspective in terms of these five elements. Before proceeding, we clarify what each element involves.

Definition. We have already presented one general definition of social problems (see page 4, above), and each of the five perspectives does, implicitly, presuppose this definition. In addition, however, each perspective includes its own more specialized definition of social problems. These more specialized definitions vary in terms of which particular aspect of a socially troublesome phenomenon they focus on in defining that phenomenon as a social problem. For example, all social problems involve expectations, alleged violations of these expectations, and reactions to the violations. Nonetheless, the five perspectives differ in terms of whether the definition of the social problem hinges on the expectations, the alleged violations, or the reactions.

Causes. Each perspective includes its own causal imagery—i.e., its own set of ideas about what types of factors produce social problems and how they do so.

Conditions. Each perspective also has something to say, implicitly or explicitly, about the conditions under which social problems emerge and develop. These are not the immediate causes of social problems. Rather, they are the more general background features out of which the causes of social problems develop.

Consequences. All five perspectives view social problems as harmful. They differ, however, in terms of how the harmful effects of social problems are described.

Solutions. Finally, each perspective includes its own implications regarding how we can solve social problems. The perspectives emerged at different points in the development of sociology. Thus, some are more explicitly concerned with social reform than are others. Nonetheless, all five perspectives have some implications for the solution of social problems, and the characteristics of the perspective determine whether the solution focuses on expectations, violations, or reactions.[6]

[6] The implications of each perspective for the solution of social problems are more thoroughly examined, and illustrated by readings, in Martin S. Weinberg and Earl Rubington, eds., *The Solution of Social Problems: Five Perspectives* (New York: Oxford University Press, 1973).

Hints about What Follows

The next five chapters each deal with one of the five perspectives. Every chapter is organized along the following lines. First, there is a brief history of the perspective, including which sociologists contributed most to its development. Next, we give a summary of the perspective—its characteristics regarding the definition, causes, conditions, consequences, and solutions of social problems. Then we present readings that explicate and illustrate the perspective, followed by a selection that criticizes it. Questions for discussion and selected references complete the chapter.

As previously noted, the five perspectives arose at different stages in the development of sociology. Thus, each has had periods of popularity and periods of relative neglect. Yet even today each is to some degree the basis for the thinking and writing of many sociologists. This, more than anything else, is the reason for this book.

Summary

Sociology began in the late 1800s with a dual mandate to study social relations, on the one hand, and social problems, on the other. Since then, there has been a recurrent tension in sociology over which of these should receive primary emphasis. In an effort to resolve this tension, sociologists have from time to time developed new perspectives for the study of social problems.

A perspective is basically a way of looking at things, and it clarifies for the sociologist the focus of his or her work. In the study of social problems, sociologists have fashioned five popular perspectives—"social pathology," "social disorganization," "value conflict," "deviant behavior," and "labeling." Each perspective has its own notion of the definition, causes, conditions, consequences, and solutions of social problems. Now, we look more closely at each of the five perspectives.

Selected References

Bernard, Jessie. *Social Problems at Midcentury: Role, Status, and Stress in a Context of Abundance.* New York: Holt, Rinehart & Winston, 1957.

A text that is extremely useful for its discussion of how middle-class reformers first formulated the concept of social problems.

Hinkle, Roscoe C., Jr., and Gisela J. Hinkle. *The Development of Modern Sociology: Its Nature and Growth in the United States.* New York: Doubleday & Co.,
1954.
One of the best discussions of the rise and development of American sociology. Admirable for the wealth of its scholarship, the brevity of its presenta-
tion.

Kitsuse, John I., and Malcolm Spector. "Social Problems and Deviance:
Some Parallel Issues." *Social Problems* 22 (June 1975), pp. 584–94.
Kitsuse and Spector argue that the task of social problems theory is to describe and explain "the definitional process in which morally objectionable
conditions or behaviors are asserted to exist, and the collective activities that
become organized around those assertions."

Nisbet, Robert A. *The Social Bond.* New York: Alfred A. Knopf, 1970.
An introductory text that defines sociology as the study of social interaction
and shows how sociological concepts are employed to analyze interaction.
Contains a useful discussion of the distinction between sociological problems
and social problems.

II.
the perspectives
2. Social Pathology

The idea that there are social problems would appear to be as old as man. But actually this is not the case at all. Though problems and suffering seem to be found in every society and every historical period, the notion that they are social problems about which something should be done is fairly recent.[1] Before examining the social pathology perspective, we consider briefly how the idea of social problems came into being.

The Concept of Social Problems

Nineteenth-century America witnessed the ushering in of the urban-industrial order. People began to migrate from farms to cities, and emigration from Europe brought additional thousands to America's burgeoning cities. As the cities swelled, a number of troublesome conditions became more and more noticeable. Near the end of the Civil War, the notion arose that these conditions of suffering, pain, social disorder, institutional malfunctioning, and the like, could be remedied. With this corrective attitude, the concept of social problems was born.

[1] According to Arnold Green, a consciousness of social problems did not arise until the latter part of the eighteenth century. Four ideas—those of equality, humanitarianism, the goodness of human nature, and the modifiability of social conditions—made this consciousness possible. See Arnold Green, *Social Problems: Arena of Conflict* (New York: McGraw-Hill, 1975).

Primarily, it was middle-class reformers who perceived situations in the cities as social problems. Impressed with scientific ideology and imbued with the humanism of the Enlightenment, they felt that scientific study, which had solved the puzzles of the physical universe, could also solve the problems of society.

Around 1865, the American Social Science Association was formed. Social reform was the overall goal of the association, and the scientific study of social problems was its immediate objective.[2] In time, however, a number of schisms took place within the association. First, several groups split off and formed more specialized associations in their respective academic disciplines—i.e., economics, political science, etc. Second, within the association itself, distinctions arose between theory, on the one hand, and application, on the other. Eventually the association was disbanded. It left a legacy, however, of social problems courses, which were soon being given in American universities by a variety of disciplines. As sociology became better established, it took over more and more of these courses.

Very much a product of its times, early American sociology dovetailed neatly with the objectives of the American Social Science Association as well as the attitudes of middle-class reformers. In particular, early American sociology was characterized by four popular beliefs of the late nineteenth century: natural law, progress, social reform, and individualism.[3] Thus, the founding fathers of American sociology believed that human behavior was governed by natural laws and that it was the task of sociology to discover these laws. Most early sociologists also believed in progress. In the course of social evolution, they thought, societies change from simple to complex, and people become freer, more rational, and happier. At the same time, however, these early sociologists saw industrialization and urbanization as the sources of some undesirable conditions, and they wanted to ameliorate those conditions. Thus, the early sociologists wanted to discover the

[2] For a more detailed discussion of the notion of social problems and the rise and fall of the American Social Science Association, see Jessie Bernard, *Social Problems at Midcentury: Role, Status, and Stress in a Context of Abundance* (New York: Holt, Rinehart & Winston, 1957), pp. 90–102.
[3] See Roscoe C. Hinkle, Jr., and Gisela J. Hinkle, *The Development of Modern Sociology: Its Nature and Growth in the United States* (New York: Doubleday & Co., 1954), pp. 7–17.

natural laws of human behavior so that they could effect social reform. Finally, these early sociologists had an individualistic conception of social life. They assumed that, although a person belongs to groups, it is ultimately one's personal interests, motives, and characteristics that determine one's behavior.

Roots of the Social Pathology Perspective

Essentially, the social pathology perspective is rooted in the organic analogy. Some early writers employed this analogy in a relatively primitive fashion; for example, some portrayed the government as the head of society, the postal service as the nervous system, the police as the "long arm of the law." Herbert Spencer, however, made a more sophisticated use of the organic analogy. In his view, society is like an organism in that it has mass, a complexity of structure that increases with its growth, interdependent parts, and a life that surpasses the life of any particular part.[4]

To the writers employing the organic analogy, persons or situations were considered to be social problems to the extent that they interfered with the "normal" workings of the social organism. In keeping with the organic analogy, such interference was viewed as a form of illness, or pathology.

The influence of the organic analogy on early American sociology can be seen in the following definition of social pathology, which appeared in an early and widely used sociology textbook.

> Since society is made up of individuals bound together in social relationships, social pathology refers to the maladjustments in social relationships. The phrase is based on the analogy of bodily maladjustment of function in the organ. . . . If carefully guarded . . . the term "social pathology" may be used to denote the social conditions which result (1) from failure of individuals so to adjust themselves to social life that they function as independent self-supporting members of society, who contribute their fair share to its stability and progressive development; and (2) from the lack of adjustment of social structure, including ways of doing things and institutions, to the development of social personality.
>
> Pathological conditions in society may result from (1) natural lack of ability in individuals to keep pace with the changing ideals and institutions of

[4] Robert L. Cameiro, ed., *The Evolution of Society: Selections from Herbert Spencer's Principles of Sociology* (Chicago: University of Chicago Press, 1967).

society; or (2) from the failure of society to keep pace in its functional machinery with the changing conditions in the world in which it lives.[5]

The early social pathologists, then, saw both individual maladjustments (such as economic dependency) and institutional malfunctioning (such as economic depression) as obstacles in the forward march of social progress. Thus, they thought that such maladjustments, whether individual or institutional, should be rooted out.

Two sociologists who helped to establish the basic outline of the social pathology perspective were Charles Henderson and Samuel Smith. Both wrote social pathology textbooks, and the line of reasoning set forth in these books dominated the field of sociology for at least a generation.[6] Central to the work of Henderson, Smith, and their many followers in the field of textbook writing was cultural borrowing. Since sociology was still a young and developing field, sociologists were inclined to borrow ideas and metaphors from disciplines that were already well established, such as medicine, philosophy, economics, and political science. The medical metaphors of pathology and the organic analogy as developed in social philosophy helped to shape this perspective. In addition, most of these writers employed popular values in their sociological writings, saturating their textbooks with the moral judgments of the day.

Most of the social pathology textbooks appeared during the first two stages of American sociology. These texts dominated the classroom for years, with revisions appearing only every seven or eight years or more. This slow, settled pace of revision, coupled with the fact that only a few textbooks were available, perpetuated and strengthened the social pathology perspective. Today, in contrast, there are numerous textbooks representing different perspectives. Also, revisions appear every three years or so, allowing more opportunity to modify perspectives.

In addition, the slow and rather steady pace of social change during the early 1900s probably made the original social pathology perspective seem more viable to early American

[5] John L. Gillin and Frank W. Blackmar, *Outlines of Sociology* (New York: Macmillan, 1930), p. 527.
[6] Charles Henderson, *Introduction to the Study of the Dependent, Defective, and Delinquent Classes, and of Their Social Treatment* (Boston: D. C. Heath, 1909); Samuel Smith, *Social Pathology* (New York: Macmillan, 1911).

sociologists than it may seem to us today. At that time, the status quo was more accepted as the normal, natural state of affairs. In such an atmosphere, it was easy for people to see anyone who deviated from the status quo as "sick." [7]

Changes in the Social Pathology Perspective

In its early form, the social pathology perspective was based on the metaphor of society as an organism. The so-called "normal" functioning of society was assumed to be "healthy," and the social pathologists occupied themselves with classifying the "ills" of society.

This simplistic and conservative strand of social pathology had its heyday before World War I, especially between 1890 and 1910. After the war, it went into slow but steady decline. In the 1960s, however, there was a resurgence of the social pathology perspective, with some sociologists again writing about the "pathology" of our existence.[8] Also, many liberals and radicals were seeing the society as "sick." Ironically, the "counter-culture" people (e.g., "hippies") who labeled society as sick were themselves the kinds of people whom the early social pathologists would have labeled "sick." Recently, however, there has been a blurring of these contrasting points of view in an attempt to make the pathology perspective more "objective" (e.g., see the selection by Kavolis in this chapter).

Characteristics of the Social Pathology Perspective

The more specific characteristics of this perspective are as follows:

[7] From a contemporary point of view, "there is little disagreement about what constitutes a healthy state of the organism. But there is much less agreement when one uses the notion of pathology analogically, to describe kinds of behavior that are regarded as deviant. For people do not agree on what constitutes healthy behavior. It is difficult to find a definition that will satisfy even such a select and limited group as psychiatrists; it is impossible to find one that people generally accept as they accept criteria of health for the organism." From Howard S. Becker, *Outsiders: Studies in the Sociology of Deviance* (New York: The Free Press of Glencoe, 1963), p. 5.

[8] See, for example, Bernard Rosenberg, Israel Gerver, and F. William Howton, *Mass Society in Crisis: Social Problems and Social Pathology*, 2nd ed. (New York: Macmillan, 1971).

Definition. Desirable social conditions and arrangements are seen as healthy, while persons or situations that diverge from moral expectations are regarded as "sick," therefore bad. Thus, in the social pathology perspective, a social problem is a violation of *moral* expectations.

Causes. The ultimate cause of social problems is a failure in socialization. Society, through its socializing agents, has the responsibility of transmitting moral norms to each generation. Sometimes, however, the socialization effort is ineffective. An early classification of deviants in the social pathology perspective portrayed them as defective, dependent, or delinquent.[9] Defectives cannot be taught, dependents are handicapped in receiving instruction, and delinquents reject the teachings. For later pathologists, social problems are the result of wrong values being learned. In this perspective's "tender" mood, the people who contribute to the social problem are viewed as "sick"; in its "tough" mood, they are viewed as "criminal." Behind both moods, however, is the notion that the person or situation is, at heart, "immoral."

Conditions. The early social pathologists considered some people to be inherently defective. And, for the most part, the "defective, dependent, and delinquent" classes tended to perpetuate themselves through inbreeding.[10] Later, however, social pathologists began to see the social environment as the important condition contributing to social pathology. Indeed, Smith himself wrote, "social disease so prevalent as to create a social problem is rarely found without a bad environment of some sort or other, and so the social student is compelled to study the causes of social disease."[11] Whereas earlier pathologists tended to focus on the immoral properties of individuals, the recent pathologists have tended to focus on the im-

---

[9] Henderson, *Introduction to Study.*
[10] Lombroso claimed there was a definite "criminal type" and that these people were born criminal. The early social pathologists were much influenced by Lombroso's work, and they generalized his position to cover a host of "problem people." These dependent, defective, and delinquent people were viewed as the source of the great bulk of social problems. A summary of Lombroso's work may be found in Marvin E. Wolfgang, "Pioneers in Criminology: Cesare Lombroso (1835–1909)," *Journal of Criminal Law, Criminology, and Police Science* 52 (November-December 1961), pp. 361–91.
[11] Smith, *Social Pathology,* p. 8.

moral properties of societies and to see problems as developing from societal forces such as technology and population density.

Consequences. In the early pathology view, social disturbances increase the costs of maintaining a legitimate social order. The early pathologists did believe, however, that ultimately the healthiest would survive. The more recent pathologists, in contrast, are morally indignant at the defects of society and are less optimistic in their prognosis. The most indignant see societal pathology as total, spreading, and likely to dehumanize the entire population.

Solutions. Both the early and the recent versions of the social pathology perspective suggest what form solutions to social problems might take. The early sociologists who dwelt on the troubles caused by "genetically" defective individuals, for example, turned to the eugenics movement as a solution. Other sociologists thought the solution to social problems lay in educating the troublemakers in middle-class morality. The recent variant, which tends to regard the society rather than its nonconforming members as "sick," has its roots in the Rousseauean view of human nature. Individuals are good; their institutions, on the other hand, are bad. Yet, even the modern social pathologists see the remedy to "sick" institutions to be a changing of people's values. Thus, according to this perspective, the only real solution to social problems is moral education.[12]

Summary

The social pathology perspective organized the thinking of early American sociologists with regard to social problems, and it has continued—in at least some quarters—to be a very influential point of view. It is rooted in the organic analogy, and its primary concern is with the ills, or pathologies, of society.

From this perspective, social problems are seen as violations of moral expectations. Their cause is thought to be socializa-

[12] For an early statement of this view see Charles A. Ellwood, *The Social Problem: A Reconstructive Analysis* (New York: Macmillan, 1919).

tion failure, which was attributed first to genetic inheritance and later to social environment. The result of such failure is moral erosion; the solution, moral education.

Social pathologists can be grouped according to their period, orientation, and politics. Earlier pathologists tended to be conservative in their orientation and politics. Later pathologists tended to be liberal or radical in their orientation and politics. Most recently, a synthesis of these approaches has appeared, but it is difficult to say what direction this perspective will take or what its influence will be in the future.

The Organic Analogy

Samuel Smith

This brief excerpt from Samuel Smith's Social Pathology *shows the considerable influence the organic analogy had on writers around the turn of the century. Like medical doctors who study physical illness, social pathologists undertook to study the "social diseases" of society. And Smith believed that just as medical doctors study disease to learn how to treat it, so social pathologists study social problems in order to learn how to "cure" them.*

Pathology in social science has a certain parallel to pathology in medical science. As the study of physical disease is essential to the maintenance of physical health, so social health can never be securely grounded without a wider and more definite knowledge of social disease. General pathology in medicine teaches that many diseases have much in common and there are morbid processes which may be discussed, as well as particular diseases.

In social pathology the interrelation of the abnormal classes is one of the most impressive facts. Paupers often beget criminals; the offspring of criminals become insane; and to such an extent is the kinship of the defective, dependent, and delinquent classes exhibited, that some have gone so far as to hold that under all the various forms of social pathology there is a

From Samuel Smith, *Social Pathology*, pp. 8–9. 1911, The Macmillan Company.

common ground in the morbid nervous condition of individuals.

Medical science classifies diseases and is not content with a study of symptoms, but seeks to find out the causes of the maladies with which it deals. Social students are coming to see with increasing clearness that the study and treatment of mere symptoms in social disease have been among the great defects of philanthropists and reformers who in times past, despite the generosity of their motives and the self-sacrifice of their labors, have failed in their task because of a lack of accurate observation and definite knowledge, which are the only foundations of wise action. The social doctrine is becoming clear and convincing to many minds that the individual can only be dealt with in his relationships. The weakness of the individual mind or will, the lack of development and the lack of self-control, are all elements in the problem but social disease so prevalent as to create a social problem is rarely found without a bad environment of some sort or other, and so the social student is compelled to study the causes of social disease.

Medical science teaches that the study of disease is only a step in the process leading to therapeutics, or the cure of disease, and instead of being the road to despair in the vast majority of physical ills, it is the only basis of hope. Nearly every disease can be cured if it is taken in time, but the crowning achievement of medical science is not in therapeutics, but in sanitation and in the prevention of disease.

Social pathology would be a gloomy study indeed if its accurate knowledge of facts and principles did not indicate pathways out of social difficulties leading to a discovery of the means by which the social causes of disease can be removed, the weak individual be socially reinforced so that finally, as an ideal at least, the social body shall exist in the minds of social workers, radiant with health, in which there is not a living being which does not share in the general glow of wholesomeness and power.

The Child Savers

Anthony M. Platt

In this excerpt, Platt discusses the evolution of the social pathology perspective. Among other things, he discusses the sources of its ideas and how these ideas changed with the development of the pathology perspective. One important source is the concept of the criminal as less than a complete human being (whether by nature or by nurture). Other features in the development of this perspective include the growth of professionalism in correctional work and the acceptance of a medical model and a "rehabilitative ideal," particularly for the treatment of "delinquent" youth.

The . . . [social pathologists'] ideology was an amalgam of convictions and aspirations. From the medical profession, they borrowed the imagery of pathology, infection, immunization, and treatment; from the tenets of social Darwinism, they derived their pessimistic views about the intractability of human nature and the innate moral defects of the lower classes; finally, their ideas about the biological and environmental origins of crime can be attributed to the positivist tradition in European criminology and anti-urban sentiments associated with the Protestant, rural ethic.

American criminology in the last century was essentially a practical affair—a curious conglomeration of pseudo-scientific theory, Old World ideas, and religious humanitarianism. Theories of crime were imported from Europe and an indiscriminating eclecticism dominated the literature. Educated amateurs, physicians, clergymen, and scholar-technicians became the experts on crime. Before 1870, there were only a few American textbooks on crime, and even the various penal and philanthropic organizations lacked specialized journals. Departments of law and sociology in the universities were rarely concerned with more than the formal description and classification of crimes.[1]

[1] Arthur E. Fink, *Causes of Crime: Biological Theories in the United States, 1800–1915* [(Philadelphia: University of Pennsylvania Press, 1938)]. Needless to say, histories of American criminological thought are hard to find.

American pioneers in criminology were either physicians, like Benjamin Rush or Isaac Ray, or at least guided by medical ideology. Their training was often based on European methods and some, like Rush, actually attended European universities. With the notable exception of Ray's work, the authoritative literature on medical jurisprudence was of English origin.[2] The social sciences were similarly imported from Europe, and American criminologists fitted their data within the theoretical framework of criminal anthropology. Herbert Spencer's writings had an enormous impact on American intellectuals and made him even more popular in the United States than he was in his own country.[3] Cesare Lombroso, perhaps the most significant figure in nineteenth-century criminology, also sought recognition in the United States when he felt that his experiments had been neglected in Italy.[4]

Spencer and Lombroso, with their emphasis on Darwinist and biological images of human behavior, provided the ideological premise for crime workers and reformers. Anthropological explanations of crime complemented social Darwinism, which, in its most simple form, suggested that life is a competitive struggle for existence whereby the fittest survive and thus elevate the whole human race. The doctrine of "natural selection" also refuted revolutionary change and characterized human progress as a slow, natural, and inevitable process of

Fink's study makes a useful bibliographical contribution to the literature by assembling and condensing a vast amount of interesting primary sources. But he rarely attempts to interpret his data other than to make the occasional bow to the evolutionary perspective. There are of course numerous modern textbooks on the history of penology—such as H. E. Barnes and N. K. Teeters, *New Horizons in Criminology* ([New York: Prentice-Hall], 1943), Max Grünhut, *Penal Reform* ([Toronto: Oxford], 1948), and George B. Vold, *Theoretical Criminology* ([New York: Oxford], 1958)—but these are essentially compiled for undergraduate reading.

[2] Isaac Ray, *A Treatise on the Medical Jurisprudence of Insanity* [(Cambridge: Belknap/Harvard University Press, 1962)]. The influence of English medical jurisprudence on American physicians is cursorily examined by Anthony M. Platt and Bernard L. Diamond, "The Origins of the 'Right and Wrong' Test of Criminal Responsibility and Its Subsequent Development in the United States," *California Law Review* 54 (1966): 1227–60. See, also, Seymour Halleck, "American Psychiatry and the Criminal: A Historical Review," *American Journal of Psychiatry* 121, no. 9 (March, 1965): i–xxi.

[3] Richard Hofstadter, *Social Darwinism in American Thought* [(Boston: Beacon Press, 1960)], pp. 31–50.

[4] See Lombroso's introduction to Arthur MacDonald, *Criminology* [(New York: Funk & Wagnalls, 1893)].

evolution.[5] As Richard Hofstadter has observed, this view of social life was "seized upon as a welcome addition, perhaps the most powerful of all, to the store of ideas to which solid and conservative men appealed when they wished to reconcile their fellows to some of the hardships of life and to prevail upon them not to support hasty and ill-considered reforms." [6]

Spokesmen for conservative Darwinism opposed welfare legislation and organized state care of the "dependent classes" on the grounds that all men, whatever their ability and resources, should engage in the competition for survival. The care and support of criminals, idiots, cripples, and the like, merely prolongs suffering, impedes human progress, and contradicts the laws of nature. The Darwinists, however, did not approve class warfare or the total elimination of the "unfit" through eugenic techniques. Hofstadter has pointed out that Spencer, accused of inhumanity in his application of biological principles to social life, "was compelled to insist over and over again that he was not opposed to voluntary private charity to the unfit, since it had an elevating effect on the character of the donors and hastened the development of altruism. . . ." [7]

Although Lombroso's theoretical and experimental studies were not translated into English until 1911, his findings were known by American academics in the early 1890's, and their popularity, as that of Spencer's, was based on the fact that they confirmed popular assumptions about the character and existence of a "criminal class." Lombroso's original theory suggested the existence of a criminal type distinguishable from non-criminals by observable physical anomalies of a degenerative or atavistic nature. He proposed that the criminal was a morally inferior human species, one characterized by physical traits reminiscent of apes, lower primates, and savage tribes. The criminal was thought to be morally retarded and, like a small child, instinctively aggressive and precocious unless re-

[5] As Charles Cooley remarked, "most of the writers on eugenics have been biologists or physicians who have never acquired the point of view which sees in society a psychological organism with a life process of its own. They have thought of human heredity as a tendency to definite modes of conduct, and of environment as something that may aid or hinder, not remembering what they might have learned even from Darwin, that heredity takes on a distinctively human character only by renouncing, as it were, the function of predetermined adaptation and becoming plastic to the environment" (*Social Process* [(New York: Charles Scribner's Sons, 1918)], p. 206).

[6] Hofstadter, *Social Darwinism*, p. 5.

[7] *Ibid.*, p. 41.

strained.[8] It is not difficult to see the connection between biological determinism in criminological literature and the principles of "natural selection"; both of these theoretical positions, according to Leon Radzinowicz, automatically justified the "eradication of elements that constituted a permanent and serious danger." [9]

Lombroso and his colleagues recognized other types of criminal behavior and even acknowledged the influence of social as well as biological factors on criminals.[10] . . .

In England, the ideas and data of the so-called Italian school of criminology had already been summarized and publicized by Havelock Ellis.[11] A similar, though much more superficial and less endurable, service was provided by Robert Fletcher in an address before the Anthropological Society of Washington, D.C., in 1891. Fletcher told his audience that criminal anthropology consisted of the study of individuals who are compelled to commit crimes as a consequence of "physical conformation, hereditary taint, or surroundings of vice, poverty, and ill example." The modern view of the criminal depicts him as a "variety of human species who had degenerated physically and morally." . . .

American penologists supported this derogatory image of criminals and enthusiastically welcomed pseudo-scientific proposals for their containment.[12] A typical medical view was expressed by Nathan Allen at the National Conference of Charities and Correction, where he observed that criminals are usually incapable of overcoming their biological fate:

All history proves that the criminal class as a body originates from a peculiar stratum or type in society—sometimes from the middle or common walks of life, but more generally from the lowest orders, especially from the ignorant, the shiftless, the indolent and dissipated. . . . If our object, then, is to

[8] An excellent critique of Lombroso's theories, findings and intellectual traditions is provided by Marvin E. Wolfgang, "Cesare Lombroso," in Hermann Mannheim, ed., *Pioneers in Criminology* [(Chicago: Quadrangle, 1960)], pp. 168–227.
[9] *Ideology and Crime* [(New York: Columbia University Press, 1966)], p. 55.
[10] This study is not the place to debate Lombroso's contributions to criminology or to measure his effect on European ideas; what I am concerned with here is how Lombroso was interpreted and simplified in the United States before 1900. It is well recognized that his later writings were more cautious and emphasized a multifactor approach.
[11] Havelock Ellis, *The Criminal* [(London: Walter Scott, 1914)].
[12] See, for example, Fink, *Causes of Crime*, pp. 188–210, on criminological attitudes toward sterilization.

prevent crime in a large scale, we must direct attention to its main sources—
to the materials that make criminals; the springs must be dried up; the
supplies must be cut off.

Allen further proposed that crime would be reduced if "certain classes of vicious persons could be hindered from propa-
gation. What right have such individuals to bring upon the
public so much misery, shame, and cost?" [13] . . .

The organization of correctional workers—through their
national representatives and their identification with the established professions, such as law and medicine—operated to
neutralize the pessimistic implications of social Darwinism, because hereditary and fatalistic theories of crime inevitably
frustrated the professional aspirations of correctional functionaries. At the same time, even though the job of guard
requires minimal training, skill, or intelligence, crime workers
did not wish to regard themselves as merely the custodians of
a pariah class.[14]

The self-image of penal reformers as doctors rather than
guards and the domination of criminological research in the
United States by physicians, helped to encourage the acceptance of "therapeutic" strategies in prisons and reformatories.
As Arthur Fink has observed, "the role of the physician in this
ferment is unmistakable. Indeed, he was the dynamic agent.
. . . Not only did he preserve and add to existing knowledge—for his field touched all borders of science—but he
helped to maintain and extend the methodology of science." [15]
Perhaps what is more significant is that physicians furnished
the official rhetoric of penal reform. Admittedly, the criminal
was "pathological" and "diseased," but medical science offered
the possibility of miraculous cures. It was, therefore, the task
of correctional agencies to make every individual self-support-
ing and independent by restraining "prodigality and extrava-
gance of expenditure of human force and substance." [16] Although there was widespread belief in the existence of a

[13] Nathan Allen, "Prevention of Crime and Pauperism," *Proceedings of the
Annual Conference of Charities (PACC), 1878,* pp. 111–24.
[14] Analogous developments in the emergence of social work as a professional career are treated by [Roy] Lubove in *The Professional Altruist*
[(Cambridge: Harvard University Press, 1965)].
[15] Fink, *Causes of Crime,* p. 247.
[16] *First Biennial Report of the Board of State Commissioners of Public Charities of
the State of Illinois,* p. 18 (Springfield, Illinois: Illinois Journal Printing Office,
1871).

"criminal class" separated from the rest of mankind by a "vague boundary line," there was no good reason why this class could not be identified, diagnosed, segregated, changed, and controlled. Crime, like disease, was revealed "in the face, the voice, the person and the carriage," so that a skillful and properly trained diagnostician could arrest criminal tendencies. . . .

Despite the wide acceptance of biological imagery, penal reformers stressed the possibility of redemption through religious and medical intervention. The desire to promote the "welfare of the community and future of the race," the stress on pseudo-scientific methods of eliminating criminality, and the ruthless, mechanistic classification of criminals had to be weighed against traditional Christian benevolence, the indulgence of the unfit, and the "optimism of Religion" (as compared with the "pessimism of Science").[17] Charles Henderson, professor of sociology at the University of Chicago and President of the National Conference of Charities and Correction for 1899, resolved this dilemma by observing that the laws of "natural selection" and the principles of educative reform were not antagonistic. To hurt the "defective classes," said Henderson, would be to hurt the social order itself; social progress must rest on the capacity of those persons who deal with this class to develop altruistic sentiments. . . .

Professional correctional workers and administrators gradually refuted monolithic explanations of crime based on biological imagery. . . . The superintendent of the Kentucky Industrial School of Reform, for example, was convinced by 1898 that hereditary theories of crime were over-fatalistic. "While I believe heredity, of both moral and physical traits, to be a fact," he told delegates to a national conference, "I think it is unjustifiably made a bugaboo to discourage efforts at rescue. We know that physical heredity tendencies can be neutralized and often nullified by proper counteracting precautions." [18] E. R. L. Gould, a sociologist at the University of Chicago, similarly objected to hereditary theories of crime, on the grounds

[17] Charles Henderson, "Relation of Philanthropy to Social Order and Progress," [*Proceedings of the National Conference of Charities and Corrections (PNCCC)*], pp. 1–15. Cf. Charles E. Faulkner, "Twentieth Century Alignments For the Promotion of Social Order," with Frederick H. Wines, "The Healing Touch," *PNCCC*, 1900, pp. 1–9, 10–26.
[18] Peter Caldwell, "The Duty of the State to Delinquent Children," *PNCCC*, *1898*, pp. 404–10.

that the empirical data was unconvincing. He criticized many so-called scientific studies for being unclear, morbid, and sentimental:

> There is great danger in emphasizing heredity, and by contrast minimizing the influence of environment and individual responsibility. Consequences doubly unfortunate must ensue. Individual stamina will be weakened, and society made to feel less keenly the duty of reforming environment. Is it not better to postulate freedom of choice than to preach the doctrine of the unfettered will, and so elevate criminality into a propitiary sacrifice? [19]

The problem confronting criminologists of "whether the man makes the circumstances or the circumstances make the man" was skillfully clarified by Charles Cooley in an address before the National Conference of Charities and Correction in 1896. He considered it unnecessary and pointless to create a dichotomy between "nature" and "nurture," inferring that there is a choice of alternatives.[20] "Like male and female, each is sterile without the other." Cooley took a dynamic and flexible position regarding the way in which social character is formed:

> The union of nature and nurture is not one of addition or mixture, but of growth, whereby the elements are altogether transformed into a new organic whole. One's nature acts selectively upon the environment, assimilating materials proper to itself; while at the same time the environment moulds the nature, and habits are formed which make the individual independent, in some degree, of changes in either. . . .

Cooley made the important observation that criminal behavior depended as much upon social experiences and economic circumstances as it did upon the inheritance of biological traits. The delinquent child is constrained by social rather than biological forces; in essence, however, he is normally constituted and the "criminal class is largely the result of society's bad workmanship upon fairly good material." Cooley criticized theories of crime based on physical peculiarities, noting that there was a "large and fairly trustworthy body of evi-

---

[19] E. R. L. Gould, "The Statistical Study of Hereditary Criminality," *PNCCC, 1895,* pp. 134–43.

[20] According to Hofstadter, "The new psychology . . . was a truly social psychology. . . . [I]nsistence upon the unreality of a personal psyche isolated from the social surroundings was a central tenet in the social theory of Charles H. Cooley. . . . The older psychology had been atomistic. . . . The new psychology, prepared to see the interdependence of the individual personality with the institutional structure of society, was destroying this one-way notion of social causation and criticizing its underlying individualism" (*Social Darwinism,* p. 150).

dence" to support the fact that many so-called degenerates could be made "useful citizens by rational treatment." [21]

. . . [Thus], the concept of the natural criminal was modified with the rise of a professional class of correctional administrators and social servants who promoted a medical model of deviant behavior and suggested techniques of remedying "natural" imperfections. The pessimism of Darwinism was counterbalanced by the spirit of philanthropy, religious optimism, and a belief in the dignity of suffering. . . .

Another important influence on nineteenth-century images of crime was a disenchantment with urban life. The city was depicted as the main breeding ground of criminals: the impact of the physical horrors of urban ghettos on unskilled, poorly educated European immigrants "created" criminals. Immigrants were regarded as "unsocialized" and the city's impersonality compounded their isolation and degradation. "By some cruel alchemy," wrote Julia Lathrop, "we take the sturdiest of European peasantry and at once destroy in a large measure its power to rear to decent livelihood the first generation of offspring upon our soil." [22] . . .

Many penal and educational reformers considered that human nature operated in a radically different way in the city compared with the country. It was, therefore, the task of reformers to make city existence more like life on the farm, where social relationships were considered wholesome, honest, and free from depravity and corruption. Jenkin Lloyd Jones, in a speech before the Illinois Conference of Charities in 1898, expressed the hope that redistribution of the population would remedy some of the serious social problems associated with industrialism:

The currents of industrial and commercial life have set in tremendously towards the city. Thither flows with awful precipitancy the best nerve, muscle and brain of the country, and the equilibrium will be permanently destroyed if there cannot be a counter current established, whereby the less competent, the unprotected, the helpless and the innocent can be passed back, to be restored and reinvigorated.[23] . . .

[21] Charles H. Cooley, " 'Nature v. Nurture' in the Making of Social Careers," *PNCCC, 1896*, pp. 399–405.

[22] Julia Lathrop, "The Development of the Probation System in a Large City," *Charities* 13 (January, 1905): 348.

[23] "Who Are the Children of the State?" Illinois Conference of Charities (1898), *Fifteenth Biennial Report of the State Board of Commissioners of Public Charities of the State of Illinois*, pp. 286–87 (Springfield: Phillips Brothers, 1899).

Children living in the city slums were described as "intellectual dwarfs" and "physical and moral wrecks" whose characters were predominantly shaped by their physical surroundings. Beverley Warner told the National Prison Association in 1898 that philanthropic organizations all over the country were

> making efforts to get the children out of the slums, even if only once a week, into the radiance of better lives. Seeing the beauties of a better existence, these children may be led to choose the good rather than the evil. Good has been done by taking these children into places where they see ladies well dressed, and with their hands and faces clean, and it is only by leading the child out of sin and debauchery, in which it has lived, into a circle of life that is a repudiation of things that it sees in its daily life, that it can be influenced.[24] . . .

Summary

Important developments in the imagery of crime at the end of the last century were (1) the concept of the criminal as less than a complete human being, whether by nature or nurture, (2) the growth of professionalism in corrections work, and (3) the acceptance of the medical model and the "rehabilitative ideal," particularly with regard to the correction of "delinquent" children and adolescents.

1. Although there was a wide difference of opinion as to the precipitating causes of crime, it was generally agreed among experts that criminals were *abnormally* conditioned by biological and environmental factors. Early theories stressed the permanent, irreversible, and inherited character of criminal behavior. To the image of natural depravity was added the image of urban corruption. Reformers emphasized the disorganized features of urban life and encouraged remedial programs which embodied rural and primary group concepts. Slum life was regarded as unregulated, vicious and lacking in social rules; its inhabitants were depicted as abnormal and maladjusted, living their lives in conflict and chaos.[25]

2. The element of fatalism in theories of crime was modified with the rise of a professional class of penal administra-

[24] Beverley Warner, "Child Saving," *Proceedings of the Annual Congress of the National Prison Association, Indianapolis, 1898*, pp. 377–78.
[25] William Foote Whyte, "Social Disorganization in the Slums," *American Sociological Review* 8 (1943): 34–39.

tors and social servants who promoted a developmental view of human behavior. The pessimistic implications of Darwinist creeds were antagonistic not only to the Protestant ethic but also to crime workers who aspired to the professional status of doctors, lawyers, and other human service functionaries. It was fortunate, as John Higham has observed, that Darwinism was flexible enough to suit both philanthropic and misanthropic views of social life.[26]

3. There . . . [was] a shift . . . in official policies concerning crime. The warrant . . . shifted from one emphasizing the criminal nature of delinquency to the "new humanism," which speaks of disease, illness, contagion, and the like. The emergence of the medical warrant is of considerable significance, since it is a powerful rationale for organizing social action in the most diverse behavioral aspects of our society.

The "rehabilitative ideal"[27] presupposed that crime was a symptom of "pathology" and that criminals should be treated like irresponsible, sick patients. The older a criminal, the more chronic was his sickness; similarly, his chances of recovery were less than those of a young person. Adult criminals, particularly recidivists, were often characterized as nonhuman. Children, however, were less likely to be thought of as nonhuman since universalistic ethics, especially the ethic of Christianity, made it almost impossible to think of children as being entirely devoid of moral significance.

Social reformers emphasized the temporary and reversible nature of adolescent crime. As Charles Cooley observed,

---

[26] ". . . the general climate of opinion in the early Darwinian era inhibited the pessimistic implications of the new naturalism. What stood out in the first instance, as the great social lesson of the theory of natural selection, was not the ravages of the struggle for survival but rather the idea of 'the survival of the fittest.' To a generation of intellectuals steeped in confidence, the laws of evolution seemed to guarantee that the 'fittest' races would most certainly triumph over inferior competitors. . . . Darwinism, therefore, easily ministered to Anglo-Saxon pride, but in the age of confidence it could hardly arouse Anglo-Saxon anxiety.

"Secondly, Darwinism gave the race-thinkers little concrete help in an essential prerequisite of racism—belief in the preponderance of heredity over environment. Certainly the biological vogue of the late nineteenth century stimulated speculation along these lines, but the evolutionary theory by no means disqualified a fundamentally environmentalist outlook. Darwin's species struggled and evolved through adaptation to those settings" ([John] Higham, *Strangers in the Land*, pp. 135–36).

[27] This term is used by Francis A. Allen, *The Borderland of Criminal Justice.* [(Chicago: University of Chicago Press, 1964)].

"when an individual actually enters upon a criminal career, let us try to catch him at a tender age, and subject him to rational social discipline, such as is already successful in enough cases to show that it might be greatly extended." [28] If, as the child savers believed, criminals are conditioned by biological heritage and brutish living conditions, then prophylactic measures must be taken early in life. Delinquent children—the criminals of the next generation—must be prevented from pursuing their criminal careers. "They are born to it," wrote the penologist Enoch Wines in 1880, "brought up for it. They must be saved." [29] Many new developments in penology took place at this time in the reformatory system where, it was hoped, delinquents would be saved and reconstituted.

A Universal Criterion of Pathology

Vytautas Kavolis

C. Wright Mills criticized the social pathology approach for cloaking the small-town values of conservative reformers in seemingly objective medical terms. In this excerpt, Kavolis argues that social pathology, carefully defined, can be a relatively objective and useful conception. Destructiveness to self or others, Kavolis holds, can be objectively identified, and such destructiveness is the core of social pathology. Thus, Kavolis believes, the study of social pathology should concern itself with people's destructive behavior and the conditions that give rise to such behavior.

The . . . [social pathology] conception of social problems . . . provides a universal criterion for evaluating social arrangements by their human costs. If it were possible to arrive at a cross-culturally valid definition of "destructive or self-destructive behavior," then conditions causally associated with such behavior could be identified as pathogenic (or having

From Vytautas Kavolis (ed.), *Comparative Perspectives on Social Problems*, pp. 2–6. Copyright © 1969 by Little, Brown and Company (Inc.). Reprinted by permission.

[28] Cooley, " 'Nature v. Nurture,' " p. 405.
[29] Enoch C. Wines, *The State of Prisons and of Child-Saving Institutions in the Civilized World* [(Cambridge: University Press, 1880)], p. 132.

pathogenic aspects), regardless of whether they were institutionalized in a society and supported by its cultural traditions or not, and whether anyone in the society in which they occurred was aware of their pathogenic effects. With this perspective on social problems, no longer would the sociologist stand theoretically helpless—as the "deviationists" must—in relation to prejudice in South Africa, slavery in the pre-Civil War American South, Nazi concentration camps, genocide under Stalin, or the pathologies arising from conformity to "normal" middle-class values.[1]

I do not accept the view that to define pathology in terms of destructiveness is a culture-bound judgment. To regard *destruction of life, health, or sense of personal identity* (a definition with a hard core and stretchable boundaries) as the universal criterion of pathological behavior constitutes the most general extension of the implications of the major ethical systems of mankind. With respect to this criterion, exceptions have to be justified, not the criterion itself; but the criterion has been frequently held to apply only to members of one's own group. What we are doing is universalizing the criterion of pathology—applying it to all societies, including those that have not generalized their moral norms sufficiently to make them applicable to outsiders as much as to themselves.

Nor can it be legitimately assumed that the social-pathology approach necessarily incorporates a conservative bias in favor of preserving existing institutions.[2] What is pathological is not behavior which deviates from established custom or disrupts social stability but that which is destructive or self-destructive in its consequences. Whenever established institutions (or innovations) promote such behavior, they must be regarded as pathogenic. Conflict, in this theoretical perspective, is not in itself pathological (unless it generates violence). Lack of conflict may be pathogenic if it perpetuates a high incidence of self-destructive behavior.

The "field" of social pathology may be defined as the study of the destructive or self-destructive behavior of individuals

[1] Erich Fromm, *The Sane Society* (Greenwich, Conn.: Fawcett Publications, 1955).
[2] An accusation that has been justly directed against an earlier generation of American social pathologists. C. Wright Mills, "The Professional Ideology of Social Pathologists," in his *Power, Politics and People*, ed. Irving Louis Horowitz (New York: Ballantine Books, 1963), pp. 525–552.

(pathological behavior) and of the social and cultural conditions, or processes, which cause or contribute to such behavior (pathogenic conditions). If the goal is to understand how particular conditions have pathogenic effects on individuals, studying one type of pathological behavior in isolation from others is insufficient. It is only by investigating the overall effects of a social condition, on all types of pathological behavior, that the social pathologist can determine to what extent and in what manner the condition is pathogenic. A theoretical framework is needed within which any given social condition can be related to all types of pathological behaviors (if a relationship can be demonstrated to exist).

In organizing the data for such a framework, it is helpful to distinguish self-directed destructiveness from other-directed destructiveness, and spontaneous pathological behavior from organized pathologies. Self-destructiveness refers to all forms of behavior by which an individual destroys or damages his own life, health, or sense of personal identity. Such forms of behavior range from suicide at the highest level of intensity, through alcoholism and neurosis at intermediate levels, to various kinds of "inauthentic" actions, alien to the "true nature" of the personality, that the individual performs either because he is forced by external circumstances or because he does not "know" himself. Only the higher and intermediate levels of intensity will be considered systematically in this article, as little reliable cross-cultural research has been done on "inauthentic" behavior, except on alienation.

Other-directed destructiveness is another umbrella term referring to all activities by which an individual destroys or damages the life, health, or sense of personal identity of another person or persons. Such activities include, at one extreme, the various forms of murder (including socially sanctioned killing, as in warfare) and, at the other extreme, the withdrawal of social esteem from a specific person or group of persons. (This may be a rational action when it has been "earned" by the specific behavior of such a person or persons, but even then it is other-destructive.) I would classify racial discrimination and most forms of crime as other-directed destructive behavior of intermediate intensity. However, racial discrimination is easily intensified to the level of genocide; and the intensity of aggression inherent in crime varies from high to low. Some activities officially designated as crimes, such as school truancy, are purely self-destructive. Some crimes do not affect either the self or others destructively (e.g., the crime of offering a glass of wine to a seventeen-year-old in Pennsylvania). On the other hand, numerous other-destructive activities have historically not been regarded as crimes (war, economic exploitation of the easily victimized).

Spontaneous pathological behavior is exhibited when an individual "chooses," in part voluntarily, to engage in a destructive or self-destructive course of action, or when he unconsciously develops, without having the ability to choose, the symptoms of a self-destructive disease. Organized pathology exists when the individual is either "morally" obligated or "politically" coerced by the group or organization to whose authority or power he is subject to commit destructive or self-destructive acts (or to encourage others to commit such acts). The purest cases of organized pathology are found in concentration camps and the institution of slavery. While the victims of these institutions are coerced into self-destructive behavior, their masters, by accepting their position within these institutions, assume the obligation to engage in other-destructive behavior, essentially (though not wholly) regardless of their personal malevolence or lack thereof. Both the victims and the masters of pathological institutions are required, by the conditions of operation of such institutions, to engage in pathological behavior.

On a lower level of intensity, but with broadly comparable psychological effects, is the organized pathology of imperialism and colonialism, the most prominent representative of which, after the virtual demise of West European colonial empires, is the Soviet Union, with its at least fifteen nations held by force in the same relationship to the Great Russians as the natives of Mozambique are to the Portuguese—"crushed with their inessentiality." [3]

Organized pathology is not necessarily, at any given time, socially disreputable. Respected organizations may require their members to participate, or unintentionally promote, pathological behavior. The Catholic church does so when it requires its clerical members, against their growing opposition, to persuade its lay members not to use effective methods of fertility control. The rationale of this requirement is moral

[3] Frantz Fanon, *The Wretched of the Earth* (New York: Grove Press, 1966), p. 30.

upgrading of the faithful. The socially relevant result is a sizable contribution to over-population, malnutrition of children, illegal abortions that damage the health or destroy the lives of pregnant women, and revolutionary political extremism, especially in Latin America. Some readers might find that the rats of Rajasthan constitute an emotionally more acceptable illustration of the point that is being made here.[4]

These examples suggest to what extent the deviance perspective may be irrelevant to understanding the causes of major social pathologies. Yet one of the measures of the rationality of a social order is the degree to which its definitions of socially unacceptable deviance correspond with what can be empirically shown to be pathological behavior. In a rational society, presumably, only the pathological would be regarded as seriously deviant, and the only socially consequential deviance would be that of demonstrably destructive or self-destructive behavior. However, since societies are not rationally organized, both the deviance and the pathology perspectives are necessary to understand their problems.

In studying social pathology, we aim at establishing the characteristics of social structure and process as well as those of cultural orientation which promote pathological behavior wherever they occur. To eliminate accidental patterns of findings that hold in a particular time and place but lack general validity, systematic cross-cultural study of the various forms of pathological behavior is necessary. Such studies should eventually lead to a theoretical integration of the knowledge of pathological behavior in preliterate, historical, and modern societies accumulated by half a dozen scholarly disciplines. It should be possible, on the basis of such a theoretical system, to predict how much of what types of pathology would be likely to occur if we constructed a society with certain specified characteristics.

[4] "Food is scarce in this desert town, as it is in much of India. . . . But the rats in this desert state of Rajasthan face no food problem. They are considered to be holy creatures, and they are fed by faithful worshippers. The rodent population of Rajasthan is said to outnumber the human population: 25 million rats to 20.1 million people." *The New York Times,* August 21, 1968, p. 16.

The Pursuit of Loneliness

Philip Slater

American culture emphasizes individualism. According to Slater, this leads to competition, denial of interdependence with one's fellows, and a heightened need for privacy. Faced with these signs of social pathology, Americans respond with increased individualism, but this only makes them feel worse, because individualism cannot cure the pathologies it has itself produced.

We are so accustomed to living in a society that stresses individualism that we need to be reminded that "collectivism" in a broad sense has always been the more usual lot of mankind, as well as of most other species. Most people in most societies have been born into and died in stable communities in which the subordination of the individual to the welfare of the group was taken for granted, while the aggrandizement of the individual at the expense of his fellows was simply a crime.

This is not to say that competition is an American invention—all societies involve some sort of admixture of cooperative and competitive institutions. But our society lies near or on the competitive extreme, and although it contains cooperative institutions I think it is fair to say that Americans suffer from their relative weakness and peripherality. Studies of business executives have revealed, for example, a deep hunger for an atmosphere of trust and fraternity with their colleagues (with whom they must, in the short run, engage in what Riesman calls "antagonistic cooperation"). The competitive life is a lonely one, and its satisfactions are very short-lived indeed, for each race leads only to a new one.

In the past, as so many have pointed out, there were in our society many oases in which one could take refuge from the frenzied invidiousness of our economic system—institutions such as the extended family and the stable local neighborhood in which one could take pleasure from something other than winning a symbolic victory over one of his fellows. But these have disappeared one by one, leaving the individual more and more in a situation in which he must try to satisfy his affiliative and invidious needs in the same place. This has made the bal-

From Philip Slater, *The Pursuit of Loneliness*, "Community and Competition," pp. 5–12, a subtitled section of Chapter 1. Copyright © 1970 by Philip E. Slater. Reprinted by permission of Beacon Press and Penguin Books Ltd.

ance a more brittle one—the appeal of cooperative living more seductive, and the need to suppress our longing for it more acute.

In recent decades the principal vehicle for the tolerated expression of this longing has been the mass media. Popular songs and film comedies have continually engaged in a sentimental rejection of the dominant mores, maintaining that the best things in life are free, that love is more important than success, that keeping up with the Joneses is absurd, that personal integrity should take precedence over winning, and so on. But these protestations must be understood for what they are: a safety valve for the dissatisfactions that the modal American experiences when he behaves as he thinks he should. The same man who chuckles and sentimentalizes over a happy-go-lucky hero in a film would view his real-life counterpart as frivolous and irresponsible, and suburbanites who philosophize over their back fence with complete sincerity about their "dog-eat-dog-world," and what-is-it-all-for, and you-can't-take-it-with-you, and success-doesn't-make-you-happy-it-just-gives-you-ulcers-and-a-heart-condition—would be enraged should their children pay serious attention to such a viewpoint. Indeed, the degree of rage is, up to a point, a function of the degree of sincerity: if the individual did not feel these things he would not have to fight them so vigorously. The peculiarly exaggerated hostility that hippies tend to arouse suggests that the life they strive for is highly seductive to middle-aged Americans.

The intensity of this reaction can in part be attributed to a kind of circularity that characterizes American individualism. When a value is as strongly held as is individualism in America the illnesses it produces tend to be treated by increasing the dosage, in the same way an alcoholic treats a hangover or a drug addict his withdrawal symptoms. Technological change, mobility, and the individualistic ethos combine to rupture the bonds that tie each individual to a family, a community, a kinship network, a geographical location—bonds that give him a comfortable sense of himself. As this sense of himself erodes, he seeks ways of affirming it. But his efforts at self-enhancement automatically accelerate the very erosion he seeks to halt.

It is easy to produce examples of the many ways in which Americans attempt to minimize, circumvent, or deny the interdependence upon which all human societies are based. We seek a private house, a private means of transportation, a private garden, a private laundry, self-service stores, and do-it-yourself skills of every kind. An enormous technology seems to have set itself the task of making it unnecessary for one human being ever to ask anything of another in the course of going about his daily business. Even within the family Americans are unique in their feeling that each member should have a separate room, and even a separate telephone, television, and car, when economically possible. We seek more and more privacy, and feel more and more alienated and lonely when we get it. What accidental contacts we do have, furthermore, seem more intrusive, not only because they are unsought but because they are unconnected with any familiar pattern of interdependence.

Most important, our encounters with others tend increasingly to be competitive as a result of the search for privacy. We less and less often meet our fellow man to share and exchange, and more and more often encounter him as an impediment or a nuisance: making the highway crowded when we are rushing somewhere, cluttering and littering the beach or park or wood, pushing in front of us at the supermarket, taking the last parking place, polluting our air and water, building a highway through our house, blocking our view, and so on. Because we have cut off so much communication with each other we keep bumping into each other, and thus a higher and higher percentage of our interpersonal contacts are abrasive.

We seem unable to foresee that the gratification of a wish might turn out to be something of a monkey's paw if the wish were shared by many others. We cheer the new road that initially shaves ten minutes off the drive to our country retreat but ultimately transforms it into a crowded resort and increases both the traffic and the time. We are continually surprised to find, when we want something, that thousands or millions of others want it, too—that other human beings get hot in summer and cold in winter. The worst traffic jams occur when a mass of vacationing tourists departs for home early to "beat the traffic." We are too enamored of the individualistic fantasy that everyone is, or should be, different—that each person could somehow build his entire life around some single, unique eccentricity without boring himself and everyone else to death. Each of us of course has his quirks, which provide a surface variety that is briefly entertaining, but aside from this human beings have little basis for their persistent claim that they are not all members of the same species.

Since our contacts with others are increasingly competitive, unanticipated, and abrasive, we seek still more apartness and accelerate the trend. The desire to be somehow special inaugurates an even more competitive quest for progressively more rare and expensive symbols—a quest that is ultimately futile since it is individualism itself that produces uniformity.

This is poorly understood by Americans, who tend to confuse uniformity with "conformity," in the sense of compliance with or submission to group demands. Many societies exert far more pressure on the individual to mold himself to fit a particularized segment of a total group pattern, but there is variation among these circumscribed roles. Our society gives far more leeway to the individual to pursue his own ends, but, since *it* defines what is worthy and desirable, everyone tends, independently but monotonously, to pursue the same things in the same way. The first pattern combines cooperation, conformity, and variety; the second, competition, individualism, and uniformity.

These relationships are exemplified by two familiar processes in contemporary America: the flight to the suburb and the do-it-yourself movement. Both attempt to deny human interdependence and pursue unrealistic fantasies of self-sufficiency. The first tries to overlook our dependence upon the city for the maintenance of the level of culture we demand. "Civilized" means, literally, "citified," and the state of the city is an accurate index of the condition of the culture as a whole. We behave toward our cities like an irascible farmer who never feeds his cow and then kicks her when she fails to give enough milk. But the flight to the suburb is in any case self-defeating, its goals subverted by the mass quality of the exodus. The suburban dweller seeks peace, privacy, nature, community, and a child-rearing environment which is healthy and culturally optimal. Instead he finds neither the beauty and serenity of the countryside, the stimulation of the city, nor the stability and sense of community of the small town, and his children are exposed to a cultural deprivation equaling that of any slum child with a television set. Living in a narrow age-graded and class-segregated society, it is little wonder that suburban families have contributed so little to the national talent pool in proportion to their numbers, wealth, and other social advantages.* And this transplantation, which has caused the transplants to atrophy, has blighted the countryside and impoverished the city. A final irony of the suburban dream is that, for many Americans, reaching the pinnacle of one's social ambitions (owning a house in the suburbs) requires one to perform all kinds of menial tasks (carrying garbage cans, mowing lawns, shoveling snow, and so on) that were performed for him when he occupied a less exalted status.

Some of this manual labor, however, is voluntary—an attempt to deny the elaborate division of labor required in a complex society. Many Americans seem quite willing to pay this price for their reluctance to engage in interpersonal encounters with servants and artisans—a price which is rather high unless the householder particularly relishes the work (some find in it a tangible relief from the intangibles they manipulate in their own jobs) or is especially good at it, or cannot command a higher rate of pay in the job market than the servant or artisan.

The do-it-yourself movement has accompanied, paradoxically, increasing specialization in the occupational sphere. As one's job narrows, perhaps, one seeks the challenge of new skill-acquisition in the home. But specialization also means that one's interpersonal encounters with artisans in the home proliferate and become more impersonal. It is not a matter of a familiar encounter with the local smith or grocer—a few well-known individuals performing a relatively large number of functions, and with whom one's casual interpersonal contacts may be a source of satisfaction, and are in any case a testimony to the stability and meaningful interrelatedness of human affairs. One finds instead a multiplicity of narrow specialists—each perhaps a stranger (the same type of repair may be performed by a different person each time). Every relationship, such as it is, must start from scratch, and it is small

* . . . Cities, small towns, and rural areas [can be used] for comparison. The small Midwestern town achieves its legendary dullness by a process akin to evaporation—all the warm and energetic particles depart for coastal cities, leaving their place of origin colder and flatter than they found it. But the restless spirit in a small town knows he lives in the sticks and has a limited range of experience, while his suburban counterpart can sustain an illusion of cosmopolitanism in an environment which is far more constricted (a small town is a microcosm, a suburb merely a layer).

wonder that the householder turns away from such an unrewarding prospect in apathy and despair.

Americans thus find themselves in a vicious circle, in which their extrafamilial relationships are increasingly arduous, competitive, trivial, and irksome, in part as a result of efforts to avoid or minimize potentially irksome or competitive relationships. As the few vestiges of stable and familiar community life erode, the desire for a simple, cooperative life style grows in intensity. The most seductive appeal of radical ideologies for Americans consists in the fact that all in one way or another attack the competitive foundations of our society. Each touches a responsive doubt, and the stimuli arousing this doubt must be carefully unearthed and rooted out, just as the Puritan must unearth and root out the sexual stimuli that excite him.*

Now it may be objected that American society is far less competitive than it once was, and the appeal of radical ideologies should hence be diminished. A generation of critics has argued that the entrepreneurial individualist of the past has been replaced by a bureaucratic, security-minded, Organization Man. Much of this historical drama was written through the simple device of comparing yesterday's owner-president with today's assistant sales manager; certainly these nostalgia-merchants never visited a nineteenth-century company town. Another distortion is introduced by the fact that it was only the most ruthlessly competitive robber barons who survived to tell us how it was. Little is written about the neighborhood store that extended credit to the poor, or the small town industry that refused to lay off local workers in hard times— they all went under together. And as for the organization men—they left us no sagas.

Despite these biases real changes have undoubtedly occurred, but even if we grant that the business world as such was more competitive, the total environment contained more cooperative, stable, and personal elements. The individual

* Both efforts are ambivalent, since the "seek and destroy" process is in part a quest for the stimulus itself. The Puritanical censor both wants the sexual stimulus and wants to destroy it, and his job enables him to gratify both of these "contradictory" desires. There is a similar prurience in the efforts of groups such as the House UnAmerican Activities Committee to "uncover subversion." Just as the censor gets to experience far more pornography than the average man, so the Congressional red-baiter gets to hear as much Communist ideology as he wants, which is apparently quite a lot.

worked in a smaller firm with lower turnover in which his relationships were more enduring and less impersonal, and in which the ideology of Adam Smith was tempered by the fact that the participants were neighbors and might have been childhood playmates. Even if the business world was as "dog-eat-dog" as we imagine it (which seems highly unlikely), one encountered it as a deviant episode in what was otherwise a more comfortable and familiar environment than the organization man can find today in or out of his office. The organization man complex is simply an attempt to restore the personal, particularistic, paternalistic environment of the family business and the company town; and the other-directed "group-think" of the suburban community is a desperate attempt to bring some old-fashioned small-town collectivism into the transient and impersonal life-style of the suburb. The social critics of the 1950's were so preoccupied with assailing these rather synthetic substitutes for traditional forms of human interdependence that they lost sight of the underlying pathogenic forces that produced them. Medical symptoms usually result from attempts made by the body to counteract disease, and attacking such symptoms often aggravates and prolongs the illness. This appears to be the case with the feeble and self-defeating efforts of twentieth-century Americans to find themselves a viable social context.

The Moral Premises of Social Pathology

Carl M. Rosenquist

> Those who employ the social pathology perspective take an attitude toward social problems like that of the physician toward physical problems. They assume that society, like the individual, is an organism, and that there are normal and abnormal conditions for that organism.
>
> Such an approach, Rosenquist argues, is untenable, for there is simply no way to define objectively states of social pathology. First of all, very often the "health" of one sector of society depends heavily on the "ill-health" of other sectors. In addition, since society is not an organism, there is no necessary set of relationships by which to define health

From Carl M. Rosenquist, *Social Problems*, pp. 10–15, 20–22. Copyright © 1940 by Prentice-Hall, Inc. Englewood Cliffs, N.J. Reprinted by permission.

(as there is, for example, between the nervous system and the digestive system). For these reasons, statements about what is "normal" or "healthy" for society reflect the ideals of the speaker, rather than any objective truth.

The most familiar explanation of social problems uses the analogy between the biological and social organisms. The study of pathology presupposes the existence of an organism in which the symptoms of disease may be observed. For the biologist the organism is a plant or an animal; for the social pathologist, a society.[1] The study of pathology further presupposes a condition of normality in the organism from which disease may be regarded as a deviation. As to the meaning of normality, it will suffice at this point to say that it ordinarily refers to the operation of the various organs in such a way as to secure or promote the welfare of the organism as a whole. Since the nature of the functions involved is dependent upon the structure of the organs, it follows that normality and, consequently, pathology, vary according to the kind of organism concerned. In the biological field, this means that each species of plant or animal has its own peculiar set of diseases; in sociology, it means that social ills differ from society to society and, since societies change, from time to time within the same society.

Normal Society

In the study of pathological manifestations, it is necessary first to know and recognize normality. . . . [It] may be assumed that society exists for its members and that they have certain ideas as to what society should provide. To the extent that these expectations are realized, society may be spoken of as normal or, for the purposes of the analogy, as healthy. This conception of normality does not necessarily find its expression in actual experience. Probably no society has ever provided complete satisfaction for all of its members. Yet the requirement remains as an ideal, from which we measure deviations, referred to as social ills.

[1] That society is not an organism in the biological sense need not concern us here, but society must be seen as a mechanism of interacting parts if the concept of pathology is to be applied to a study of its ills.

When this concept of normality is compared with that of biology, a conspicuous difference is at once apparent. The animal organism is in health when as a whole it is functioning perfectly; the social organism is in health when all of its members are functioning perfectly. . . . It must be emphasized that the social organism exists for the benefit of the individuals who compose it, rather than for itself alone. Conceivably, a society might be healthy according to standards similar to those used in biology—that is, the group as a whole might be wealthy, successful in war, increasing in size, and long of life—but if the internal organization is based upon a system of exploitation in which some of the people make life miserable for the rest, the society is sick according to the usually accepted sociological viewpoint.

The Meaning of Pathology

. . . The discussion of pathology as ordinarily carried on makes it appear that disease is an enemy of the biological organism, existing outside the organism and always waiting for a favorable moment to launch an attack, just as a wolf prowls around a flock of sheep, waiting for the shepherd to relax his vigilance long enough to permit a raid on his charges. This notion has doubtless been strengthened by the discovery that micro-organisms are found in connection with many types of disease. To the human mind, with its strong predilection for personification, the minute organisms have appeared in the role of an attacking army bent on the destruction of its victims. Actually, the picture thus presented is far from the facts.

> Diseases are not entities: the classification of diseases is purely a matter of convenience: what are known as diseases are the results of what happens when the organism comes in contact with inimical agents.[2]

The word disease, then, does not properly refer to an attacking force, but to the response of the organism to certain conditions threatening its safety. The response consists of a series of physiological changes, described as the symptoms of the disease. They are but the indications that the organism has suffered from an injury or infection and is attempting to re-

[2] William A. White, *The Meaning of Disease*, p. 171. Baltimore: The Williams and Wilkins Company, 1926.

pair the damage. The symptoms are beneficent in character in
the sense that they show active resistance on the part of the organism. To attempt to remove them may harm the organism
instead of benefiting it. Disease may be tentatively defined
therefore as a process of readjustment. . . .

The Concept of Normality

Since biologists invariably define disease in terms of deviation from a state of health, it becomes imperative to define
health also. The definition of health as freedom from disease,
is, of course, of no value. Substitution of the word "normality"
does not remove the difficulty, for normality has no more specific meaning than health. It cannot mean the average condition of the organism, for perfect health is rarely if ever observed. Since normality does not exist as an actual condition, it
must obviously refer to an imaginary condition, found only in
the observer's mind. A brief inquiry shows this to be the case.
Health or normality is an ideal state unattained and probably
unattainable, but regarded as eminently desirable. It is taken
for granted that good health and, consequently, a long life,
are among the chief objectives of man, and that anything
which militates against its attainment is pathological. This
points plainly to the subjective and hedonistic elements in the
definition of normality. From his own experience, the individual comes to certain conclusions regarding his own welfare.
Sympathetically transferring his personal feelings to others, he
produces a general notion of the kind of physical condition he
considers ideal. To this he gives the name of normality. Not
satisfied with this, he extends his anthropomorphism to all
other forms of life, postulating norms for them as well as for
himself. With these norms established for a given species, he
can proceed at once to a study of its pathology. This is not to
say that normality thus determined is without value. On the
contrary, the results have amply justified working from postulates of this sort, as the triumphs of pathologists have shown
many times; but it can hardly be maintained that the procedure is scientific, if by scientific we mean objective. . . .

This fairly well describes the status of the "pathology" which
sociology has borrowed from biology. . . . As a basis for the

study of social pathology, a "healthy" society is set up as a norm, from which deviations are observed. Unhappily for the comfort of sociologists, it appears to be much more difficult to arrive at an agreement as to the health of societies than as to the health of individuals. In this connection society is, of course, contemplated in its organic aspects, that is, it is considered as a whole composed of interrelated parts. Yet it is impossible to overlook the fact that there can be no social "health" apart from the health of individual members of society, and the further fact that the nature of the organization of society is determined by the members themselves. For example, it is possible to find described in history societies which have proved themselves very able in conflict with other societies and with nature, so that they have flourished and endured over long periods. From the viewpoint of society as an organism such a group might well be considered "healthy" or normal, whereas its internal organization might be of such a sort as to keep the vast majority of the members in a state of social degradation. On the other hand, it is possible to find societies which, because of looser controls, are less efficient and less secure, but in which the individual members find life highly agreeable. There can be hardly a doubt as to which society the ordinary individual would prefer to live in, and probably we cannot consider that society diseased which is, from the individual's point of view, the most desirable of all. . . .

What then is the most desirable society? What are we to take as the norms or ideals from which we may diagnose our social ills? The answers offered us in the numerous utopias in our literature are by no means unanimous. Some have war and others have peace; some are capitalistic and others are communistic; some are religious and others are unreligious. All have forms of family and community life. Each of them reflects its author's ideas as to what was wrong with the society he lived in. The variety presented makes instantly clear the fact that even in the planning of a new society, in which the authors are limited only by the powers of their own imagination, no agreement in form is possible. And if we were to question all the people in the world as to which of the several existing societies they would prefer, we should probably find no conclusive vote for any. . . .

Conclusion

In view of all these difficulties, it may well be wondered how social problems can be studied at all. Obviously we have no norm, real or imaginary, upon which we can agree. Nor is it likely, in view of the constantly changing character of society, that a norm can be established. How can we know what in society is really pathological? The only answer is: we do not and cannot know.

There is, however, a way in which social problems may be studied without answering these questions. They may be treated, not as the study of variations from a norm, but as manifestations of society itself. From this viewpoint popular recognition of any social condition or process as bad, followed by an attempt to eliminate or cure it, serves as the criterion for its inclusion in a study of social problems. The writer merely accepts the judgment of public opinion. . . . The question to be answered is not, then, whether poverty or any other condition is bad for society, and if so what is to be done about it, but what are the conditions of society which large numbers of people regard as harmful and remediable. Is poverty found among them? If so, what are its manifestations? How does it affect the individual? What is being done to remedy it? To these matters we address ourselves. Social problems are nothing more nor less than those conditions or aspects of society which considerable numbers of people are trying to change.[3]

Questions for Discussion

1. Smith's statement appeared in 1911; Slater's, in 1970. What are the major differences between their statements?
2. What role did correctional workers play in the development of the social pathology perspective?
3. Does Rosenquist's critique apply to the contemporary social pathology approach exemplified by Slater and Kavolis? How does it apply or not apply? In what ways do you agree or disagree with Rosenquist?

[3] "A social problem . . . is determined by group sanction, being the judgment of a group concerning the efficiency of a type of social organization in its structure or function. It is within the realm of folkways, mores, and opinions." George A. Lundberg, Read Bain, and Nels Anderson, Editors, *Trends in American Sociology;* Harold A. Phelps, "Sociology and Social Work," p. 332. New York: Harper and Brothers, 1929. Reprinted by permission of the publishers.

4. What are some of the implications of the social pathology perspective for sociology in general? What do you yourself think about the approach?

Selected References

Gillin, John L. *Social Pathology*. 2nd ed. New York: D. Appleton-Century, 1939.
Gillin's book represents the turning point in pathology texts. This was perhaps the first social pathology book to "attempt to treat social maladjustments in a framework of sociological theory." The middle-class bias is less pervasive in Gillin's book than in other texts, and the theory is more eclectic. (For an example of the prominence of the middle-class bias in some social pathology textbooks, see Stuart Alfred Queen and Jennette Rowe Gruener, *Social Pathology: Obstacles to Social Participation*, 2nd ed. New York: Thomas Y. Crowell, 1940.)

Henderson, Charles Richmond. *Introduction to the Study of the Dependent, Defective, and Delinquent Classes, and of Their Social Treatment*. Boston: D. C. Heath & Co., 1909.
Henderson coined the expression "dependent, defective, and delinquent classes." The expression was quite popular in social pathology books for at least a generation. Henderson's book is typical of those that blame the characteristics of the individual for any violation of social rules.

Kavolis, Vytautas, ed. *Comparative Perspectives on Social Problems*. Boston: Little, Brown & Co., 1969.
Kavolis, particularly in the preface of this book, seeks to revive the term "social pathology" and give it a set of objective indices. Kavolis claims that the problems he includes in his collection are all (a) universally troublesome and (b) measurable in their consequences.

Mills, C. Wright. "The Professional Ideology of Social Pathologists." *American Journal of Sociology* 60 (September 1942), pp. 165–80.
A widely celebrated essay on the sociology of sociology. Mills points out that most writers on social pathology came from small towns and were middle-class in their outlook, pragmatic in their approach, and conservative in their politics. He attacks their studies for being atheoretical and heavily biased.

Rosenberg, Bernard, Israel Gerver, and William Howton, eds. *Mass Society in Crisis: Social Problems and Social Pathology*. 2nd ed. New York: Macmillan, 1971.
A book of readings compiled in the framework of the more recent perspective on social pathology. Included is "A New Look at Mills' Critique," by Emil Bend and Martin Vogelfanger.

3. Social Disorganization

The social disorganization perspective arose after World War I in response to a particular set of circumstances in both the larger society and the field of sociology. In this chapter, we look at the circumstances that gave rise to the social disorganization perspective, the sociologists who formulated it, and the basic features of the perspective.

Problems of Society

Migration, urban living, and factory work are certainly nothing new. The ancestors of the American Indians, for example, migrated from Siberia across the Bering Strait and down into the Americas. The ancient Greeks and Egyptians lived in cities. And the ancient Romans are said to have established some of the earliest factories.

After World War I, however, these processes—migration, urbanization, and industrialization—began to occur in the United States at an unprecedented pace. And as they did so, many previously recognized social problems such as poverty, delinquency and crime, mental illness, and alcoholism seemed to become more and more prevalent.

Migration, for example, produced considerable culture conflict both for European immigrants and for native American migrants (e.g., people moving from the rural South to the Northern cities). The European immigrants, for example, were likely to find considerable conflict between their native culture and the prevailing culture in their new home. Of course, many soon became "Americanized." Others, however, were less successful in the "Americanization process," and these people soon came to be seen as the source and substance of most American social problems. Urbanization also contributed to the sense of increasing social problems. The cities, for instance, included deviant subcultures that were not found in more rural areas—delinquent gangs, for example. Finally, industrialization brought with it many social problems. For example, working conditions were often poor, and technological advances put many people out of work.

Taken together, then, these three factors—migration, urbanization, and industrialization—established a broad social and cultural base for a host of undesirable conditions. Outgrowths of these conditions—such as crime, mental illness, alcoholism, drug addiction, and juvenile delinquency—all came to be treated in the social problems textbooks of the day. When these problems had been smaller in scale, the social pathology perspective had seemed adequate. As they increased, however, the pathology perspective seemed less useful. Concomitantly, sociology was facing new problems as a discipline. In coping with these problems—both in society and in sociology—sociologists fashioned the social disorganization perspective.

Problems of the Discipline

Any fledgling discipline faces a number of difficulties. It has to state a rationale for its existence, it has to formulate what it will do that other disciplines do not do, and it has to make clear what its relationship to other disciplines will be. During its formative period (up to 1918), sociology had not yet resolved these issues.

When the Frenchman Auguste Comte coined the term "sociology," he envisioned it as the queen of the sciences, encompassing all the other scientific disciplines.[1] But Emile Durkheim, battling two generations later to establish sociology as a university discipline in France, took a quite different tack: he

[1] Auguste Comte, *Positive Philosophy*, trans. Harriet Martineau (London: George Bell & Sons, 1896).

set out to make sociology a science with its own concepts and subject matter.[2]

Throughout its formative period, American sociology remained a hodgepodge of history, political science, economics, psychology, and social philosophy. It dealt with issues that overlapped these older disciplines or that they chose to ignore. Thus, some of the early critics called sociology a "science of leftovers." Throughout these years, sociology's concern with order, progress, and the philosophy of history ran strong.

As American sociology moved into its second period (1918 to 1935), it centered more and more on the formation of a scientific policy. Heavy emphasis was placed on the development of concepts and definitions, and much of this conceptual and definitional effort centered on showing how the subject matter of sociology differed from that of other disciplines.

The emergence of the social disorganization perspective during the 1920s reflects this effort to develop sociology as a scientific discipline. The very concept of social disorganization springs from a then-developing network of ideas centering on the concept of social organization. The notion of social organization implies, first of all, that there is a whole whose parts stand in some ordered relationship to one another. Secondly (and secondarily), it implies the concept of social disorganization—i.e., that the various parts can get out of phase with one another.

Central to this entire conceptualization, implicitly or explicitly, is the notion of *rules*. Rules define not only the different parts of society but also how they interrelate. And by focusing on rules, sociologists succeeded in defining their subject matter as different from that of any other discipline.

The social disorganization perspective emerged from this developing sociological viewpoint, and in time it came to be the most popular way of studying social problems. To be more specific, sociologists began to see social problems as an index of social disorganization; as they developed a body of sociological concepts to deal with social organization, they also developed sister concepts to describe and explain social disorganization. In any case, sociology began to bloom as a discipline with its own subject matter, its own concepts, and its own way of describing reality.

[2] Emile Durkheim, *The Rules of Sociological Method,* trans. Sarah Solovay and John Mueller (Chicago: University of Chicago Press, 1938).

Differences Between the Pathology and Disorganization Perspectives

Compared with the earlier social pathology perspective, the social disorganization perspective is more complex, more intellectually distinct, and considerably more systematic—benefiting, of course, from the greater maturity of sociology as a discipline at the time it developed. It is instructive, at this point, to compare these two perspectives in terms of their subject matters, vocabularies, methods, and concerns with practical applications. The social pathologists, it will be recalled, studied social problems by looking at the failings of individuals and institutions. Their concepts and vocabularies, however, were borrowed from other disciplines, most notably medicine. Their methods were more philosophical than scientific. Finally, they wanted action; they wanted to apply their discoveries to the solution of social problems.

Writers using the social disorganization perspective, in contrast, studied social problems by examining social rules. They developed their own conceptualizations and vocabularies. They became more concerned with development of theory and with precision in methodology. Finally, their emphasis on theory led them to be more concerned with acquiring knowledge than with finding practical solutions to social problems.

This comparison of the pathology and disorganization perspectives brings up the chronic division of opinion in sociology regarding whether sociologists should themselves make moral judgments or should merely study the moral judgments of others. Pathologists made moral judgments with regard to institutions and individuals alike. Disorganization writers, in contrast, chose to study moral judgments in a more detached, "objective" manner. (The social disorganization perspective, however, has since been criticized for not being objective. Critics have charged that nonconforming ways of life are often called disorganized when, in reality, they simply represent a different form of social organization. See, for example, the Clinard reading in this chapter.)

The Major Social Disorganization Theorists

The social disorganization perspective as we know it today stems largely from the writings of Charles H. Cooley, W. I.

Thomas and Florian Znaniecki, and William F. Ogburn. To be sure, the idea of social disorganization has been considerably refined since these men first wrote about it. However, the major influences on current social disorganization writers can all be traced back to these four. All were primarily theorists, and all sought to explain why individuals sometimes fail to obey rules. And as the following discussions show, they all pictured social problems as a function of social disorganization.

Cooley. A very early but still influential writer, Cooley made some important conceptual contributions to the social disorganization perspective. First, he formulated the distinction between primary and secondary group relations. Primary relations refer to personal and enduring face-to-face relationships.[3] Secondary relationships, on the other hand, denote less frequent, impersonal contacts. Given this distinction, sociologists quickly saw that the movement from rural to urban areas was accompanied by a breakdown in primary group controls. Second, Cooley conceptualized social disorganization as the disintegration of traditions. He argued that the worst aspect of social disorganization is that "the absence of social standards is likely to lower . . . [a person's] plane of achievement and throw him back upon sensibility and other primitive impulses." [4]

Thomas and Znaniecki. In their major work on the Polish immigrant to America,[5] Thomas and Znaniecki defined social disorganization as the breakdown of the influence of rules upon the individual. The bulk of their work consists of letters written by Polish immigrants to friends and relatives back home in Poland. The letters all give testimony to the conflict of cultures, ethnic as well as generational. According to Thomas and Znaniecki, the Polish immigrant faced either no rules or too many rules. In the case of a paucity of rules, the immigrant had no means of defining his or her situation. In the case of a plenitude of rules, the rules were either unclear or in conflict with each other. Thus, the immigrant often did not know how to behave in America and lacked mutual under-

[3] Charles Horton Cooley, *Human Nature and the Social Order* (New York: Charles Scribner's Sons, 1902).
[4] Charles Horton Cooley, *Social Organization: A Study of the Larger Mind* (New York: Charles Scribner's Sons, 1909), p. 348.
[5] William I. Thomas and Florian Znaniecki, *The Polish Peasant in Europe and America,* 2 vols. (New York: Alfred A. Knopf, 1927).

standing with native Americans. In their study of Polish immigrants, Thomas and Znaniecki conceptualized the experiences of millions who immigrated into the United States. They
also indicated that a variety of social problems (e.g., delinquency, crime, mental illness, and alcoholism) could be attributed in large part to the failure of the immigrant family to
control its members.

Ogburn. Ogburn's contribution lies primarily in his notion of
cultural lag.[6] The different parts of a culture are interdependent, Ogburn said, and when different parts change at different rates, one part can get out of phase with another and
produce disorder. Usually, Ogburn observed, people accept
new tools more readily than new ideas; thus, material culture
changes much faster than nonmaterial culture. Stated another
way, changes in customs and rules tend to lag behind those in
technology, which is what Ogburn means by "cultural lag."
The principal source of social disorganization, according to
Ogburn, is this uneven rate of cultural change.

Characteristics of the Social Disorganization Perspective

People who work with this perspective view society as a social system—a complex, dynamic whole whose parts are coor-
dinated. When events change one part of the system, there is a
corresponding need for adjustment in other parts. "Social disorganization" refers to lack of adjustment, or poor adjustment, between the parts. The major elements of the social disorganization perspective are as follows:

Definition. Social disorganization is conceived of as a failure of
rules. Three major types of disorganization are *normlessness,
culture conflict,* and *breakdown.* With normlessness, no rules
exist on how to act. With culture conflict, at least two opposing
sets of rules exist on how to act. In such situations, persons
who act in terms of one set of expectations may in so doing violate another set of expectations. Breakdown is a variation on
this same theme. Here rules exist, but conformity to them ei-

[6] William F. Ogburn, *Social Change with Respect to Culture and Original Nature*
(New York: B. W. Huebsch, 1922), pp. 199–280.

ther fails to produce the promised rewards or yields punishments instead.

Causes. The root cause of social disorganization is, broadly speaking, social change. As changes occur, the parts of the social system get out of tune with one another.

Conditions. The parts of a social system are never perfectly in tune. Nevertheless, there is usually a dynamic equilibrium. Any condition that upsets the equilibrium may precipitate social disorganization. Such conditions include technical, demographic, or cultural changes that generate social change (i.e., a change in social relationships).

Consequences. The social disorganization perspective predicts outcomes for the system and for persons in it. For persons, social disorganization produces stress, which in turn produces "personal disorganization"—e.g., mental illness, alcoholism.[7] For the system, social disorganization may have three types of consequences. First, there can be change in the system (i.e., some response or adaptation may bring the various parts of the system back into equilibrium). Second, the system can continue to operate in a steady state (i.e., the disorganization may remain but the system continues to function anyway). Third, the system may break down (i.e., the disorganization may be so disruptive that it destroys the system).

Solutions. Attempts to reduce social disorganization can be put into effect once the proper diagnosis has been made. Thus, parts of the system that are out of phase can be brought back into equilibrium—e.g., technical changes can be slowed down.

Summary

After World War I, American sociologists strove to establish sociology as an independent scientific discipline with its own concepts and subject matter. At the same time, migration, urban growth, and technological change seemed to be produc-

[7] See, for example, Robert E. L. Faris and H. Warren Dunham, *Mental Disorders in Urban Areas: An Ecological Study of Schizophrenia and Other Psychoses* (Chicago: University of Chicago Press, 1939).

ing a number of social problems, and sociologists worked hard to devise a set of terms to describe and explain these problems.

Cooley taught a generation of sociologists to look for the signs of a breakdown of traditions, especially as reflected in the decreased hold of small, intimate groups on their members. Thomas and Znaniecki devised an important set of concepts and, in their study of Polish immigrants to America, showed how moving to a strange city in a foreign land disrupts families, sharpens generational conflict, and increases chances of criminality and mental illness. Ogburn examined the effects of technology on social organization, developed his influential theory of cultural lag, and fostered a whole school of technological determinists.

Briefly stated, social disorganization denotes a failure of rules. Social change is usually viewed as the cause, and technological, demographic, and cultural changes are viewed as the precipitating conditions. Personal disorganization and disequilibrium of the social system are seen as consequences of social disorganization, and the solution for disorganization is to bring the features of the social system back into equilibrium.

The Rules of the Game

Albert K. Cohen

Many writers have used the concept of social disorganization simply to describe situations that violate their own personal values. Cohen, in the valuable statement below, tries to develop a more analytically useful notion of social disorganization.

According to Cohen, in order to understand social disorganization one must first examine the components of social organization. The basic conditions of social organization are the existence of rules to define events and the motivation of people to follow the rules. With regard to the first condition, social disorganization results from no

From Albert K. Cohen, "The Study of Social Disorganization and Deviant Behavior," Chapter 21 of *Sociology Today*, edited by Robert K. Merton, Leonard Broom, and Leonard S. Cottrell, Jr., pp. 474–83. Copyright © 1959 by Basic Books, Inc. Reprinted by permission of the publisher.

rules, vague rules, or conflicting rules. With regard to the second con-dition, social disorganization may result, Cohen implies, from inad-equate socialization or a failure in social control. Cohen also points out the differences between social disorganization and deviant behav-ior and concludes that deviant behavior does not necessarily produce social disorganization.

The sociology of social disorganization is in an even worse state than the sociology of deviant behavior. Few terms in soci-ology are defined so variously and obscurely as social disorga-nization. Values intrude themselves so persistently and in-sidiously into definition and usage that the concept is often regarded as a term of evaluation and therefore unscientific. It is difficult to determine what, if any, is the line of demarcation between social disorganization and deviant behavior. Some sociologists even question whether social disorganization exists and suggest that there are only different kinds of organiza-tion. However, we believe that social disorganization can be defined in a way that is value-free, that is independent of the definition of deviant behavior, and that, at the same time, des-ignates a set of crucial theoretical problems. (This definition owes a great deal to a paper by Dr. Harold Garfinkel.[1])

Let us begin by noting what we consider to be some ex-amples of social disorganization. A children's ball game is disrupted when their only ball falls into the creek. A meeting of a learned society is disrupted when some members of the local Chamber of Commerce appear and announce that the room has been reserved for their use during that hour. A mili-tary mission is disrupted when the leader is killed and no one steps forward to assume command. In all these situations some activity has been going on and has been disrupted or in-terrupted. Our task now is to formulate a general definition of an activity or of an interaction system which enables us to mark the boundaries, as it were, between one activity and another, to state whether a particular act is or is not constitu-tive of a particular activity, and to determine whether an activ-ity is or is not in progress, has or has not been disrupted.

We shall begin, as does Garfinkel, with the game as our paradigm of an activity or interaction system and show that

[1] Harold Garfinkel, "Trust as a Condition of Stable Concerted Action," paper delivered at the annual meetings of the American Sociological Society, 1957.

those characteristics which define organization and disorganization for a game are equally applicable to nongame activities.

The Game

In the first place, the names of games are taken from the
language of the participants. They designate sets of events
which the participants perceive as belonging together and
jointly constituting one thing, a certain kind of game. Therefore, to determine whether a particular kind of game is going
on, we must use the participants' own criteria for defining that
sort of game.

These criteria are given by the rules of the game, which designate certain classes of events and state the standards for assigning events to these classes. All events which can be so classified and only those events are possible game events. Thus a
swing that misses and a hit ball that goes out of bounds both
fall in the class "strike" in the game "baseball." Game events
may include not only actions of the players but also events in
the situation of action. For example, the advent of darkness
during a baseball game is a game event if it is anticipated by
the rules and a class of situations exists to which it is assigned
by the rules.

Furthermore—and this is crucial—the rules specify an order
among these classes of events; to constitute the game in question, events must conform to that order. Many concretely different sequences may conform to the order of a given kind of
game. At a given stage of the game, a player on second base
may steal third or stay on second. He may not proceed directly
to bat, for this would not be a game event in the game of baseball. Note that the order of events enters into the definition of
an event. For example, whether or not hitting a ball out of
bounds is a strike depends on how many strikes a batter already has against him.

The rules also provide a criterion for determining whether
the game is in progress or has been interrupted. If the "constitutive order of events"—an order conforming to the constitutive rules—is interrupted, the game is interrupted or, as we
shall use the word, disorganized. If the game terminates in accordance with the rules of the game—that is, if it culminates in

a state of affairs defined by the rules as "the end of the game"—we simply say that the game is over. But if the constitutive order of events is breached at any other point, if the game is neither over nor in progress, it is disorganized. If, for example, a brawl develops in which all the players become involved, the game is disorganized. (A brawl, in turn, can be regarded as a game subject to disorganization on its own terms; for example, police may break up a "rumble.")

Deviant Behavior and Disorganization

A property of the rules of the game which is of the most fundamental importance is the fact that these rules are definitional statements. They do not tell us what is the right or the wrong thing to do; they merely tell us whether what we are doing is part of a given game. There are also rules of right conduct, morality, fair play—what we have called institutionalized expectations. But violations of these rules of right conduct, if they are covered by the rules of the game, are themselves game events and need not constitute a breach in the constitutive order of events. It may, for example, be forbidden to step over a certain line, to strike another player, to spit on the ball. If the constitutive rules designate such events as "fouls" or "cheating" and prescribe a penalty, events and penalty are part of the constitutive order. In short, deviant behavior is not defined by the same rules that define game events and therefore does not, merely by virtue of being deviant, constitute disorganization.

This is not to say that deviant behavior may not precipitate disorganization. If a player, in clear violation of the rules of good sportsmanship, stalks off the field and the constitutive rules have failed to anticipate such situations, if the rules prescribe that there shall be a certain number of players on both sides and there are no replacements available, or if the rules are obscure and there is disagreement as to how the situation is to be defined, the resulting situation is, at worst, meaningless and, at best, ambiguous. In any case, it creates at least temporary disorganization. Deviant behavior, therefore, may or may not precipitate disorganization, but it is not *ipso facto* disorganization.

Games and Nongames

What we have said of games may be said of the nongame activities of everyday life as well, although the constitutive rules are less likely to be labeled rules and codified, and they may not command the same measure of agreement. The set of constitutive rules of a military operation is the plan of the operation. (Many of its details are provided by an implicit context of army regulations, field manuals, and the subculture of the military unit concerned.) This plan sets forth a sequence of events the fulfillment of which constitutes the operation. In like manner, the operations of a railroad, an industrial organization, a public utility, or a family resolve themselves into sets of recurrent and interlocking activities, each of which is defined by its respective constitutive rules. The range of alternatives possible at any given stage of an activity, and therefore the variety of concrete sequences that are compatible with the constitutive rules, varies from one type of activity to another. The definition of a church service, for example, may require adherence to a rather rigid order of events; the definition of a seminar can be met by a wide range of concretely different sequences.

The matter becomes clearer when we consider how the same set of interactions can be analyzed into different activities. In a basketball game, one of the teams may have a particular strategy, a concerted plan which takes certain contingencies into account and prescribes appropriate action for designated players in the event of those contingencies. Such a strategy has the characteristics of the rules of the game. The order prescribed by the strategy may be breached if the opposing team creates a situation that is not contemplated by the plan. In this case, the execution of the strategy has been disorganized. Nothing has happened, however, that is incompatible with the constitutive rules of basketball; the basketball game, therefore, has not been disorganized. Similarly, the strategy of management or of labor in a collective-bargaining process may be disorganized without disorganizing the collective-bargaining process itself. Again, the disruption of the operations of a commercial firm or even the failure of the firm as a result of unanticipated changes in the market need not imply any interruption in the market as a system defined by its own constitutive rules. It follows, therefore, that in speaking of organization or disorganization we must be careful to specify the game, activity, or interaction system in question.

An activity may consist in an order among lesser or included activities, each of which can be defined in terms of its own constitutive rules and is subject to disorganization on its own terms. Disorganization of one of these included activities, however, may or may not result in disorganization of the constitutive order that defines the more inclusive activity. For example, the operations of one plant of an industrial concern or one unit of a fire department may be disorganized as a result of a natural disaster. If, however, another plant or another unit can be mobilized to do the same job as the disorganized member of the system, there may be no breach of the organization of the larger activity.

Different activities may be interdependent and even interpenetrating in a variety of ways. It is possible to draw up rules for two games to be played simultaneously on the same checkerboard such that every physical event that is a move in one game is a move—that is, a game event—in the other. A winning move in one game may be a losing move in the other, but the continuity of neither game is disorganizing with reference to the other. In a perfectly organized society, all activities would be so organized that every event in one activity would be a possible event in others or would help to create the conditions necessary for the continuity of other activities. As a matter of fact, in every viable social system there must be some approximation to this state of affairs. However, this kind of articulation is always problematical. Every system requires time, space, personnel, and equipment for the unfolding of its constitutive order, but different systems compete for these resources, and the availability of these resources to one system may depend upon their denial to another system to which they are equally necessary. Thus, the execution of a business operation or the very survival of a business may depend, on the one hand, upon the continued orderly functioning—that is, functioning in accordance with their own constitutive rules—of the firms from which it buys and sells and, on the other hand, upon the denial to its competitors of the materials and customers upon which their own operations or survival depend.

The foregoing definition of social disorganization is, we think, congruent with usage. In describing military routs and

natural disasters—situations in which there is consensus that
the word disorganization is relevant—we say that people
"freeze," "panic," "flounder," "give up," "run away," "change
their plans," or "stand around helplessly." All these behaviors
disrupt or at least threaten the constitutive order of the ongoing activity; therefore, they are themselves, or at least they
precipitate, disorganization—a fact generally recognized by
making these behaviors synonymous with disorganization in
ordinary English usage.

Disorganization as we have defined it can occur on a less
dramatic scale and with less dramatic consequences in any
social setting—in the family, on the job, in the classroom.
More than this, in every interaction system, no matter how stable and tranquil, the threat of disorganization, like the threat
of deviant behavior, is always present, and the mechanisms for
averting it and nipping it in the bud pose a problem that is ev-
erywhere relevant. As a matter of fact, our definition of organization as an order of events conforming to a set of constitutive rules implies our definition of disorganization as a breach
of that order. The two terms, therefore, define a single field—
organization-disorganization—as do conformity and deviant
behavior.

The poverty of theory in the area of social disorganization
reflects the lack of clarity and agreement with respect to the
demarcation of the field. For this reason we have devoted a
good deal of space to defining disorganization, to clarifying its
relationship to deviant behavior, and to showing how the use
of the concept as here defined helps us to analyze more
rigorously and, we think, more fruitfully the sequences of behavior that are ordinarily described as "social disorganization."
The test of any definition, including that presented here, will
lie, of course, in the amenability of the field, as demarcated by
that definition, to systematic theory.

The Conditions of Disorganization. Implicit in any definition of a
field is a way of formulating its outstanding problems. The
problem of clarifying the conditions under which disorganization occurs can be approached by first asking: What are
the preconditions of *organization*? If organization is an order
of events conforming to a set of constitutive rules, then organization implies two conditions. First, it presupposes that action unfolds in such a way that, at any stage or phase of the

system, the situations that the participants confront and the alternative possibilities of action can be defined by the rules. Secondly, it presupposes that the participants are motivated to "play the game"—that is, to assume the perspectives provided by the rules and to select their actions from the constitutive possibilities designated by the rules. Conversely, disorganization must arise when one or both of these two conditions are not satisfied. First, it arises when the situations that the participants confront cannot be defined as system events or when there is no clear definition of the constitutive possibilities of action. This is a situation of normlessness, anomie, or meaninglessness. Secondly, it arises when the participants are not motivated, when their values, interests, and aims are not integrated with the requirements for continuity of the interaction system.

Localized conditions of anomie or failure of motivation, however, are not, in and of themselves, disorganization. Nor do all events which fall outside the constitutive order necessarily breach that order. For example, an individual soldier may panic and start running about wildly, an event which is not contemplated by the plan and which falls outside the scope of the plan. Yet the loss or defection of one soldier may not affect the orderly development called for by the plan. By contrast, however, the failure of one battery in one radio, if that radio is the only means of communication with a command center, may result in complete confusion and disorganization. In the absence of instructions, the situation and the behavior it calls for from each participant cannot be defined. There is a general state of anomie and a complete breach of the constitutive order.

The broader systemic repercussions of an event depend upon the way in which it is articulated with the rest of the system. Local conditions of anomie or failure of motivation may spread, involving more and more areas of the system, until they reach a vital spot and destroy the minimal conditions necessary for the continuity of the events called for by the plan. On the other hand, systems may have mechanisms for walling off the affected areas so that contagion cannot spread to involve those events that are definitive of the constitutive order. Systems may have mechanisms for restoring organization—for example, by sending in replacements for confused, incompetent, or disaffected personnel—or for reinforcing motivation by bringing powerful sanctions to bear. Systems may have alternative arrangements for producing certain events that are necessary for the constitutive order, which arrangements go into effect when some segment of the system breaks down. All these mechanisms, in turn, depend upon mechanisms for gathering and transmitting information so that incipient or threatening disorganization can be spotted and the appropriate steps taken to halt or avert it.

Anomie and Failure of Motivation. Anomie and failure of motivation are of such central importance to a theory of disorganization that certain additional comments are called for. Anomie may take a number of forms: confrontation by a situation for which there are no relevant rules, vagueness or ambiguity of the relevant rules, or lack of consensus on which rules are relevant and on the interpretation of rules. However, anomie depends not only on the structure of the set of constitutive rules but also on the situations which the system encounters. No set of rules covers all the situations which might conceivably arise. The fact that the rules do not cover certain conceivable situations spells anomie *only if those situations do in fact arise.* Control of anomie, therefore, may depend on one of two conditions. On the one hand, given the situation, it depends upon the existence and clarity of the relevant rules. On the other hand, given the rules, it depends upon the extent to which the system, in interaction with its environment, generates situations for which the constitutive rules provide definitions. This implies that a system capable of maintaining organization only under a narrowly limited set of conditions may nonetheless be very durable, provided that it has sufficient control over its environment to guarantee to itself the conditions it requires, or that some other system, through *its* functioning, can guarantee those conditions. The "wisdom of the body" in maintaining the constancy of its "internal environment" is an appropriate analogy.

One other property which a system of rules may possess should be noted. When a given situation may be defined in more than one way—that is, when there is more than one relevant rule—the rules themselves may specify priorities among rules or other criteria for resolving the ambiguity. When situations are ambiguous or meaningless, the rules may provide rules for making rules—for example, by designating leaders whose definitions are, by the rules, authoritative and valid for all participants.

The theoretical problems implied in failure of motivation and in mechanisms for averting that failure also need clarification. Here we shall limit ourselves to some observations on institutional elements in motivation.

Deviant behavior and conformity, we have said, are not definitive of disorganization and organization. This is not to say that moral considerations are not highly relevant to organization and disorganization through the part they play in motivation. It is difficult to conceive of a system in which the incentive to assume one's role and play one's part in accordance with the constitutive rules does not require, to some extent at least, the backing of a sense of moral obligation and the assumption that others also feel morally bound. Hobbes' Leviathan, the most impressive attempt to conceive such a system, is empirically impossible.

However, a sense of moral obligation is only one factor in motivation. Presumably, even a Nazi concentration camp could not function without some moral discipline among the jailers themselves, but the stability and viability of its constitutive order do not presuppose that the prisoners share the moral sentiments of their jailers. The relevant question for a theory of social disorganization, therefore, is this: How does the relative importance of different types of motivation—for example, moral obligation, force, and coercion—vary with the type of system, the sector within the system, and the situation within which the system functions?

But the relationship between motivation and conformity to institutionalized expectations is more subtle than this. There may well be situations in which deviant behavior is organizing and conformity disorganizing. Under certain conditions, choice of the institutionally sanctioned constitutive possibility may lead to organizational breakdown, and choice of an institutionally condemned alternative can alone avert this breakdown. For example, the procurement of certain supplies may be essential for the continuity of a certain activity. This procurement may be regulated by certain institutionalized expectations which, under the range of conditions ordinarily encountered, serve their purpose quite well. Under other conditions, however, conformity to these institutionally prescribed procedures will not work or will result in fatal delays in procurement. What used to be called "moonlight requisitioning" in the Army was at times the only method of procurement compatible with the execution of a mission or even the routine functioning of some operation. Too delicate a G.I. conscience was destructive of organization.

There is much more to be said about motivation, but our object is only to indicate in a general way the complexity of the relationship of motivation, and especially institutional elements in motivation, to social organization and disorganization, and the nature of the problems to be explored.

Moral Norms Without Enforcement

George C. Homans

In this study of a small town called "Hilltown," Homans demonstrates that moral norms, to be effective, must be backed by social control. Traditionally, frequent social contact among Hilltowners reinforced their moral norms, mainly through gossip. As changes in life style made contact less frequent, however, Hilltowners lost their sense of clearly agreed upon right and wrong. They became increasingly indifferent to their neighbors, and they lost interest in small-town gossip. Without reinforcement, the traditional norms lost their status in Hilltowners' eyes, and the eventual result was normlessness.

. . . We shall look first at changes in the environment in which Hilltown as a group has survived. All these changes have been mentioned; we need only cite them briefly. In the first place, the Hilltowners themselves brought about important changes in their physical environment. The land was cleared; the barns and houses built. The soil, once quite rich but always shallow, became depleted beyond the possibility of recovery by ordinary Yankee methods of farming. The forests were cut off, only timber for cordwood remaining.

Many other important changes, outside the control of Hilltowners, took place in the physical and technical environment. In particular, transportation was improved in scope, speed, and carrying capacity far beyond anything known at the beginning of the nineteenth century. Perhaps the most important event in the social history of Hilltown, and even in that of New England, was the opening of through railroads to the Great Lakes and the Ohio Valley. This meant that the products of Hilltown farms and shops had to compete in a national market with the products of richer areas. Later the appearance of the hard-surfaced road, the automobile, and the truck hastened the same process, but at the same time enabled Hilltowners to sell perishable produce, such as milk and chickens, more widely than they had before, and, with the rise of factory towns in the neighborhood, allowed them to sleep in town but work and play outside.

The physical and technical changes in the nation at large stimulated change in another field, the national standard of living. By a national standard of living we do not mean actual expenditures for different kinds of goods, but the scale of expenditure that many people feel to be appropriate: the standard of living is one of the norms of a society. Suppose the people of one part of the country—Hollywood is a good example at the present day—are able to buy certain kinds of houses, clothes, gadgets, and entertainment that other people have not yet enjoyed. The knowledge of this fact is then, in one way and another, transmitted to, and acts as an influence on, the people of hundreds of other communities. They develop a new level of aspiration for the enjoyment of material goods. Certainly the rising standard of living of the nineteenth and twentieth centuries taught the Hilltowners to aspire to something better than subsistence farming. And national standards in such matters as road maintenance, poor relief, and children's schooling became so high that Hilltown could not meet those standards without help from outside. A concomitant of a rising standard of living is an increase in the scope and power of state and national government.

Finally, the Hilltowners were communicants in what the anthropologists would call New England culture. Its norms, far from checking the influence of rising living standards, encouraged Yankees to attain them. This effect of the cultural environment may be hard to describe but it cannot be ignored. We have said that the Yankees were, in effect, mere squatters on the land, content to till the soil only so long as no better opportunity presented itself. Unlike the French-

Canadians, they were not indoctrinated in devotion to family, land, church, and tradition. Instead, their spiritual leaders, from John Wycliffe through Calvin to Emerson, had taught them for centuries the value of self-reliance and individual decision in the conduct of life. Translated from the spiritual plane to the half-conscious assumptions of everyday life, conveyed from parent to child, from teacher to pupil, from minister to churchgoer and even, for the Yankees were readers and their literature was flourishing, from writer to reader, this doctrine encouraged a conviction that every person should "make something of himself," "get ahead in the world," and submit to no group controls that might prevent his attaining these ends. At times Yankees seemed to believe, not that wealth came next to godliness, but that the two were identical. We are not arguing that even the kind of norms taught to French-Canadians will keep men subsistence farmers in the face of a rising standard of living. After all, a norm alone is not enough to preserve behavior unchanged; controls must back up the norm. We are arguing that the norms instilled in Yankees positively encouraged them to pursue the characteristic goals of American civilization in the nineteenth and twentieth centuries.

In short, the changes in the technical and physical environment made Hilltowners poorer, in comparison with other people, than they had once been, while the changes in the cultural environment made them anxious to get richer.

The External System

We turn now from the environment to the external system of social relationships in Hilltown, that is, the relationships determined by the survival of the group in its environment. We will remember that the sentiments entering the external system are those that men bring to a group rather than those that result from their membership in the group. These sentiments are often called individual self-interest. It is clear that in the course of Hilltown's history, *the number and strength of the sentiments that led members of the group to collaborate with other members had declined.* When the land had been cleared, and the barns and houses raised, the need for neighbors to work together became much less than it had been. As transportation improved, local industry declined, and mill towns grew up round about, the interests of Hilltowners led them to take part in organizations, such as markets and factories, outside the town rather than inside it.

At the same time, *the number of activities that members of the group carried on together decreased.* It is revealing just to count the number of activities in which Hilltowners collaborated with their fellow townsmen in the early part of the nineteenth century and then to count the ones that were still carried on in 1945. The farm bees had gone; farming itself was in decline; the local industries, first the small shops and then the factories, had been unable to survive; the general stores, once their customers began to trade in larger centers, lost money until finally only one of them was left. Though town government and town meeting remained, their activities were greatly curtailed. Militia training and the management of church affairs had vanished altogether; control of highways, schools, and relief was greatly reduced. Hilltown no longer sent its own representative to the state legislature—it was merely part of a larger electoral district. Finally, the church itself had been broken by schism.

This does not mean, of course, that individual Hilltowners had nothing to do. It does mean that they had much less to do with other Hilltowners. As the number of activities that members of the group carried on together declined, *so the frequency of interaction between members of the group decreased.* The sentiments, activities, and interactions of Hilltowners had become centrifugal rather than centripetal.

The Internal System

The decline in the external system was accompanied by a decline in the internal. In studying the Bank Wiring Observation Room, we saw that when the wiremen were "thrown together" in the room, they soon developed "social" sentiments, activities, and interactions, over and above those necessary for the accomplishment of the wiring job itself. But if the process can run in one direction, it can also run in the other. *As the frequency of interaction between the members of a group decreases in the external system, so the frequency of interaction decreases in the internal system.* If we had known this rule and had

been watching Hilltown at the turn of the century and af-
terwards, we should have been able to predict what happened.
In a comparison of the Hilltown of 1850 or even 1900 with
the Hilltown of 1945, even the crudest observations reveal an
enormous impoverishment of social life. At the later date,
there was much less informal visiting, and there were fewer
parties. The decline was so great that some persons, particularly in the upper group, saw almost nobody outside of business. The fraternal orders disappeared, and the men stopped
spending the time of day in the general store. The social occasions, such as church suppers, connected with the formal
organs of Hilltown life, were much less frequent than they
had once been. Even town meeting and church services were
sparsely attended. Once again, it is important to state, in order
to avoid misunderstanding, that this does not necessarily
imply any lack of social life on the part of individual Hilltowners. It does imply that a citizen of the town today has
fewer contacts with other Hilltowners than his ancestor had in
the past. And it may imply something more, namely that, inside Hilltown or outside, the social life of an individual is
made up of fewer occasions at every one of which substantially
the same persons appear. There are fewer groups that come
near being exclusive.

Just as an increase in the frequency of interaction between
the members of a group will bring about an increase in the intensity of the sentiments they feel toward one another, *so a
decrease in the frequency of interaction will bring about a decrease in
the strength of interpersonal sentiments.* In Hilltown this rule
seems to have held good for sentiments of antagonism as well
as for sentiments of friendliness. Both retreated toward some
neutral value. The words of informants suggest that, if there
was less mutual good feeling in 1845 than in 1945, there was
also, in certain fields, less mutual bad feeling. Certainly the attitudes of a townsman toward a member of a church different
from his own were much more moderate. People were more
nearly indifferent to one another. Again, this does not mean
that people did not talk about one another. There is no evidence that gossip was in abeyance, but the gossip did not carry
the same emotional tone.

This we should have been able to predict from what we
know already. We have seen in the Bank Wiring group, and it
is a commonplace of small-town life, that a sharp division into

subgroups is quite compatible with a definite unity of the group as a whole. We should expect then that, if the unity of the group as a whole disintegrates, the division into subgroups disintegrates too. Something like this we find in Hilltown. If, in 1945, there was less positive antagonism dividing one sub-group from another than there had been in 1845, this did not bring positive good feeling within the group as a whole but rather emotional indifference, that is, the absence of social or-ganization.

Norms and Social Class

The emotional indifference of persons toward one another may increase through two processes, one direct and the other indirect. Sheer decline in the frequency of interaction may be one: a man may have a hard time feeling strongly about some-one he does not see. But the decline may also affect sen-timents through the medium of norms. No more than other aspects of the social system do norms exist in a vacuum. Norms—notions of proper forms of behavior—are not left un-touched by real behavior. The degree to which norms are held in common by the members of a group must bear a relation to the frequency of interaction of the members, and the definite-ness of norms, to the frequency with which the activities, whose standard form they describe, are repeated. Thus in Hilltown, as elsewhere, *a decrease in the frequency of interaction between the members of a group and in the number of activities they participate in together entails a decline in the extent to which norms are common and clear.* In Hilltown this process is best illustrated in the decay of the Protestant churches, the guardians of the most important norms. The disintegration of the community led to a weakening of the norms and this in turn to a weaken-ing of the churches. But the circle is vicious, and the weaken-ing of the churches led to a further weakening of the norms. Through ritual and preaching, churches drill people in norms, so that any decline in the churches contributes to social disintegration, since fewer people get the old thorough train-ing in social standards. We can recognize this process at work in Hilltown, while still admitting that a general decline in the attitudes supporting the Protestant churches in America con-tributed to the decline in this single community. At least one point is clear: in the Hilltown of 1945 one important factor in the indifference of persons toward one another was their lack of an accepted standard for judging one another's behavior. A person is ready to look down on someone who has acted wrongly, but what if there is no definition of wrong? . . . .

Social Control

. . . Social control is not a separate department of group life; it is not a "function" that the group performs, or that someone performs for it. Instead, control, to a greater or lesser degree, is inherent in the everyday relationships between the members of the group. Now it is clear that social control was weaker in the Hilltown of 1945 than in the Hilltown of the nineteenth century. We do not have as much evidence as we should like, but we have enough. Reactions to the sexual irresponsibility of the young and to the misappropriation of town funds were very different in the two eras. When the tax collector, a few years ago, went off with town money, he was, to be sure, caught and put in jail, but so far as the town was concerned, nothing happened. The townspeople did nothing to catch him, and no one in town felt bound to make good the loss. When he got out of jail, he came back to town and was received as though everything was the same as before; no one was indignant and refused to associate with him; his social standing did not suffer. In short his action had none of the social consequences it would have had in an earlier generation. Yet it is a definition of stable equilibrium in a group that when a norm is violated something does happen. If a change takes place in a single element of behavior, there is a change in the other elements, and that of a certain kind: one tending to restore the previous state of the system. In the example we are using, the mere return of the funds would not have been enough to restore the previous state. If that had been enough, the equilibrium of Hilltown could have been preserved by a bonding company. Something more was needed: the supremacy of the violated norm should have been re-established, and this certainly did not take place.

The reaction of the town to the pregnancy of young women before marriage was of much the same kind. But let us be perfectly clear. Although we use, for convenience, such words as "decline" and "disintegration," we are not taking a moral stand here. The point we are making is not that sexual continency in the young is, by absolute standards, a particularly valuable norm, but rather that it had once been a Hilltown norm and in 1945 was one no longer. There are plenty of societies in which the young people enjoy sexual freedom before marriage and in which, at the same time, social control is strong. The norms of these societies are not those of old-time New England, and yet a breach of the norms, such as they are, is at once met by a strong reaction. Hilltown, on the contrary, had been losing its old norms, and the controls associated with them, without acquiring others to take their place. No doubt we exaggerate, but this seems to have been the general direction of change.

We observe the fact that social control had weakened; *if, moreover, social control is implicit in the relationships of the social system, any change in the strength of control must be determined by changes in the relationships.* And this is just what we can begin to see in Hilltown. Control ultimately is a matter of the punishment or reward of individuals. If social interaction is rewarding to a man, then loss of social interaction will hurt him. But if loss of social interaction—that is, avoidance—does not follow a breach of a norm, where is the punishment, especially when, as in Hilltown, the frequency of interaction is low to start with? If the good opinion of his neighbors is a reward to a man, then a loss of their good opinion will hurt him, but if this loss does not follow a breach of a norm, where is the punishment? And how can it follow, when the norms themselves are not well defined? If social ranking in the community is not established, how can a man suffer loss of social rank? In short, the social system of Hilltown has become such as to bring very little automatic punishment upon a man if he departs from his existing degree of obedience to a norm.

Moreover, a decline in control to such an extent that a man who commits a serious offense is not driven out of town probably implies also that a good citizen is less apt to be kept in. If reward is the other side of punishment, a group that cannot induce the bad to leave cannot induce the good to stay. If a man enjoys working with others in a common enterprise, and cannot find one; if he wants to gain, by achievement, the good opinion of his neighbors, and there is no foundation, in a common body of norms, for that good opinion, then, in effect, his social system will not reward him sufficiently, and he will be apt to leave it. Emigration from Hilltown, which was partly determined by changes in environmental conditions, must also have been determined in part by changes in the social system. What we can see is that interaction, activity, sentiment, and norms in Hilltown, unlike some other groups we have studied, were not working together to maintain the *status quo* or to achieve further integration of the group. Instead the relationships between the elements of behavior were such as to lead, in time, toward the condition Durkheim called *anomie,* a lack of contact between the members of a group, and a loss of control by the group over individual behavior. Let us hasten to add, lest we be accused of a conservative bias, that changes in the *status quo* are not, in our view, always and necessarily in the direction of *anomie.*

Many people would see the problem of Hilltown as a moral one: a weakening of the moral fiber of its inhabitants or, in some way, an increasing flabbiness in the community considered as a person. But surely we have learned that conscience itself is, in part at least, a function of the social circumstances in which conscience develops, and that for conscience to decide on action in accord with community norms, the community must make conscience more, rather than less, easily able to choose right. Because Hilltown still has a name, geographical boundaries, and people who live within the boundaries, we assume that it is still a community and therefore judge that it is rotten. It would be wiser to see that it is no longer, except in the most trivial sense, a community at all.

The decline of a community means decreasing control by that community over individual behavior. Since the group can support the individual and help him to maintain his personal equilibrium under the ordinary shocks of life, this decline in control may mean damage to individual personalities, provided the individuals are members of no other community that will take up the slack. Extrapolating from Hilltown to modern America, or indeed to the modern world, we recognize that what we have been studying is very common. Civilization has fed on the rot of the village. This in itself is not the problem. It becomes a problem only when the organizations to which the former Hilltowners go, such as the big new industries, fail to develop some of the characteristics that Hilltown once had. If they do fail, then the disorders of personal behavior increase. To this question, the leaders of these organizations have, on the whole, failed to address themselves.

Primary Groups and Secondary Contacts

Robert E. L. Faris

In this study, Faris shows the social disorganization that existed for many immigrants who came to America's cities from small towns in other countries. First of all, the immigrants settled in neighborhoods that offered no sense of tradition or history. Second, the social heterogeneity of the residents in these areas tended to discourage the formation of cohesive neighborhood life. And when contact between neighbors is not recurrent and sustained, gossip loses its force as a means of social control. Moreover, without the stability provided by a strong local organization, the family also breaks down. Generational as well as cultural splits occur, and the family loses control of its young people.

In this excerpt, Faris captures the viewpoint of a whole generation of sociologists who worked with the idea that social control arises from organized primary groups and that social disorganization involves the decline of group control over the individual.

The general association of high juvenile delinquency rates with the slums—the deteriorated urban areas near industrial sites where low-income and unassimilated populations constitute a majority of inhabitants—has been thoroughly and methodically demonstrated.[1] Sociologists have examined the rate patterns in most large American cities, and without exception the findings are that the high delinquency rates are thus concentrated, almost regardless of the racial or nationality composition of the population. The few exceptions are furnished by small, self-isolated groups, like the Orientals in certain west coast cities, or members of religious sects, which are able to

From Robert E. L. Faris, *Social Disorganization,* first edition, pp. 128, 131–36. Copyright © 1948 by The Ronald Press Company, New York. Reprinted by permission of the publisher.

[1] The leadership in these investigations has been taken by Clifford R. Shaw *et al.* Their *Juvenile Delinquency and Urban Areas* (Chicago: University of Chicago Press, 1942) provides an adequate sample of the evidence on this matter.

live for a time in the midst of a high-delinquency region and resist the disorganizing influences. . . .

The aspects of slum life which are important in relation to the high development of delinquency are the general conditions of social life—that is, the social disorganization that is prevalent in the area. The disorganization, while not a positive influence in the direction of criminality, is the most important permissive circumstance, for the two most important primary groups that normally control the behavior of children and prevent serious delinquency—the family and the neighborhood—are unable to function effectively.

Neighborhood Disorganization

In a settled village where there is little or no social disorganization, the people of a neighborhood constitute an effective primary group which is a powerful agency of social control. Most of the members have known one another all their lives. Newcomers are subjected to inspection and exchange of information which soon assimilates them into the primary group. There is little privacy—personal interest is strong, and through the natural channels of neighborly gossip any information known to one is as a rule shortly known to all others. Each person knows that whatever he does that is in any way a departure from the conventional will inevitably be discovered by neighbors and will not only be spread to all but will be perpetuated in the unwritten history of the community. Not only is his own reputation at stake, but also that of his family, including the wider circle of relatives. For those who are not often subject to temptations to depart from established ways of acting, this enveloping supervision is not oppressive, but it does furnish a visible force in opposition to unconventionality. Children are warned not to act in certain ways for various reasons, but among them is the consideration "What would the neighbors think?" [2]

The mobility of urban slum neighborhoods operates against

[2] An informant recalls a childhood incident which illustrates the operation of this supervision. A boy five years old, wondering what cigarette smoke would taste like, picked up a lighted stub from the sidewalk and tried it for a moment. Hours later, at the supper table, his father mentioned that an acquaintance had told him that his son was seen smoking on the downtown

the establishment of such a neighborhood consensus. There is no local history—not enough persons remain long enough to preserve a collective memory. Before persons have an opportunity to build up a thorough acquaintanceship with neighbors, one or the other moves away. In a situation of such frequent moving, most persons abandon the attempt to make acquaintances on a basis of proximity, even when it occasionally becomes possible. Each family lives in a world of strangers and cares little for the opinions these strangers form of them, for there is no collective force of opinion and no public reputation to build up and cherish.

The heterogeneity of the residents of these areas also tends to discourage the formation of neighborhood life. Persons surrounded by a mixture of racial and national groups experience a sense of futility in the development of primary acquaintanceships. Normal ethnocentrism and traditional intercultural hostilities interfere with friendliness and mutual understanding. Members of one group do not seek the approval of peoples of whom they themselves disapprove.[3]

The collective life with which the immigrant peoples were familiar in their lands of origin is not subject to transplantation without a great amount of disruption. The life of the European peasant cannot be lived in the modern American industrial city, and when many central features of the old culture are necessarily abandoned, the whole fabric of the culture is weakened. The mechanisms of control of individual behavior are not sustained apart from a whole integrated culture, and thus general culture shock is a cause of some individuation of persons. These slum persons, especially children and youth, whose habits have not been set by years of experience, are thus left unguided by a stable social organization and are consequently more responsive to the surrounding influences of urban life.

---

streets. Not only the "wayward" boy but also the other children in the family were impressed by the omnipresence of adult supervision of their behavior and so became increasingly conscious that each of their public actions involved the reputation of the whole family.

[3] There do exist in some of the largest cities some small and relatively unmixed communities, as in the Japanese sections of west coast cities, or the pockets of highly orthodox Jews in eastern cities. In these it generally does occur that a primary neighborhood life is developed and social disorganization is avoided. Most of the neighborhoods inhabited by foreign-born populations, however, contain a mixed group of nationalities.

Family Disorganization

Patterns of delinquency develop most readily in the first generation of children born in the city. In most families the parents of foreign birth are not criminal and are in fact dismayed by the prospect of having criminal children. The typical foreign-born father attempts to prevent the delinquency of his children, often employing violent physical discipline, and is bewildered at his failure. The primary reason for the difficulty of control is the cultural gulf between Old World parents and American-born children.

Foreign-born adults seldom are assimilated to any great extent into American culture. They hold to many old habits, preferences, and loyalties. Their speech reflects foreign origin in accent and idiom if they acquire the English language at all. The atmosphere in the home, the furnishings, the diets, and the family customs, have a strong imprint of the land of origin. The children, on the other hand, acquire the new language without perceptible foreign traces and, through their playmates and school life, learn to prefer the American costumes and mannerisms and to hold in contempt the foreign aspects of their home life. They may even be ashamed of the apparent ignorance of their parents and may lose respect for their abilities and their judgment.

There thus grows such a split between the generations that there is little mutual understanding between them and little basis for the control of children through family sentiment and loyalty. Attempts at control by corporal punishment alone usually fail, producing hostility that increases the split between the generations.

Shaw and McKay have presented a case study which furnishes an admirable illustration of this form of intrafamily conflict and its relation to the loss of control of the behavior of children.[4]

Nick, a fourteen-year-old Greek boy, was brought to the Juvenile Court on a delinquency petition, charged with various forms of misconduct, including theft from his home, running away, use of abusive and obscene language, quarreling with parents and sister, and similar behavior. According

[4] Clifford R. Shaw and Henry D. McKay, *Report on the Causes of Crime*, Vol. 2, No. 13. Washington: National Commission on Law Observance and Enforcement, 1931. The following material is adapted and condensed from this report.

to his mother, "Nick no wanta work. He big man, fourteen, and wanta play ball all day. Father say, 'You go today and work in restaurant and work with uncle, for he pay you and you learn the business.' What does he say? He makes faces, cusses, laughs, and runs out to play ball. . . . He tell me to 'go to hell,' 'shut your mouth,' 'why don't you holler all the time.' . . . He get up at noon and go out and play ball. That not right. I go out to the ball game and say, 'Nick come home with me from these bad boys and work.' He laugh at me, make a face, tell me to go home and to mind own business. He like nothing but ball. He gets very mad and breaks the chairs, smashes the house, and falls on the floor kicking and saying bad names to me. The father work hard. Have heart trouble. Nick ought to help. His father work hard when he was only eleven years old. That would be right way for Nick."

Nick did not share with his parents the expectation that his occupational career should begin at fourteen, for this was not the pattern among the boys he knew. In the culture with which he was familiar, this was an age for playing baseball with other boys, and he resented the efforts of his parents to deprive him of this phase of his life. He put his position as follows, "I've had a lot of trouble at home. They all fight me and hate me. They don't want me to play or have any fun with the fellows. They say I ought to work all day and then only play a little at night. The other fellows my age don't work, and I don't see why I have to if they don't. . . .

"All was going well until I stole two dollars from my mother and bought a baseball glove. When my mother found out she gave me a beating and sent a note to my eighth-grade teacher, stating that I had robbed two bucks. She asked me why I robbed them. I told her the reason and I never robbed again. . . .

"The other night when I was playing ball with the guys out in the street my ma came out, began scolding me, broke up the game, and made me come in. Then she whipped me with a big stick. The next time I met the guys they made fun of me and asked me if I asked my ma if I could come out. I whaled into Irish and beat him up, but I got a black eye. Then my dad beat me for fighting and for not asking my ma if I could go out and play.

"That's the way they are all against me. I feel like I don't belong there. They tease me and nag me and I get mad and feel like I could kill them. That's why I hit them with a chair or anything. I can't have any fun. If I work hard they still fuss at me and don't give me any money. I get filled up with mad feeling and tear into them, I can't help it. They all think I am a liar and thief. I get blamed for everything. I wish I wasn't living with them. They don't want me to have any fun. I don't tell the guys I have to work all the time."

The population of the neighborhood in which Nick's family lived was predominantly of Irish and German-American extraction. There were no other Greeks in the vicinity, and thus there was little basis for understanding between Nick's parents and the neighbors, who spoke of Nick's people as "foreigners" and even "dagoes," and regarded them as outcasts. One neighbor stated, . . . "That's a dago family or some other foreigners. They fight most of the time. The oldest girl has a sharp tongue. You can hear her all the time laying somebody out. The kid seems purty nice; he'd be all right if they wouldn't beat him all the time. I guess they are like all foreigners, just fighting all the time. They have a madhouse all night. They pound Nick around, want him to work and support his family, I guess. I don't blame the kid. I told him he didn't have to work and that it was against the law for him to work yet. These foreigners want their kids to work before they're out of the cradle. You ought to throw the old folks in the pen instead of the kids. They don't belong in this country; they don't know how to live here. I wish they'd move out of here, but they own those houses so I guess they are here to stay. We don't have much to do with them, only I side with the kids. I like the boy. He's a nice chap. Too young to work. I told him I'd leave that dump if I was him."

Nick's parents reveal their alien culture and their failure to comprehend American ways in their statements of their points of view. The father stated, "I was born in Europe. My father was a strict man. He beat his kids if they did not mind. At the age of eleven I started to work as an apprentice in a machine shop, for I didn't want to go to school. All boys there except the rich ones begin to work. I worked hard, but I didn't get no pay. That is the way things are there. The boy works and learns a trade to make a living; that is a good way, that is the only good way. In America things are not good for a boy. He don't learn a trade, nothing else; just wants to bum around. It is good for a boy to work hard. He is some good then and knows lots when he gets big and can make his own living without stealing. I had to mind my father. I couldn't do anything else; if I didn't I got beat up. Many time I got beat up. The father whips lots in the old country. That is the reason their kids mind and don't get into bad things. He was the boss, and I couldn't argue him. Here in America the kids don't have to mind. They only laugh at the father and fight him and play all day.". . .

Nick's mother is less articulate, but takes the same view as the father. "I was born in Europe. My father and mother poor people, no nothing to eat and have to work hard. I no went to school. They keep me home and I work hard with my brothers and sisters. If I want to be bad my father lick me hard and make me work harder. . . . In America kids curse father and call him 'old man' and make faces at him and gets mad and fights when father licks him. That is not right. Kids are bad and need licking, lots licking. But father can do nothing, just lick and lick, but kids only fight."

While the culture conflict between generations, as illustrated in the case of Nick, is common among immigrant populations of the slum areas, there are other aspects of family disorganization which also involve loss of control over the behavior of children. Absence of a parent, dissension between parents, parental demoralization and indifference to children, and even in some cases actual criminality of parents may be found.

A Disorganizing Concept

Marshall B. Clinard

Social disorganization started out as a sensitizing concept for sociologists, and those of the first generation who used the concept were able to understand a changing society better by means of the notion. The next generation of sociologists, however, often found the idea baseless and confusing. In this excerpt, Clinard summarizes the problems with the concept. Subjectively, writers tended to be unclear, whimsical, or biased when using the idea. Objectively, they tended to confuse change, deviant behavior, subcultures, and human variation with social disorganization.

. . . A state of disorganization is often thought of as one in which there is a "breakdown of social controls over the behavior of the individual" and a decline in the unity of the group because former patterns of behavior and social control no longer are effective.[1] There are a number of objections to this frame of reference. (1) Disorganization is too subjective and vague a concept for analyzing a general society. Effective use of the concept, however, may be made in the study of specific groups and institutions. (2) Social disorganization implies the disruption of a previously existing condition of organization, a situation which generally cannot be established. Social change is often confused with social disorganization without indicating why some social changes are disorganizing and others not. (3) Social disorganization is usually thought of as something "bad," and what is bad is often the value judgment of the observer and the members of his social class or other social groups. For example, the practice of gambling, the patronage of taverns, greater freedom in sex relations, and other behav-

[1] Contemporary use of the concept "social disorganization" comes largely from W. I. Thomas and Florian Znaniecki, *The Polish Peasant in Europe and America* (New York: Alfred A. Knopf, Inc., 1927). For criticisms of this concept see John F. Cuber, Robert A. Harper, and William Kenkel, *Problems of American Society* (New York: Holt, Rinehart and Winston, Inc., 1956), Chap. 22; [Edwin M.] Lemert, *Social Pathology* (New York: McGraw-Hill, 1951), Chap. 1; and [Frank E.] Hartung, "Common and Discrete Values," *Journal of Social Psychology*, 38:3–22 (1953).

ior do not mean that these conditions are naturally "bad" or "disorganized." (4) The existence of forms of deviant behavior does not necessarily constitute a major threat to the central values of a society. The presence of suicide, crime, or alcoholism may not be serious if other values are being achieved. American society, for example, has a high degree of unity and integration despite high rates of deviant behavior if one considers such values as nationalism, a highly developed industrial production, and goals of material comfort. (5) What seems like disorganization actually may often be highly organized systems of competing norms. Many subcultures of deviant behavior, such as delinquent gangs, organized crime, homosexuality, prostitution, and white-collar crime, including political corruption, may be highly organized. The slum sex code may be as highly organized and normative regarding premarital relations in one direction as the middle-class sex code is in the other.[2] The norms and values of the slums are highly organized, as Whyte has shown in his *Street Corner Society*.[3] (6) Finally, as several sociologists have suggested, it is possible that a variety of subcultures may contribute, through their diversity, to the unity or integration of a society rather than weaken it by constituting a situation of social disorganization.[4]

Questions for Discussion

1. What does Cohen see as the two basic conditions of organization? Is there any relationship between these two conditions?

2. Apply Cohen's conceptualizations of social disorganization (a) to Hilltown and (b) to Nick and his family. How well do you think they fit?

3. How does rapid social change precipitate social disorganization? Discuss the articles in this chapter in this light.

4. Do you agree with Clinard's critique of the social disorganization perspective? Is there any way a social disorganization analysis can avoid Clinard's criticisms? How so or why not?

[2] William F. Whyte, "A Slum Sex Code," *American Journal of Sociology*, 49:24–32 (1943).
[3] William F. Whyte, *Street Corner Society* (Chicago: University of Chicago Press, 1943). Also see Marshall B. Clinard, *Slums and Community Development: Experiments in Self-Help* (New York: The Free Press, 1967).
[4] See Robin Williams, Jr., "Unity and Diversity in Modern America," *Social Forces*, 36:1–8 (1957).

Selected References

Cooley, Charles Horton. *Social Organization: A Study of the Larger Mind.* New York: Charles Scribner's Sons, 1927, pp. 342ff.
Discusses the effects of disorganization—namely, chaos and lack of discipline in the lives of individuals.

Cottrell, W. F. "Death by Dieselization: A Case Study in the Reaction to Technological Change." *American Sociological Review* 16 (June 1951), pp. 358–65. A useful study of how changes in railroad technology disorganized a whole town centered around railroading.

Elliott, Mabel A., and Francis E. Merrill. *Social Disorganization.* 4th ed. New York: Harper, 1961.
An encyclopedic text on the interrelationship of personal and cultural problems in society. The authors make a vigorous effort to include all types of deviant behavior under the rubric of social disorganization.

Faris, Robert E. L., and H. Warren Dunham. *Mental Disorders in Urban Areas: An Ecological Study of Schizophrenia and Other Psychoses.* Chicago: University of Chicago Press, 1939.
An application of Burgess's concentric zone theory of the city. Near the heart of the city is the most socially disorganized area—the "zone of transition." Faris and Dunham show that, for certain mental illnesses, the rates are highest in this zone.

Ogburn, William F. *Social Change with Respect to Culture and Original Nature.* New York: B. W. Huebsch, 1922.
Ogburn presents his theory of cultural lag. Social disorganization arises out of a failure of groups to adapt to technological change.

Thomas, William I., and Florian Znaniecki. *The Polish Peasant in Europe and America.* 2 vols. New York: Alfred A. Knopf, 1927.
In the introduction, Thomas and Znaniecki state that social disorganization consists of a breakdown in social rules. This famous book then presents letters written by recent immigrants from Poland to America, piling up abundant evidence of the anomalous situation they face in America.

Wirth, Louis. "Ideological Aspects of Social Disorganization." *American Sociological Review* 5 (August 1940), pp. 472–82.
A distinguished American sociologist indicates that the term "social disorganization" frequently conceals a set of vested interests or special pleading.

4. Value Conflict

During the first two stages of American sociology's development (1905 to 1935), a number of theorists pointed to the prominence of conflict in society.[1] In addition, these early theorists were social critics. They found much that was wrong with American society, and they argued for basic changes in its structure.[2] Since American sociology was only in its infancy, however, all these writers addressed a reform-minded audience that was outside the academic setting.

During the 1930s and throughout the third period (1935 to 1954), American sociologists were to fashion a different role for themselves and were to begin addressing a different kind of audience. They became more concerned with developing sociology as a scientific discipline, and other academics became their audience. Instead of espousing social reform on behalf of an explicit set of values, they became more "objective" and detached in their analyses of social problems. And because the social disorganization perspective seemed the most congenial to the development of sociology as a scientific discipline, most sociologists subscribed to that perspective. Nonetheless, the conflict perspective was not forgotten, and during the third period in the development of American sociology the value conflict perspective was resurrected.

[1] Early American conflict theorists included Albion Small, Edward Ross, Lester Ward, Thorstein Veblen, and Robert Park.
[2] Lewis A. Coser, *The Functions of Social Conflict* (New York: The Free Press, 1956).

Conflict Theorists and the Formulation of the Value
Conflict Perspective

The value conflict perspective grew out of a synthesis of European and American theories of conflict. Among early European sociologists, conflict theorists abounded.[3] Karl Marx, for example, described history in terms of a struggle between the classes, and Georg Simmel analyzed conflict as a form of social interaction.[4] Americans had studied European masters such as these and developed their own notions about social conflict,[5] but until the 1920s and 1930s, they did not apply the conflict perspective to the study of social problems. In 1925, Lawrence K. Frank advocated the value conflict approach to the study of social problems; applying this perspective to housing problems, Frank showed how a variety of social interests were entangled in housing questions and how changes introduced to solve the problems of the urban slum would entail a host of groups in endless conflicts of interests.[6]

The major formulation of the value conflict approach to social problems, however, was accomplished more than a decade later by Richard C. Fuller and Richard R. Myers. In two seminal papers published in 1941 [7] (and reprinted in this chapter), Fuller and Myers held that conflicts of values usually figure in all phases of most social problems, regardless of the

[3] For example, Ludwig Gumplowicz, Karl Marx and Friedrich Engels, Gustav Ratzenhofer, and Georg Simmel.

[4] See, for example, Karl Marx and Friedrich Engels, *Selected Works*, 2 vols. (Moscow: Foreign Languages Publishing House, 1965); and Georg Simmel, "The Sociology of Conflict," trans. Albion Small, *American Journal of Sociology* 9 (1903–04), pp. 490–525, 672–89, 798–811.

[5] In America, the most important early conflict theorists were Albion Small and Robert Park. Small is largely responsible for introducing Simmel's writings to American sociologists. In addition, Small treated conflict as an important social process in his own writings. Park was also greatly influenced by Simmel. He treated conflict as one of the basic forms of interaction, and he used the notion of conflict at great length in his writings on community, city, and race relations. See Albion W. Small and George E. Vincent, *An Introduction to the Study of Society* (New York: American Book Company, 1894); Robert E. Park and Ernest W. Burgess, *Introduction to the Science of Sociology* (Chicago: University of Chicago Press, 1921).

[6] Lawrence K. Frank, "Social Problems," *American Journal of Sociology* 30 (January 1925), pp. 463–75.

[7] Richard C. Fuller and Richard R. Myers, "Some Aspects of a Theory of Social Problems," *American Sociological Review* 6 (February 1941), pp. 24–32; Richard C. Fuller and Richard R. Myers, "The Natural History of a Social Problem," *American Sociological Review* 6 (June 1941), pp. 320–28.

specific issues involved. They argued that all problems have a natural history with three stages—awareness, policy determination, and reform—and that at each of these stages, the values and interests of different groups clash.

The formulation of the value conflict perspective reflected the times. Fuller began to develop the approach during the Depression,[8] and his and Myers's papers were published during World War II.[9] The Depression and the War revived interest in conflict theory. In contrast to the disorganization perspective, conflict theorists assumed that there is nothing wrong (or "disorganized") about people upholding their own interests and values against the competing interests and values of other groups.

In addition, when the nation went to war, sociologists found a patriotic rationale for injecting social values into their sociology. In the early 1940s, two articles criticized the social disorganization perspective in a way that indirectly supported this school of thought. In these articles, the term "disorganization," like "pathology," was criticized for violating the norm of value neutrality.[10] More recently, as mentioned in the preceding chapter, what was labeled "disorganization" was said to reflect simply the sociologist's failure to recognize organization among people who did not have middle-class life styles.[11] Thus, it was suggested that sociologists using the disorganization approach were only deluding themselves when

[8] Richard C. Fuller, "Sociological Theory and Social Problems," *Social Forces* 15 (May 1937), pp. 496–502; Richard C. Fuller, "The Problem of Teaching Social Problems," *American Journal of Sociology* 44 (November 1938), pp. 415–28; Richard C. Fuller, "Social Problems," Part I, in R. E. Park, ed., *New Outline of the Principles of Sociology* (New York: Barnes & Noble, 1939), pp. 3–61.

[9] Fuller and Myers, "Some Aspects of Theory"; and Fuller and Myers, "Natural History."

[10] Louis Wirth, "Ideological Aspects of Social Disorganization," *American Sociological Review* 5 (August 1940), pp. 472–82; C. Wright Mills, "The Professional Ideology of Social Pathologists," *American Journal of Sociology* 49 (September 1942), pp. 165–80.

[11] See, for example, Marshall B. Clinard, *Sociology of Deviant Behavior*, 2nd ed. (New York: Holt, Rinehart & Winston, 1968), pp. 41–2; Albert K. Cohen, "The Study of Social Disorganization and Deviant Behavior," in Robert K. Merton, Leonard Broom, and Leonard S. Cottrell, Jr., eds., *Sociology Today: Problems and Prospects* (New York: Basic Books, 1959), p. 474. Two classic field studies refute the claim that slums are examples of social disorganization. See William Foote Whyte, *Street-Corner Society: The Social Structure of an Italian Slum*, 2nd ed. (Chicago: University of Chicago Press, 1955); and Gerald D. Suttles, *The Social Order of the Slum: Ethnicity and Territory in the Inner City* (Chicago: University of Chicago Press, 1968).

they claimed to deal with social problems in a value-free and
"objective" manner. By pointing out that value judgments
were implicit even when sociologists tried to avoid them, these
critiques gave solace to those sociologists who believed that
they *should* inject their values into their sociology.

Consequently, the formulation of the value conflict perspective included the notion that sociologists' concern should be
with service to society rather than scientific appearances. Fuller, for example, pointed out that the social problems course is
a "service" course.[12] Most students who take it do not intend
to go on to graduate work in sociology; thus what they need is
a textbook and a point of view that will help them as citizens to
understand, analyze, and take action regarding the social
problems they are bound to face after graduation. (Fuller
himself was planning a textbook along these lines when he
died.) The notion of applied sociology was also echoed in
another work of the period, a famous study of race relations,
which argued, among other things, that social scientists should
labor explicitly in the service of their society.[13]

The first social problems textbook to be organized around
the value conflict perspective appeared in 1948.[14] This book
built on the papers by Fuller and Myers and by sociologists of
the early 1940s. The authors of this book differed from Fuller
and Myers and others in the value conflict perspective, however, by seeking to make the sociologist a detached analyst
(and not, in addition, a therapist) of social problems. Thus,
even within a perspective, there can be dissension regarding
how sociology should fulfill its dual mandate.

Characteristics of the Value Conflict Perspective

Value conflict, as a perspective, is considerably sharper in
focus than the social pathology perspective, yet less complex
than the social disorganization perspective. Its essential characteristics are as follows:

[12] Fuller, "Problem of Teaching."
[13] Gunnar Myrdal, *An American Dilemma: The Negro Problem and Modern De-
mocracy* (New York: Harper, 1944).
[14] John F. Cuber and Robert A. Harper, *Problems of American Society: Values
in Conflict* (New York: Henry Holt, 1948).

Definition. Social problems are social conditions that are incompatible with the values of some group whose members succeed in publicizing a call for action.

Causes. The root causes of social problems are conflicts of values or interests. Various groups, because they have different interests, find themselves in opposition. Once opposition crystallizes into conflict, a social problem is born.

Conditions. Background conditions affecting the appearance, frequency, duration, and outcome of social problems are competition and contact between groups. When two or more groups are in competition and in particular types of contact with one another, a conflict cannot be avoided. A number of different kinds of social problems have arisen under these conditions. And once the problem has arisen, the competing groups can also be in conflict over how to resolve the problem.

Numerous writers have pointed out that social problems consist of an objective condition and a subjective definition. The objective condition is contact and competition; the subjective definition reflects different ways of defining and evaluating contact, competition, and the distribution of goods and rights. The social problem, then, emerges out of the volatile mixture of objective condition and subjective definition.

Consequences. Conflicts can be abrasive and costly. Sometimes they result in the sacrifice of higher values on behalf of lesser-ranked values. More often, they result in abortive stalemates or in loss by the weaker party in the conflict. They also produce a tradition of "bad feeling" between the groups. In addition, however, as more liberal observers point out, conflicts can have the positive effect of helping groups clarify their values.

Solutions. The value conflict perspective suggests three ways in which social problems arising out of clashing interests and values may be resolved: consensus, trading, and naked power. If the parties can resolve the conflict on behalf of a set of higher values shared by both parties, then consensus wins the day. If the parties can bargain, then a trade of values—all in the spirit of democratic process—can take place. If neither consensus nor trading works, then the group with the most power gains control.

Summary

Conflict has always figured in the thinking of important European and American sociologists. But as American sociologists sought to develop sociology as a science, they began to focus on social order and seemed to forget about conflict as a basic fact of social life and a major component of many social problems.[15] The Depression years, together with World War II, rekindled interest in conflict theory and in making sociology more "relevant" to society. Fuller and Myers produced the outstanding formulation of this view, which continues to be popular among sociologists.

From this perspective, social problems are seen as arising from conflicts of values. Competition and particular types of contact among groups are the conditions under which such conflicts develop. Value conflicts frequently lead to the polarization of groups and a clarification of their values. "Solutions" take the form of exerting power, bargaining, or reaching a consensus.[16]

[15] John Horton, "Order and Conflict Theories of Social Problems," *American Journal of Sociology* 71 (May 1966), pp. 701–13.

[16] A conflict perspective that has recently become popular among many sociologists is that of critical theory. Although derived from different philosophical roots, critical theory resembles the value conflict perspective in that it recognizes conflicts of interests and emphasizes the role of the sociologist as a critic of society. One of the major differences between the two perspectives is that sociologists working in the pure conflict perspective see conflict as a basic feature of social life in any society, while the critical theorists attribute conflict primarily to the workings of capitalist society (assuming, for example, that conflict would not appear in the right type of socialist system). In a sense, the critical sociologists merge the conflict perspective with the pathology perspective, explicitly or implicitly labeling various features of capitalist society as pathological. See, for example, Richard Quinney, *Critique of Legal Order: Crime Control in Capitalist Society* (Boston: Little, Brown & Co., 1974).

The Conflict of Values

Richard C. Fuller and Richard R. Myers

Fuller and Myers, the two main theorists of the value conflict perspective, posit three kinds of social problems: the physical, the ameliorative, and the moral. The distinctions revolve around whether or not people agree on the undesirability of the condition and on what actions should be taken. With physical problems (such as tornadoes or hurricanes), people agree that the condition is undesirable and that nothing can be done about the physical cause of the problem. (They may disagree, however, about how to deal with the consequences of the event.) With ameliorative problems (such as crime or poverty), people agree that the condition is undesirable and that the condition can be corrected, but they disagree about what action should be taken. With moral problems (such as abortion or gambling), people do not agree about whether the condition is undesirable or about what action, if any, should be taken. As society changes, problems can shift from one category to another. Nonetheless, Fuller and Myers maintain, central to all social problems are "conflicts in the value scheme of the culture."

Social problems courses have too often fallen into disrepute because sociologists have had no clear understanding of the nature of the social phenomena out of which problems arise. Because of this lack of understanding, courses have been "informational" in character, the teaching lopsided and incomplete, and the textbooks primarily compendia of unrelated facts.

"Social Problems" has been a convenient heading under which a mass of data pertaining to crime, divorce, immigration, insanity, and the like, has been assembled and presented to the student in unsystematic and undigested form. In this lumping together, the contribution of the sociologist as such has been negligible. He has borrowed from the fields of history, economics, medicine, psychiatry, penology, and social work and has condensed findings from these various disciplines into a series of separate courses in miniature, but has added to the totality very little distinctly sociological analysis.

What justification is there for preserving in the sociology curriculum a course which surveys differentiated and discrete

From Richard C. Fuller and Richard R. Myers, "Some Aspects of a Theory of Social Problems," *American Sociological Review*, Vol. 6, February 1941, pp. 24–25, 27–32. Reprinted by permission.

problems, catch-as-catch-can, without a unifying and systematic sociological interpretation? It may be that there is some
place in the college curriculum for a survey course which considers a variety of social problems from a variety of view-
points—biological, medical, economic, political—but a course
of that type should be presented in collaboration by a number
of different specialists. There is no reason why a sociologist
should have any special competence to handle so many varied
kinds of data with so many different scientific analyses.

Some may object that social problems do not have enough
in common to be dealt with by one central thread of sociological theory. If such be the case, then each separate problem
must be interpreted with a different set of sociological concepts and the only excuse for considering a number of problems together would be that of practical expediency—to satisfy
students who desire a survey course because they have not the
time or interest for more specialized study.

It seems worthwhile, therefore, to inquire whether sociology
can work out a common orientation for the treatment of diverse social problems as "sociological phenomena," and
whether this central thread of analysis can be maintained consistently throughout a course or textbook.

Attempts to achieve such common orientation have been
made by certain textbook writers. The most popular climate of
theory has been the application of cultural lag and social disorganization analyses to social problems.[1] We find this theory
set up in skeleton form in first and last chapters of textbooks,
but rarely, if ever, consistently applied throughout the book to
all the problems with regard to which the author presents factual data. The result is that the theoretical discussion of the
concept "social problem" is of little practical use to the student
and is relegated to a minor role in the introduction or conclusion of the course.

The failure of sociologists to develop a workable sociological
orientation stems from their inability to free themselves from
the traditional concept "social problem" which is unrealistic
because it is incomplete. Traditionally, sociologists have dealt
with social problems as "givens," rather than as phenomena to
be demonstrated. They have assumed certain conditions as in-

[1] For a discussion of some of the limitations of the social disorganization
theory in the analysis of social problems, see Richard C. Fuller, "The Problem of Teaching Social Problems," *Amer. J. Sociol.*, Nov. 1938, 415–25.

evitable social problems, either to suit their own scheme of values, or because such conditions have historically been discussed as problems in the textbooks.

A social problem is a condition which is an actual or imagined deviation from some social norm cherished by a considerable number of persons. But who is to say whether a condition is such deviation? The sociologist may say so, but that does not make the condition a social problem from the point of view of the layman. Sociologists, nonetheless, have been content to take deviations for granted, without bothering to consult the definitions of conditions which laymen make. . . .

A common sociological orientation for the analysis of all social problems may thus be found in the conflict of values which characterizes every social problem. These conflicts are mirrored in the failure of people to agree that a given condition is a social problem, or assuming such agreement, failure to reach an accord as to what should be done about it. It is exactly this disagreement in value-judgments that is the root cause of all social problems, both in the original definition of the condition as a problem and in subsequent efforts to solve it. May we suggest, tentatively, a threefold classification of social problems on the principle of different levels of relationship to the value-scheme? [2]

At the first level, we have what we may call the *physical* problem. The physical problem represents a condition which practically all people regard as a threat to their welfare, but value-judgments cannot be said to cause the condition itself. This is perhaps best demonstrated by such catastrophic problems as earthquakes, hurricanes, floods, droughts, locust plagues, and so forth. That these are "serious" problems from the standpoint of the people which they affect, we can have no doubt. However, we may raise the question whether or not they are "social" problems, since they do not usually occur because of conflicts in the value-scheme of the culture. We find no public forums debating the question of what to do about preventing earthquakes and hurricanes. There is no controversy over how to stop volcanic eruptions and cloudbursts. The causation is thought of as nonhuman, resting in natural forces outside the control of man. Perhaps we may call such causation noncultural or precultural.

[2] The elements of this classification were stated by Richard C. Fuller in the article, "The Problem of Teaching Social Problems," 419–20.

Here, we must distinguish between the condition itself and the effects of the condition. While the earthquake itself may involve no value-judgments, its consequences inevitably will call for moral judgments and decisions of policy. People will not agree on how much should be spent in reconstruction, how it should be spent, or how the funds should be raised. There may be serious questions as to whether people in other unaffected areas of the same society should come to the aid of the stricken area. However, the earthquake itself is not a social problem in the same sense as illegitimacy and unemployment. The latter have cultural elements in their causation.

In the case of the physical problem, there is scientific ignorance of causation and control, and we cannot say that the value-judgments of the people are obstructing the solution of the problem. There is no social disorganization involved, no clash of social values, no lag between public opinion and scientific opinion. If scientific knowledge has ascertained the causes of the condition and for some reason the value-judgments of the people interfere with the acceptance and application of this knowledge, then we can say that value-judgments are a part of the causal pattern of the problem and that the problem is truly "social" and no longer belongs at our first level. Thus, if we may anticipate the time when scientists can tell us how to prevent earthquakes, control hurricanes, and make rain for drought-stricken areas, we may imagine some elements of the population who will oppose the application of scientific techniques on the ground that they are too costly and threaten budget-balancing, or that they interfere with nature and God's will, or for some other reason. At this point in the evolution of the culture, we do have a man-made problem, since the will of certain groups is a causal element in the occurrence of the condition itself.

Most diseases have at one time or another constituted physical or medical problems rather than social problems. Many years ago, the bubonic plague, small-pox, and syphilis were far beyond medical knowledge of prevention and control. Today, if the bubonic plague and small-pox should again sweep the world, they would not be essentially "medical" problems since medicine now knows how to deal with them. They would be "social problems" since their recurrence could be traced to the breakdown of our educational techniques, popular resistance against vaccination, confusion as to public policy in public health matters, or some other man-made situation. Likewise, the control of syphilis is now definitely a social problem. Medical knowledge of prevention and control is very nearly perfected, but the problem of changing social attitudes and removing social inertia is very much with us. . . .

As for locust plagues and floods, it is perhaps debatable whether or not they belong at this first level of the physical problem. To the degree that we know how to check boll weevil and grasshopper invasions and avoid floods, these things are social problems. To the degree that we lack such knowledge, they are merely technical, engineering, or physical problems.

At the second level, we have the *ameliorative* problem. Problems of this type represent conditions which people generally agree are undesirable in any instance, but they are unable to agree on programs for the amelioration of the condition. The essence of the ameliorative problem is one of solution and the administration of reform rather than original agreement that the condition constitutes a social problem which must be eradicated. Crime and delinquency fall in this category. Though there are individuals who offend the dominant community mores by robbing, murdering, raping, and petty thieving, there are no interest groups who openly in forum and legislature seek to perpetuate the interests which these individuals represent. All "right-thinking" people, regardless of race, nationality, religion, or economic status, look upon the ameliorative problem as intolerable. Among other problems which we may place in this class are most physical diseases, mental deficiency and insanity, and industrial and automobile accidents.

In contrast to the physical problem at the first level, the ameliorative problem is truly "social" in the sense that it is a man-made condition. By this we mean that value-judgments not only help to create the condition, but to prevent its solution. In the case of crime, certain moral judgments of our culture are to a large extent responsible for the criminal act in the first place. To the degree that our mores of conspicuous consumption enter into the motivation of crimes for pecuniary gain, there is a cultural responsibility for such criminal acts. Or again, traditional prison policies based on our belief in severity of punishment may become part of the causal pattern of further criminal behavior in the prisoner after his liberation. These same cherished notions of retribution in punishment of criminals operate to dissuade legislatures from adequately financing probation and parole systems, juvenile delinquency clinics, and the schools for problem children.

At this level, also, we have those physical and mental diseases where traditional beliefs obstruct the application of medical and psychiatric knowledge to the prevention and treatment of individual deficiencies. Certainly illness, disease, and industrial accidents among the low income groups reflect the failure of our culture both in preventing high incidences of risk to these people and in adequately insuring them against the costs of such risks. Specifically, the uneven distribution of wealth and income throughout our various social classes serves both to expose wage-earners and their families to malnutrition, disease, and accident, and to deprive them of the means to meet the economic costs of such disasters. . . .

It is true that all our ameliorative problems have their technical, medical, or engineering aspects similar to those involved in the physical problem. Venereal disease, tuberculosis, insanity, and automobile accidents all necessitate investigation by scientific specialists. The point is, of course, that in the case of such problems, even when the specialists have isolated the cause and are agreed upon programs of control, laymen still are hopelessly divided over questions of policy.

At the third level we have what we will call the *moral* problem. The moral problem represents a condition on which there is no unanimity of opinion throughout the society that the condition is undesirable in every instance. There is no general agreement that the condition is a problem and thus many people do not feel that anything should be done about it. With the moral problem, we have a basic and primary confusion in social values which goes much deeper than the questions of solution which trouble us in the ameliorative problem.[3] Of course, the ameliorative problem reflects confusion in the value-scheme and thus contains real elements of moral conflict, but such conflict centers more around techniques and means of reform than around fundamental agreement on objectives and ultimate values. Hence, though all "right-thinking" people regard such conditions as crime, insanity, and disease as bad, there are interest groups openly defending and

[3] The term "moral problem" is used by Stuart A. Queen and Jennette R. Gruener in their *Social Pathology*, 38–42, New York, 1940. The moral problem, as they define it, pertains to questions of fundamental right and wrong.

perpetuating the conditions classified as moral problems. Witness the problems of child labor and low wage and hour standards. We have only to read the record of newspaper and Congressional debate on the recently enacted Fair Labor Standards Act to learn that many individuals and groups not only objected to the specific solution attempted in the legislation, but also refused to admit that the conditions themselves were problems over which we should be concerned. In one of the first cases heard under the child labor legislation, one Michigan judge defended the labor of a newsboy on the ground that when he was a boy such work was regarded as excellent character development and training in individual qualities of initiative and self-discipline. Certainly employers in the beet sugar fields of the middle-western states who rely heavily on the labor of children do not define the condition, insofar as it pertains to them, in terms of a social problem. In those families where the labor of children is considered necessary to the maintenance of the family budget, parents and children alike have a stake in the continuance of the condition so abhorred by others. Religious groups have even frowned on government control of child labor as an unjustifiable invasion of the home and a threat to the prerogatives of the church. As to long hours and low wages, the opposition of some dominant groups in the southern states to the enactment of the federal legislation indicated no "problem-conscious" attitude on their part. Classical economists and employers have been known to look upon unemployment and low wage and hours standards as the inevitable, if not the necessary, mechanics of competition in the labor market. . . .

The utility of this classification is in its relativity. The purpose is not to pigeonhole the different problems with finality at any one level, but rather to give us a working basis for observing the position of each problem relative to other problems, and to the value-scheme as a whole. Note that problems will move from one category to another with changes in the state of scientific knowledge and with shifts in the value-scheme. When the physical problems cease to be essentially problems of engineering and medical knowledge, and come to involve questions of social policy, they will move over into alignment with the ameliorative problems at the second level. As indicated, venereal disease has seemingly made this transition though infantile paralysis has not. When problems now

classed as moral come to have wide disapproval throughout
our culture as conditions which must in every instance be
done away with, they will become essentially problems of solution rather than agreement on basic values and will be dealt
with as ameliorative problems. Some day child labor may be
looked upon as criminal in the same sense that robbery and
murder are now regarded as criminal. Conceivably, war may
sometime be defined as wrong as venereal disease.

Nor is there any finality about the problems tentatively classified as ameliorative. Many crimes, such as political corruption, gambling, liquor offenses, and traffic violations are con-
doned, tolerated, and even participated in by respected and
otherwise responsible members of the community. White-
collar crimes are conspicuous in this category. Crimes of this
sort reflect the same fundamental confusion of values as the
problems which we discussed as moral. Before such offenses
can be said to be merely problems of police detection and
judicial enforcement, the citizens of the community must get
together and agree that something should be done.

It may well be that there are very few contemporary problems which can be said to be purely ameliorative in nature,
since most of them reflect no underlying clarity of definition
and moral evaluation. If such be the case, it is a revealing com-
mentary on the absence of any firm tissue of cultural integration in the value-scheme. Cultural integration itself is a matter
of degree. There is always more or less, but never complete
integration. A complete homogeneity of social values would
mean we would have no social problems at all unless we include only the purely physical problems discussed at the first
level.

The Stages of a Social Problem

Richard C. Fuller and Richard R. Myers

*Social problems, according to Fuller and Myers, follow an orderly
"career." The authors argue that all social problems go through the
three stages of awareness, policy determination, and reform. In the*

From Richard C. Fuller and Richard R. Myers, "The Natural History of a
Social Problem," *American Sociological Review*, June 1941, pp. 320–29. Reprinted by permission.

first stage, groups begin to see a particular situation as a threat to important values. In the second stage, people choose sides, redefine values, and offer proposals for action. In the third stage, some group or groups succeed in rallying action on behalf of their values. Thus, Fuller and Myers argue, values are clearly involved in all phases of the history of a social problem.

It is our thesis that every social problem has a natural history and that the natural history approach is a promising conceptual framework within which to study specific social problems.

Let us first clarify our usage of the terms "social problem" and "natural history." The concept "social problem" as used in this paper can be stated in a series of propositions.

1. A social problem is a condition which is defined by a considerable number of persons as a deviation from some social norm which they cherish. Every social problem thus consists of an objective condition and a subjective definition. The objective condition is a verifiable situation which can be checked as to existence and magnitude (proportions) by impartial and trained observers, e.g., the state of our national defense, trends in the birth rate, unemployment, etc. The subjective definition is the awareness of certain individuals that the condition is a threat to certain cherished values.

2. The objective condition is necessary but not in itself sufficient to constitute a social problem. Although the objective condition may be the same in two different localities, it may be a social problem in only one of these areas, e.g., discrimination against Negroes in the South as contrasted with discrimination in the North; divorce in Reno as contrasted with divorce in a Catholic community. *Social problems are what people think they are* and if conditions are not defined as social problems by the people involved in them, they are not problems to those people, although they may be problems to outsiders or to scientists, e.g., the condition of poor southern sharecroppers is a social problem to the braintrusters of the New Deal but not to many southern landowners.

3. Cultural values play an important causal role in the objective condition which is defined as a problem, e.g., the objective conditions of unemployment, race prejudice, illegitimacy, crime, divorce, and war come into being, in part at least, because people cherish certain beliefs and maintain certain social institutions which give rise to these conditions.

4. Cultural values obstruct solutions to conditions defined as social problems because people are unwilling to endorse programs of amelioration which prejudice or require abandonment of their cherished beliefs and institutions, e.g., one possible "solution" to illegitimacy would be social acceptance of contraception and abortion, practices which in themselves are now defined as violations of the mores.

5. Social problems thus involve a dual conflict of values: first, with regard to some conditions, people disagree as to whether the condition is a threat to fundamental values, e.g., race prejudice, divorce, child labor, war, unorganized labor; second, with regard to other conditions, although there is a basic agreement that the condition is a threat to fundamental values, because of a disparity of other values relative to means or policy, people disagree over programs of reform, e.g., crime, mental and physical disease, motor car accidents.

6. In the last analysis, social problems arise and are sustained because people do not share the same common values and objectives.

7. Sociologists must, therefore, study not only the objective condition phase of a social problem but also the value-judgments of the people involved in it which cause them to define the same condition and means to its solution in different ways.[1]

The specific analytical frame which we have called the "natural history" is derived from the above conception of what constitutes a social problem. In our concept "social problem,"

---

[1] The basic idea that the social problem is a conflict of values is not a new one. See Lawrence K. Frank, "Social Problems," *Amer. J. Sociol.*, 1925, 30:463–473, page 468 for Frank's definition; Harold A. Phelps, *Contemporary Social Problems*, rev. ed., 737, New York, 1938; Willard Waller, "Social Problems and the Mores," *Amer. Sociol. Rev.*, 1936, 1:922–933; Kingsley Davis, "The Sociology of Prostitution," *Amer. Sociol. Rev.*, 1937, 2:749–755, and "Illegitimacy and the Social Structure," *Amer. J. Sociol.*, 1939, 45:215–233; Richard C. Fuller, "The Problem of Teaching Social Problems," *Amer. J. Sociol.*, 1938, 44:415–425, and [with Richard R. Myers], "Some Aspects of a Theory of Social Problems," *Amer. Sociol. Rev.*, 1941, 6:24–32; Stuart A. Queen and Jennette R. Gruener, *Social Pathology*, 38–42, New York, 1940; Louis Wirth, "Ideological Aspects of Social Disorganization," *Amer. Sociol. Rev.*, 1940, 5:472–482. Talcott Parsons, *The Structure of Social Action, passim*, New York, 1937, and "The Role of Ideas in Social Action," *Amer. Sociol. Rev.*, 1938, 3:652–664, and Robert K. Merton, "Social Structure and Anomie," *Amer. Sociol. Rev.*, 1938, 3:672–682, have also analyzed the concepts of social problem and social disorganization from a general sociological point of view.

we have attributed to all social problems certain common characteristics. These common characteristics imply a common order of development through which all social problems pass, consisting of certain temporal sequences in their emergence and maturation. The "natural history" as we use the term is therefore simply a conceptual tool for the examination of the data which constitute social problems.

Social problems do not arise full-blown, commanding community attention and evoking adequate policies and machinery for their solution. On the contrary, we believe that social problems exhibit a temporal course of development in which different phases or stages may be distinguished. Each stage anticipates its successor in time and each succeeding stage contains new elements which mark it off from its predecessor. A social problem thus conceived as always being in a dynamic state of "becoming" passes through the natural history stages of awareness, policy determination, and reform. As we proceed to discuss the qualitative differences between these stages, we will refer by way of illustration to data gathered by graduate students on the residence-trailer problem in Detroit.

Awareness

The genesis of every social problem lies in the awakening of people in a given locality to a realization that certain cherished values are threatened by conditions which have become acute. Definitions of alarm emerge only as these group values are thought to be involved. Without awareness or "problem consciousness" in certain groups of people, be they scientists, administrators, or likeminded neighbors, no identifiable problem can be said to exist. Before a social problem can be identified, there must be awareness on the part of people who express their concern in some communicable or observable form.[2] The outstanding characteristic of this initial phase of awareness inheres in the constantly recurrent statements of people involved in a challenging situation that "something ought to be done." As yet, these people have not crystallized their definition sufficiently to suggest or debate exact measures for amelioration or eradication of the undesirable condition. In-

[2] As yet, we have not perfected research techniques which can penetrate covert mental states very satisfactorily.

stead, there is unsynchronized random behavior, with protest expressed in general terms.

The objective condition aspect of the residence-trailer problem is the residence-trailer camp or community. The earliest record of such a community in Detroit goes back to the spring of 1920. This was a small camp of eight or ten families located on the periphery of the city; the residents were industrial workers living in homemade trailers. At this time, no discernible residence-trailer problem existed in Detroit. The three Detroit newspapers contain no reference to the situation and the records of the police, health department, and social work agencies are equally silent. Although neighbors remember the camp, they insist it was "no trouble at all." However, the objective condition grew rapidly in proportions. By 1930, there were four well-established camps within the city limits and by 1935 the number had increased to nine. In five of these nine communities, the inhabitants made no pretense of temporary camping, but removed the wheels from their trailers, mounted them on saw horses and two-by-fours, and settled down to a semipermanent existence. As the visibility of trailers and trailerites increased, there came the dawn of a social problem awareness as measured by newspaper items, gossip of neighbors, formal complaints of neighbors to the press and to civic authorities, and the official utterances of these civic authorities.

A sampling of the three Detroit newspapers reveals no comment on the situation either in the form of news or editorials until January, 1925, when we have an item in one paper noting a "brawl" which occurred in one of the camps. During the next decade, 1925–35, there was a steadily increasing number of items and in the two-year period 1936–37, the items reached their greatest frequency. If a qualitative interpretation of these items is permissible, we can say that up to 1930 their tone was one of curiosity and amusement rather than alarm. Before 1930, the editorial columns and "letters to the editor" section gave very little attention to the situation. After 1930, the editorial departments of all three papers made frequent comment and "letters to the editor" became quite common. In both straight news reporting and in editorial page comment, the tone of the items rapidly took on a note of concern and alarm. In 1936–37, over one half of the items were editorials or letters to the editor; the remainder were news items concerned with crime, disease, fires, accidents, and humorous incidents in the camps. The letters to the editor were principally from people living in the neighborhoods close to the trailer communities, from school authorities, from real estate dealers, and from social workers.

Complaints of neighbors were articulated on the grounds of the unsightliness of the camps, noises, odors, immorality, crime, and property depreciation in the surrounding districts. The response of neighborhood groups to the condition was measured not only by formal complaints to police, health officials, and newspapers, but also by the participant observations of students living in local areas near trailer camps. One student reported:

"At first, none of us paid much attention when a number of families moved into the big open lot on the next corner below us. They were poor factory workers and the depression was pretty tough in 1932. They did not have to pay much rent. Most of us thought they would only stay a month or two and then be on their way. But after a year there were more trailers there than ever and neighbors began to say, 'Well, it looks as if they were here to stay.' But no one seemed to think that the camps were hurting any of us. Then we all began to miss certain small articles around the house. Newspapers, milk bottles, and tools began to disappear. We laid it to the trailer kids and blamed their parents for letting them run wild. Then someone said, 'Why aren't these kids in school? That will keep them out of trouble.' A neighbor wrote a letter to the truant officer about it but nothing came of it at first."

[Another typical comment] "Dad said Mother thought the trailer children were a bunch of sex perverted brats, but Dad said he did not worry half so much about that as how he would ever sell his house unless they got the campers out of the district. And Dad was always saying that he had nothing against the trailerites themselves. They could not help being poor, he said, but it was a 'hell of a note why that should mean we all must be poor.'" [This statement referred to the situation in 1932.]

Awareness was registered in the official statements of organized civic authorities, such as health agencies, the police, and school functionaries, almost as soon as protests were being registered by local neighborhood groups. The health authorities were the first governmental unit to show concern in public statements and their information was given them first by social workers called into the camps to administer relief. The chief complaints of health inspectors to the Common Council were: families averaged two to each trailer and accommodations were scarcely large enough for one; several of the camps had no toilet accommodations and there was little or no privacy in such matters; water supply was low and residents were often dependent on sources outside the camp; in winter, the heating accommodations were deficient, small gas stoves serving most trailers and others had no heating whatsoever; garbage disposal was indiscriminate and dumping on nearby vacant lots was the usual expedient.

The police, as another organized official group, came to view trailer camps as potential danger spots, presenting a new challenge to the preservation of law and order. This awareness definition reflected in official police reports emerged as the police were increasingly called in to quell brawls, apprehend delinquents, and investigate reports of indignant neighbors.

School authorities became aware of the residence-trailer problem because the stability and routine of the school were affected. Some schools did not have the accommodations for the incoming trailer children, day to day attendance of the newcomers was extremely irregular, and, because of the impermanence of the trailer community, many children would depart before the school year was completed.

Thus, the stage of progressive awareness for Detroit's residence-trailer problem covered the approximate period of 1925–35, and is measurable by newspaper indexes as well as by the definitions of citizens and government officials who felt that group values of health, education, private property, and morals were threatened by the existence of the objective condition.

Policy Determination

Very soon after the emergence of awareness comes debate over policies involved in alternative solutions. Ends and means are discussed and the conflict of social interests becomes intense. People who propose solutions soon find that these solutions are not acceptable to others. Even when they can get others to agree on solutions, they find agreement as to means a further difficulty. The stage of policy determination differs significantly from the stage of awareness in that interest groups are now concerned primarily with "what ought to be done" and people are proposing that "this and that should be done." [3] Specific programs occupy the focus of attention. The multi-sided protests have become organized and channelized.

Policy determination on the residence-trailer problem in Detroit indicated discussion on at least three interrelated levels: first, discussion by neighbors and other interested but unorganized groups; second, discussion by organized interest or pressure groups such as taxpayers, trailer manufacturers, real estate organizations, parent-teacher associations, women's clubs, and men's clubs; third, discussion among specialists and administrators in government or quasi governmental units— the police, health officials, Common Council, social workers, and school boards. The interinfluence and cross-fertilization of debate among and between these three levels of participating discussants represent the dynamics of policy determination.

Policy determination was preoccupied both with broad questions as to ends and with narrow, more specialized questions as to means. As to ends, should the trailer camps be prohibited entirely and expelled from the community, should they only be licensed, taxed, or otherwise restricted in growth, or should they be let alone in the hope that the situation would right itself? As to narrower questions of means, the more established, organized, and official the group, the more likely it was to agree on ends but to disagree on means. For instance, health officials debated periodic inspection, which would be costly but more efficient, as against sporadic inspection on complaints received, which would be less costly but involve more risk to the health of the community at large. Similarly, school officials debated the pros and cons of expansion, the pros and cons of vigorous truant officer activity, the pros and cons of a special class for trailer children. Police had to decide whether or not special details and augmented forces were nec essary for trailer camp areas and whether a tough or lenient policy of arrest should be applied to trailer inhabitants.

Conflicts over policy determination can best be observed by

[3] Newspaper comment on the residence-trailer problem subsequent to 1935 reveals this transition in emphasis from simple alarm to concrete proposals.

charting the alignments of different interest groups who have various stakes in the solution of the difficulty. These groups represent certain institutional values, many of which appear incompatible with each other, all of which must be reconciled or compromised before the community can go ahead on a collective policy of reform. The official groups (police, health, school, social workers) can be said to be perpetuating basic organizational mores pertaining to the protection of private property, public health, education, and relief of the distressed. Then there are the special interest groups such as the real estate operators, hotel owners, and neighborhood taxpayers who want elimination or restriction of the homes on wheels because their pecuniary values of survival and status are threatened.

Lined up on the other side is the Coach Trailer Manufacturers' Association, a pressure group seeking the protection of the interests of trailerites, also motivated by self-interest and the profit mores. Then there are the interests of those who live in trailers. Though these trailer communities consist of low-income groups of migrant and transient workers, the casually employed, the chronic unemployable, factory wage earners, and the like, some of them are identified with an interest group of their own—The Mobile Home Owners' Association of America. This organization contends that trailer homes are the solution to the housing problems of the low-income family. With property and rental values held beyond their means, what is left for these people but the trailer house? There are citizens who are in sympathy with the position of trailer-residents, and although they favor some public control, they oppose abolition of these communities. Labor unions, civil rights groups, and other liberal organizations also are on record as championing the survival of trailer communities.

It seems, then, that the dynamics of policy determination on the residence-trailer problem, which became intensified during the approximate period of 1935–37, can be represented as an alignment of certain humanitarian interests with certain organizational interests to combat other humanitarian interests aligned with other organizational interests.

Reform

The final stage in the natural history of a social problem is that of reform. Here we find administrative units engaged in putting formulated policy into action. General policies have been debated and defined by the general public, by special interest groups, and by experts. It is now the task of administrative experts specially trained in their jobs to administer reform. This is the stage of action, both public and private. The emphasis is no longer on the idea that "something ought to be done" or that "this or that should be done" but on the fact that "this and that are being done." Public action is represented in the machinery of government bodies, legislative, executive, and judicial; and in the delegated authority of administrative tribunals, special supervisory officers and boards. This is the institutionalized phase of the social problem in the sense that we have established policies carried out by publicly authorized policy-enforcing agencies. Reform may also be private in character, as witnessed by the activities of private clubs and organizations, private charities and other benevolent associations, and church groups.

Decisions of policy remain necessary at the reform stage, but such decisions usually involve quite technical matters pertaining to means and fall within the special bailiwick of the experts concerned with such questions. Of course, such policy questions may be taken out of the hands of the administrators whenever the general public exercises its powers of censorship, veto, or referendum. The already established public agencies may prove sufficient for the administration of reform in connection with a new community problem or it may be necessary to establish new agencies of administration.

The residence-trailer problem in Detroit is just beginning to enter the reform stage in its natural history. Although police and sanitation officials had sporadic contacts with the camps prior to 1937, their activities were not concerned with carrying out any special policies established for trailer communities. They were merely acting on community policies already established pertaining to crime and public health, wherever and whenever conditions called for bringing such old policies into action. Beginning about 1937, however, the Common Council enacted legislation which placed the trailer camps within the city under certain prohibitions and restrictions. These camps were absolutely prohibited from certain areas and allowed to survive only in specially designated areas. Also, special requirements as to licensing, inspection, and supervision of the camps were enforced on owners and/or leasees of the real estate where the camps were located. The health officials and sanitation inspectors were ordered to establish special rules of public health for the trailer communities. Reform has only begun, and many knotty legal problems remain to be ironed out before collective action can proceed further. There is no indication that the school authorities have taken any official action. The problem seems to be on the border of transition from policy determination to reform.

It should be fairly obvious from the statement of the residence-trailer problem that the stages in the natural history are not mutually exclusive and that they tend to overlap. For conceptual purposes, however, the three general phases may be set off from each other; in practical reality, the state of development of a problem at any one time usually contains elements of all three stages.

Is the natural history technique equally adaptable to all types of social problems? The residence-trailer problem is a situation which can be observed on a local and emergent basis in specific neighborhoods and communities. The factors of localism and emergence offer the investigator a delimited area and a timeliness of observation which permit a current, intimate focus on the items of awareness, policy determination, and reform. The data are fresh and immediate and the participant observer technique is available. Such problems are often transitory—that is, awareness, discussion, and conflict cease permanently with some arrangement for compromise or removal of the difficulty; or the abatement of conflict may be only momentary and the issue flares up again and again.

What of the traditional, older, more pervasive problems which have occupied the attention of teacher and student in social problems texts for the past fifty years or more? What of crime, poverty, insanity, war, family disorganization, prostitution, illegitimacy, and race prejudice? Obviously, we cannot go back into antiquity to record the first awareness of social groups defining such conditions as problems. We cannot trace the earliest conflicts over policy and the first attempts at solution. Anthropological, historical, and contemporary data may be used to demonstrate to the student the universal aspects of these problems in space and in time. Such materials, however, are inadequate in that they do not bring the student face to face with the dynamics of the problem. If the student is to understand why these old established problems persist and defy solution, he must examine the values of our social organization which bring the undesirable conditions into existence and which obstruct efforts to remove them. His laboratory for the study of these realities is the local community where the cross-sectional conflicts at the core of the problem can be observed most intimately.

The important fact which the textbooks overlook is that the old traditional problems are given relative emphases in the local community. At the awareness stage, a problem such as crime may be receiving very little attention in community *A*, whereas in the neighboring community *B* it is the all-absorbing focus of interest. Similarly, there may be no discussion of policies relative to race discrimination in *B*, whereas the people of *A* are intensely occupied with such discussion. The administration of relief for unemployment may be in an advanced stage in *B*, whereas little if anything is being done in *A*. Thus, even these problems which are persistently national in scope do not blanket the country with the same stage of development. Such conditions are only latent, dormant, or potential problems in the local area, and before they rise to local consciousness, debate, and control, a local issue is essential to set the natural history going. Although the conflicts of social values which make up the problem, once it has evolved, are much the same in all communities, the natural history technique provides a specific focus on these conflicts as they function in the concrete reality of a local situation.

Conclusion

We have presented the "natural history" interpretation of social problems as a broad conceptual frame for the examination of the dynamics of specific social problems. Obviously, before the natural history technique can be made a precise tool of research, the many implications of our statement must be refined and explored by further analysis.

Within our experience as teachers, the natural history approach has proved most valuable in bringing students to grips with the realities of social problems. These realities, as we see them, are the cross purposes at which people find themselves because they cherish incompatible and inconsistent objectives. The very norms of organization which give the community a working routine tend to produce conflicts of cultural values which create and sustain conditions defined as social problems.

In the search for temporal sequences in the "becoming" of a social problem, the student does not take problem conditions for granted, as objective "evils" caused by "evils." He seeks to explain social problems as emergents of the cultural organization of the community, as complements of the approved values of the society, not as pathological and abnormal departures from what is assumed to be proper and normal. As such, the natural history technique is a sociological orientation rather than a social welfare orientation. If social problems theory is to come of age, it must cease being a poor relation of sociological theory and become sociological theory in its own right.

Words Without Deeds

Willard Waller

In this classic statement on the role of values in social problems, Waller discusses the basic tension between humanitarian and organizational mores. People make value judgments on the basis of humanitarian mores. But, at the same time, they are often constrained in eliminating the problematic conditions because of the costs that would result vis-à-vis institutions that are important to them. Hence, many people can object to a situation without wanting to do what is necessary to change it. In terms of Fuller's and Myers's scheme, awareness and policy determination can exist without necessarily leading to reform. Thus, Waller claims, "social problems are not solved because people do not want to solve them."

If we are to treat social problems scientifically, we must try to understand why we consider them problems. We must subject to analysis our judgments of value as well as the social

From Willard Waller, "Social Problems and the Mores," *American Sociological Review*, December 1936, 924–30. Reprinted by permission.

phenomena upon which these judgments are passed. We may do this by applying the concept of the mores to the problem of social problems as we have defined it. Social problems exist within a definite moral universe. Once we step out of our circle of accustomed moralities, social problems cease to exist for us. Likewise, if we consider the possibility of revolutionary change, social problems lose most of their complexity. A simple formulation of our standpoint, which we advance as roughly accurate for most social problems, rests upon the assumption of two conflicting sets of mores. Social problems result from the interaction of these two groups of mores, which we may call the *organizational* and the *humanitarian* mores.[1]

The organizational, or basic, mores, are those upon which the social order is founded, the mores of private property and individualism, the mores of the monogamous family, Christianity, and nationalism. Conditions of human life which we regard as social problems emanate from the organizational mores as effective causes. Indeed, the fact that a certain condition is in some sense humanly caused is an unrecognized but essential criterion of the social problem. We are all, as Galsworthy remarked, under sentence of death, but death is not a social problem; death becomes a social problem only when men die, as we think, unnecessarily, as in war or by accident or preventable disease. Not all the miseries of mankind are social problems. Every condition which we regard as a social problem is in some sense a result of our institutions or we do not concern ourselves with it.

Alongside the organizational mores there exists a set of humanitarian mores; those who follow the humanitarian mores feel an urge to make the world better or to remedy the misfortunes of others.[2] Probably the humanitarian impulse has always existed, but it has apparently attained group-wide expression at a relatively late period in our history, following the breakdown of primary group society. Social problems in the modern sense did not exist when every primary group

[1] I have limited the present paper to discussion of the interaction of these mores at the present time. A lengthier treatment of the subject would have to pay considerable attention to the historical interrelations of these sets of mores.
[2] While an explanation in terms of psychopathology would account for the fact that certain persons rather than certain others are the ones to pass value judgments, we must assume humanitarian mores in order to account for the fact that anyone passes them.

cared for its own helpless and unfortunate. Social problems as we know them are a phenomenon of secondary group society, in which the primary group is no longer willing and able to take care of its members. It was this breakdown which called group-wide humanitarianism into existence; it was this situation which brought it about that we were asked to feel sympathy for those whom we had never seen. Humanitarian mores are frequently expressed, for they are highly verbal, and they command the instant assent of almost any group.

The formula which crystallizes in our minds as we approach social problems from the angle of the mores is this: Social problems are social conditions of which some of the causes are felt to be human and moral. Value judgments define these conditions as social problems. Value judgments are the formal causes of social problems, just as the law is the formal cause of crime. Value judgments originate from the humanitarian mores, which are somewhat in conflict with the organizational mores. Social problems are moral problems; they are like the problems of a problem play. The existence of some sort of moral problem is the single thread that binds all social problems together. Any important social problem is marked by moral conflict in the individual and social conflict in the group. It is thus that the strain for consistency in the mores expresses itself.[3]

When someone has expressed a value judgment upon some condition of human life which originates from the organizational mores, and begins to reflect upon possible courses of action, he is at last in a position to understand the sense in which social problems are complex. For the same mores from which the deplored conditions originate continue to operate to limit any action which one takes in order to remedy them.

[3] I should not like to be understood as making a claim for the originality of this conception of social problems. My interpretation is apparently not very far from Sumner's. L. K. Frank, in the paper quoted and in some other writings, appears to have anticipated my statement almost completely. Burgess makes use of a similar conception in one of his papers. (See E. W. Burgess, "Social Planning and the Mores," *Pub. Amer. Sociol. Soc.*, 29, No. 3, 1–18.) In numerous writings Woodard has attacked the same problem by means of a different type of analysis; I have in fact borrowed some terminology and certain interpretations from him. The Marxian conception of dialectic seems closely related to my interpretation; so, I am informed, are certain passages of Bergson. It appears, then, that a great many thinkers have converged upon what is essentially the same interpretation, a fact which should serve, at any rate, to give the interpretation a certain added cogency.

Frank illustrates this limiting action of the organizational mores by showing how difficult it would be to explain our housing problem to a man from Mars.

We should have to delegate an economist, a lawyer, a political scientist, a sociologist, and a historian to explain about the system of private property, the price system, popular government, congestion of population, transportation, and so on. And when they had severally and jointly expounded the complexities of the situation, pointing out that we cannot just build houses, but must rely upon individual initiative and private enterprise to enter the field of building construction, that we must use the "price system" to obtain the needed land which is someone's private property, to buy the necessary materials and to hire the skilled labor, that we must borrow capital on mortgages to finance these expenditures, paying a bonus to induce someone to lend that capital and also pay interest on the loan, together with amortization quotas and then we must contrive to rent these dwellings in accordance with a multiplicity of rules and regulations about leases and so on—after all these sundry explanations showing that to get houses built we must not infringe anyone's rights of private property or freedom to make a profit, and that what we want is to find a way of getting houses without interfering with anyone's customary activities, our visitor would suddenly exclaim, "Yes, I begin to see; have you any other such difficult problems, for this is exceedingly interesting?" [4]

In every social problem seek the moral problem; try to discover the complex processes of conflict, supplementation, and interference in our own moral imperatives. That is the principle which should guide the sociologist as he seeks to study social problems scientifically. Let us attempt to sketch the outlines of this conflict of mores with regard to a few typical social problems. Poverty is a social problem, when it exists in the midst of plenty, or in a world in which universal plenty is a technological possibility. The value judgment passed on poverty defines it as at least in part socially caused and as something which ought to be remedied. A simpleton would suggest that the remedy for poverty in the midst of plenty is to redistribute income. We reject this solution at once because it would interfere with the institution of private property, would destroy the incentive for thrift and hard work and disjoint the entire economic system. What is done to alleviate poverty must be done within the limits set by the organizational mores.

A slightly different type of conflict appears when a value judgment is passed, not upon the conditions of someone's life, but upon his behavior. An unmarried girl has a baby; her

[4] L. K. Frank, "Social Problems," *Amer. J. Sociol.*, 30, Jan., 1925, 465–466.

family and community take harsh and unreasoned action
against her. The humanitarian comes in to save the pieces, but
he cannot make things too easy for the girl or try to convince
her family and community that she is not guilty of moral tur-
pitude for fear of encouraging illegitimacy and injuring the
morality upon which the monogamous family is founded.
Likewise, venereal disease becomes a social problem in that it
arises from our family institutions and also in that the medical
means which could be used to prevent it, which would unques-
tionably be fairly effective, cannot be employed for fear of al-
tering the mores of chastity. The situation is similar when it is
a question of adjusting family relationships; Kingsley Davis
has supplied a penetrating analysis of the "family clinic" as an
agency operating within a circle of conflicting moral demands.[5]

Confusing conflicts of mores appear in those situations,
frequent enough in unemployment relief, in which human
misery and misbehavior are intermingled. When people suffer
privation, the humanitarian mores dictate relief. If these people are willing to work, if the old live in strict monogamy and
the young do not contract marriage until they are off the
relief rolls, if they obey the law, if they do not conceal any as-
sets, if they spend absolutely nothing for luxuries, if they are
grateful and not demanding, if the level of relief does not
approach the income of the employed, relatively few objections are raised to the giving of relief. But let any of the above
violations of the organizational mores defining the situation of
the recipient of charity arise, and the untrained investigator
will quite possibly cut off relief in a storm of moral indignation. Herein he is in agreement with the moral sense of the
greater part of the community. The trained social worker attempts at this point to bring the investigator over to a more
broadly humanitarian point of view.[6]

It is necessary to remember that in all this the humanitarian
is simply following his own mores, which he has received irra-
tionally and which he obeys without reflection, being supported in this by the concurrence of his own group. When the
social worker says, "One must not make moral judgments,"

[5] Kingsley Davis, "The Application of Science to Personal Relations, A Critique of the Family Clinic Idea," *Amer. Sociol. Rev.*, 1, April, 1936, 236–247.
[6] For a delightful discussion of a number of these situations, see the column,
Miss Bailey Says, edited by Gertrude Springer, in *The Survey*.

she means that one must not make moral judgments of the conventional sort, but that it is perfectly all right to pass a moral judgment on the cruel judge or to hate the man who hates the Negro. Often the humanitarian has all the prejudices of his society upside down, and one who talks to him is reminded that there is still "a superstition in avoiding superstition, when men think to do best when they go furthest from the superstition formerly received." Among the sociologists, those who teach so-called "attitudes courses" are particularly likely to fall into this type of confusion.

A few further complications may be noted. The humanitarian often argues for his reforms on the basis of considerations which are consonant with the organizational mores but alien to the spirit of humanitarianism; he advocates a new system of poor relief, saying that it will be cheaper, while really he is hoping that it will prove more humane. As all of us must do sometimes, in order to communicate truth he has to lie a little. Great confusion is caused in the field of criminology by shuttling back and forth between practical and humanitarian universes of discourse. Orthodox economists have recognized the humanitarian impulse in an almost perverted manner; they owlishly assure us that prevalent economic practices are not what they seem to be, but are in the long run ultra-humanitarian.

Certain implications of this interpretation of social problems on the basis of conflict in the mores seem very clear. I should venture to suggest the following point:

The notion of conflict of mores enables us to understand why progress in dealing with social problems is so slow. Social problems are not solved because people do not want to solve them. From a thousand scattered sources the evidence converges upon this apparently unavoidable conclusion, from the history of reform movements, from the biographies and autobiographies of reformers, from politics, from the records of peace conferences, from the field of social work, from private discussions, and even from the debates of so-called radical groups. Even those who are most concerned about social problems are not quite at one with themselves in their desire to solve them. Solving social problems would necessitate a change in the organizational mores from which they arise. The humanitarian, for all his allegiance to the humanitarian mores, is yet a member of our society and as such is under the sway of its organizational mores. He wishes to improve the condition of the poor, but not to interfere with private property. Until the humanitarian is willing to give up his allegiance to the organizational mores, and in some cases to run squarely against them, he must continue to treat symptoms without removing their causes.[7]

Frequently the liberal humanitarian is brought squarely up against the fact that he does not really want what he says he wants. The difficulty which he faces is that the human misery which he deplores is a necessary part of a social order which seems to him good. A cruel person may amuse himself at the expense of humanitarians by suggesting simple and effective means to secure the ends which they believe they value above all others, or a cynical person may use this device to block reform. The means suggested, if adequate to the ends, are certain to involve deep changes in our society, and their cost terrifies the humanitarian so that he feels compelled to make excuses. The pacifist is sincerely concerned about war, and he will even assent to the general proposition that permanent peace requires, among other things, a redistribution of world population. But suggest that the United States should make a start by ceding the Philippines and Hawaii to Japan and opening its doors to Oriental immigration, and the pacifist usually loses heart! Indeed, one wonders whether there are many pacifists whose pacifism would not be shattered by a Japanese invasion of Mexico or Canada. The pacifist does not really want peace at its necessary price; he wants peace with the continuation of things in the present order which necessitate war. He wants a miracle. Lincoln Steffens tells how the shrewd but illiberal Clemenceau defeated Wilson by showing him the costs of peace; the incident is valuable, at any rate, as showing how the two men might have behaved.[8] Professing to be completely in sympathy with Wilson's ideals, Clemenceau stated that peace would involve giving up empire and the thought of em-

---

[7] Frank makes his intelligent Martian say: "If it is not indelicate of me to remark, every social problem you describe seems to have the same characteristics as every other social problem, namely, the crux of the problem is to find some way of avoiding the undesirable consequences of your established laws, institutions, and social practices, without changing those established laws, etc. In other words, you appear to be seeking a way to cultivate the flower without the fruit, which, in a world of cause and effect is somewhat difficult, to say the least." (*Op. cit.*, p. 467.)

[8] Lincoln Steffens, *The Autobiography of Lincoln Steffens*, pp. 780–781.

pire; for England it would involve the loss of colonies; the French would have to come out of Morocco; the United States would have to surrender island possessions, give up spheres of influence, abrogate the Monroe doctrine, and so on. When Wilson replied that America was not ready to go quite so far, all at once, Clemenceau retorted that in that case the conference did not want peace, but war, and that the best time for France to make war was when she had one of her enemies down. One is reminded of Bacon's saying, "For it is the solecism of power to think to command the end, and yet not to endure the mean."

When one considers the conditions under which the humanitarian impulse comes to expression, he must realize that the urge to do something for others is not a very important determinant of change in our society, for any translation of humanitarianism into behavior is fenced in by restrictions which usually limit it to trivialities. The expression of humanitarian sentiments must remain almost wholly verbal, and because of this situation which is inherent in our acquisitive and possessive society: No one loses by giving verbal expression to humanitarianism or by the merely verbal expression of another, but many would lose by putting humanitarianism into practice, and someone would certainly lose by any conceivable reform. From the powerful someone who is certain to lose comes opposition to reform.

A Critique of the Value Conflict Perspective

Kenneth Westhues

Westhues makes three major criticisms of the value conflict perspective. First, it is class-biased, for it simply accepts the judgments of the more powerful social classes in defining what conditions are social problems. Second, the value conflict perspective does not contribute to a theoretical understanding of society; it tells us nothing about the structure of a society, how it works, and what it produces in the way of social problems. Third, Westhues claims that the perspective does not

From Kenneth Westhues, "Social Problems as Systemic Costs," *Social Problems* 20:4 (Spring 1973), quotations from pp. 419, 422–26, 428–29. Reprinted by permission.

tell us how to resolve social problems. Westhues does suggest, however, that the sociologist can overcome these three shortcomings by studying cross-culturally the systemic costs of different forms of social organization.

Even when social pathology was still a respectable name for the social disorganization approach, various sociologists were discontented with it. The organic model of society on which it was based and its obvious bias toward the existing order led to a search for alternative approaches. Virtually all of those that have resulted choose "public opinion," "significant groups," or "a majority of people" as the actor with respect to whom the social problem is defined. The expert analysis of the sociologist is rejected as the criterion of what is or is not a social problem; instead the sociologist studies what others say are social problems. He then applies the tools of social science to the particular problems he is given; and the sociology of social problems proceeds in the same way as if its object were education, religion, the family, or any other facet of the given society.

Fuller, both alone (1937, 1938) and with Myers (1941a, 1941b), developed one early alternative to the social disorganization approach. In his "natural history" approach, the problem is defined by "a considerable number of persons." Then the job of the sociologist is to bring sociological theory to bear on the social problem and to study the stages through which the social problem passes, from initial formulation to eventual solution. Related to Fuller's approach is Blumer's (1970) portrayal of social problems as collective behavior; he argues (in contrast to the social disorganization proponents) that social problems are not objective phenomena but rather the result of subjective definition by some collectivity.

For Fuller and Blumer, the study of social problems becomes the study of *problematization,* the processes by which various publics define and solve problems; it is a field close to that of social movements. This orientation has the effect of insulating the sociologist from the kind of political implications with which the social disorganization approach is necessarily involved. It enhances the sociologist's claim that as sociologist he is free of evaluative biases and instead only an objective student of society. The study of social problems becomes another substantive course in the curriculum. . . .

Three problems of the plebiscitary approaches may be pointed out. First is that they are without a sophisticated theory of society or of history. This is not to say that a large number of logically-interrelated and empirically-supported hypotheses have not been accumulated. It is to say only that the theory has been mostly on the micro or social psychological level. There is no theoretically and empirically sound portrayal of what kind of society the United States (or any other society) is, as compared to alternatives. For this reason the plebiscitary approaches remain within the walls of the given society and do not result in policy-relevant theory.[1]

A second problem with plebiscitary approaches is that the definition of social problems is still largely dictated by the given society (this criticism has been developed at length by Liazos, 1972). If "significant groups" are relied upon to define what the social problems are, it is most likely that these are also the powerful groups who sit in central positions of the *status quo*. If—in order to become more democratic (see Finnigan, 1971)—representative samples of the population at large are asked to decide what the social problems are, the answers obtained are largely determined by the current whims of the mass media, which are in turn greatly influenced by the public opinion makers, namely those in power. In either case, as Liazos points out, the problems studied in the sociology of social problems are those given to the field by the existing order. As a result, plebiscitary approaches share at root the same biases as the social disorganization approach.

The third problem of approaches of this kind is that students are seldom satisfied to see the social problems course redefined as a substantive area, whether collective behavior or deviance. Students expect that the social problems course will

---

[1] This criticism has been developed at length against Gouldner's moralism by Bredemeier (1971). The point is only that liberal values cannot substitute for careful societal theory. Becker (1963), for example, attributes American anti-marijuana legislation largely to the "moral entrepreneurship" of Harry Anslinger, one-time head of the Federal Narcotics Bureau. Becker's social-psychological explanation is happily biased toward the pot-smoker, but the sympathetic reader is left with no policy conclusion except to try to get rid of Harry Anslinger. Dickson (1968), on the other hand, has offered an organizational analysis to explain the anti-marijuana legislation. Not only is his analysis more convincing, it is grounded in macro-level theory. The reader is left with some insight into how bureaucratic societies function; he learns something about the *structure* of his society, not just about personalities within it.

be geared toward policy-relevant or applied sociology; they want to come out of the social problems course with knowledge they can use. . . .

Systemic Costs

[An alternative] approach to the sociology of social problems can be termed the systemic costs approach, in which problems are defined as costs of the particular form of sociocultural organization a given society manifests. This approach, like the social disorganization approach, conceptualizes the given society as an ordered structure or system. Instead, however, of defining as problems those phenomena which do not fit into or satisfy the given order, problems are defined as those qualities or aspects of the given order that do not satisfy some outside criterion. Such a criterion is the actor with respect to which the problems are defined. The question raised in this approach is fundamentally, out of all possible gratifications, what does it cost members of a given society to be gratified according to the structure of their society. What this approach calls into question is not the behavior of deviants or dysfunctional sectors of the society; rather it calls into question the society itself, and asks what one has to forego in order to live in it, and why.

This approach is suggested to some extent in the social problems text of Bredemeier and Toby (1960:x), in which they "emphasize those aspects of American society which (we believe) produce problems, and necessarily, we ignore aspects of American society which (we believe) are achievements of the human spirit." The costs (their term) which they study are withdrawal from, submission to, relentless self-reliance upon, or rejection of what Bredemeier and Toby define as the four governing principles of American society. Congruity between these governing principles and people's behavior appears as the criterion or yardstick against which American society is evaluated. Thus, even while their approach is critical of the existing order, the perceptive student using the book cannot help but conclude that if only people were not frustrated there would be no problems. Even while they adopt a critical approach, Bredemeier and Toby's yardstick is not external to

American society. Hence, their analysis of social problems remains trapped within the boundaries of American society.

Another example of a systemic costs approach is Mishan's (1967) *The Costs of Economic Growth*. He calls into question the compulsion for growth and the cult of efficiency which are integral to the workings of industrial societies and points out their undesirable effects. Although an economist, he does not limit himself to studying costs that can be quantified monetarily. The costs (or problems) he reviews are "the ways in which the organized pursuit and realization of technological progress themselves act to destroy the chief ingredients that contribute to man's well-being" (1969:165). The yardstick by which Mishan evaluates industrial society is a humanistic model of man. Unfortunately, his book does not systematically describe what that model of man is.

In a similar vein is Lindenfeld's (1968:3) collection of readings, *Radical Perspectives on Social Problems*. This reader is grounded in the notion that "the sociologist's biases show through precisely in *what he takes for granted*." Lindenfeld is determined not to take the existing order for granted. The criterion by which the readings evaluate it varies from the Marxist model to other utopian ideals; in some articles the criterion appears simply as moral man, who is expected to be incensed at a portrayal of the United States as a garrison society or at the existence of an "Other America." While Lindenfeld's reader does take a critical approach, it risks being perceived as a collection of potshots at America, some of them hardly social scientific, that appeal to readers who already believe America is bad.

The most useful and policy relevant form of a systemic costs approach, it seems to me, is one in which the yardstick for assessing costs (and defining problems) is another existing society, or at least one that has existed at some point in time. Careful and systematic comparative analysis of alternative societies calls one's own society into question and at the same time prevents unrealistic utopian criticisms by forcing empirical thinking.

Comparative approaches to social problems are not unknown. Eisenstadt (1964:v) has produced a reader of this kind, prefaced with a statement of the utility of a comparative approach:

Second, the recognition that social problems are inherent in any social system, in any social organization, necessarily increases the importance of studying their manifestations and incidence in a variety of societies—be they primitive, historical, modernizing, or modern—and analyzing them in terms of these social structures.

Unfortunately, Eisenstadt limits his comparative approach largely to the conventional list of popularly regarded social problems: suicide, alcoholism, mental illness, family stability, etc. While a reader cannot be expected to offer a theoretically integrated framework, Eisenstadt's book does suggest the need for such frameworks for comparative analysis. The same can be said for Gerson's (1969) reader in social problems; while it takes a cross-cultural approach, its list of problems is quite conventional.

A good, albeit limited, example of a systemic costs approach is Faunce's (1968) *Problems of an Industrial Society.* The principal cost of industrial society on which Faunce concentrates is worker alienation. In the beginning of his book he analyzes the social structure of a Guatemalan peasant society, and later on he systematically compares craft production systems with mechanized and automated production systems. In this way he uses empirically observable alternative societies to evaluate the structure of work and production in modern industrial societies.

The matter of which problems should be chosen for study in a social problems class or for research priority outside the classroom is up to the sociologist himself in the systemic costs approach. Depending on which alternative society he might choose as the yardstick by which to measure costs, virtually any aspect of the given society can be regarded as a cost or problem. In choosing which costs or problems to examine, the sociologist may be aware of what the major problems are according to public opinion, but he may also decide upon problems not currently in the public vocabulary. He may, as it were, make students and readers aware of what they are missing and then explain with careful analytic techniques why they, in this particular society, are missing it.

The political implication of the systemic costs approach is social change. Through a theoretically integrated comparative analysis of his own and other societies, the students come to understand how variation in culture and social structure account for variation in the social problems experienced. Such a theory, provided it has an empirical basis, lends itself to effective social action in the manipulation of the cultural and structural variables which govern the particular area studied.[2] To the extent that students are given such a theory they are given power. Even if, by virtue of their social position, they lack the power to manipulate the variables that cause the particular social problem, at least they know that the problems are not inevitable or solvable only by the manipulation of personality variables. Such knowledge is itself a form of power, just as ignorance of social process is a form of powerlessness. . . .

Conclusion

A month or two before the beginning of each semester, literally thousands of sociologists have to choose what they will teach in their social problems classes. . . .

The choice is made to a great extent according to how one views the given society at present and the sociologist's role within it. If the given society is seen as good, and if the sociologist sees himself like Nisbet (1966:16) as one "interested in making the protection of society his first responsibility," then the social disorganization approach (or one of its surrogates) will be chosen. If, whatever the evaluation of the given society, the role of sociologist is seen as one removed from the arena of public policy, then one of the plebiscitary approaches can be taken. If, finally, society is seen as in need of structural change, and the sociologist as one whose professional expertise can be used for that purpose, then the systemic costs approach is appropriate.

It is true that many critical sociologists, especially in the United States, have little interest in comparative research. Cannot their evaluation of given structures by the yardstick of utopian models or native deviant subcultures or the given society's stated ideology result in progressive and change-oriented thinking? The answer is certainly yes. The question, however,

---

[2] This is not to say that the systemic costs approach limits its analysis to variables that are manipulable—to applied sociology in the sense in which Gouldner (1957) has used the term. A comprehensive theory includes variables of both kinds, theoretical or pure, manipulable or applied. The role of the social problems teacher, as I see it, is to present comprehensive theory, realizing at the same time that not all the variables in the theory will be relevant for political action.

is whether this means is most effective. Utopian models risk
on the one hand being too visionary to put into practice; on
the other hand, utopian models which find their way into
practice tend to be rather nasty and oppressive. With regard
to the deviant subcultures, the problem is that they have been
born out of reaction to the dominant order and are likely to
be greatly conditioned by its way of doing things. To rely on
deviant reactions for new ideas may result in ideas which appear much newer than they are. Evaluation of the given society by the yardstick of its own ideology may indeed disclose
grievous problems, but why should the sociologist restrict his
yardstick to a single society when he has a worldful to choose
from? . . .

The reason why American sociologists in particular, and
others in general, tend to limit themselves to their own society
is that sociologists, like everybody else, internalize the values
of their society and learn to take them for granted. The task
of unlearning is not only the demand of personal growth but
of good sociology and particularly of sociology that would lead
to structural change. In the case of American sociologists, this
is an even greater problem, since the careers of almost all
American sociologists have been developed during the period
of ascendancy of the United States in the international community. American culture, of which American sociologists are
a part, has grown to take for granted the contention of *For-
tune* magazine in 1940, "less by definition than by achievement, the United States is the greatest nation on earth." Given
such a belief, American sociologists could scarcely need cross-
cultural analyses of the kind that would call their own system
into question: what could possibly be learned? Now that the
knowledge has become more common, even within the United
States, that this country is not in a class apart from all others,
but rather lags behind on a range of indices, perhaps a comparative, systemic costs approach to the study of social problems will gain in popularity.[3] . . .

[3] It is interesting that two prominent "left-wing" sociologists, Howard
Becker and Irving L. Horowitz, in a 1972 article on the differences between
radical political positions and radical sociological research, still fail to suggest
the need for comparative analysis of the United States with other sociocultural systems. Again and again they write of "society" as if the United States
were the only one or as if all societies were alike. They propose, for example, studying communal living groups from a sympathetic point of view,
while they seem unaware that other societies have produced forms of family

References

Becker, Howard. 1963. *Outsiders: Studies in the Sociology of Deviance.* Glencoe: Free Press.

Blumer, Herbert. "Social problems as collective behavior." *Social Problems* 18 (Winter):298–306.

Bredemeier, Harry C. 1971. "Banfield, Gouldner, and 'Social Problems'." *Social Problems* 18 (Spring):554–568.

————— and Jackson Toby. 1960. *Social Problems in America.* New York: John Wiley and Sons.

Dickson, Donald. 1968. "Bureaucracy and morality: An organizational perspective on a moral crusade." *Social Problems* 16 (Fall):143–156.

Eisenstadt, S. N. (ed.). 1964. *Comparative Social Problems.* New York: Free Press.

Faunce, William A. 1968. *Problems of an Industrial Society.* New York: McGraw-Hill.

Finnigan, B. W. 1971. "The relevance of sociological theory to Canadian social problems," paper presented at the Annual Meeting of the Western Association for Sociology and Anthropology, Calgary.

Fuller, Richard C. 1937. "Sociological theory and social problems." *Social Forces* 15 (May):496–502.

————— 1938. "The problem of teaching social problems." *American Journal of Sociology* 44 (November): 415–435.

Fuller, Richard C. and Richard R. Myers. 1941a. "The natural history of a social problem." *American Sociological Review* 6 (June):320–328.

————— 1941b. "Some aspects of a theory of social problems." *American Sociological Review* 6 (February):24–32.

Gerson, Walter M. (ed.). 1969. *Social Problems in a Changing World.* New York: Thomas Y. Crowell.

Gouldner, Alvin W. 1957. "Theoretical requirements of the applied social sciences." *American Sociological Review* 22 (February):92–102.

Liazos, Alexander. 1972. "The poverty of the sociology of deviance: Nuts, sluts and preverts." *Social Problems* 20 (Summer):103–120.

---

and kinship which the United States might possibly find instructive, perhaps even more instructive than the deviant life-styles of its own sons and daughters. The fact that Horowitz has himself done considerable research outside the United States, it may also be noted, illustrates the fact that cross-cultural research does not necessarily lead to comparative frameworks that question the structure of one's own society.

Lindenfeld, Frank (ed.). 1968. *Radical Perspectives on Social Problems*. New York: Macmillan.

Mishan, E. J. 1967. *The Costs of Economic Growth*. Middlesex: Penguin.

Nisbet, Robert A. 1966. "The study of social problems," pp. 1–25 in R. K. Merton and R. A. Nisbet (eds.), *Contemporary Social Problems*. New York: Harcourt Brace and World.

Questions for Discussion

1. What type of social problem would Fuller and Myers consider the issue of equal rights for women to be? Why? Discuss the natural history of this problem.
2. What are the similarities between the natural history of the contemporary women's-rights issue and the natural history of present-day racial problems?
3. What are the "organizational mores" involved in the problems of equal rights for women and for blacks? How do organizational mores contribute to these problems? How do humanitarian mores "cause" social problems? Be specific.
4. Westhues presents three basic criticisms of the value conflict approach. Do you agree that these features are necessarily characteristic of the value conflict approach? Do you think these features are necessarily weaknesses? Why or why not? What perspective does Westhues employ?

Selected References

Becker, Howard S., ed. *Social Problems: A Modern Approach*. New York: John Wiley, 1966, pp. 1–31.
A useful statement that succinctly presents the Fuller-Myers approach in terms of symbolic interaction. Most useful for people who subscribe to the value conflict approach.

Chambliss, William J., ed. *Problems of Industrial Society*. Reading, Mass.: Addison-Wesley, 1973.
A recent collection of social problems readings organized around the value conflict perspective.

Cuber, John F., William F. Kenkel, and Robert A. Harper. *Problems of American Society: Values in Conflict*. 4th ed. New York: Holt, Rinehart & Winston, 1964.
This textbook first states the Fuller-Myers position, then goes on to examine a series of social problems from this point of view.

Dahrendorf, Ralf. *Class and Class Conflict in Industrial Society*. Stanford, Calif.: Stanford University Press, 1959.
An important statement of conflict theory.

Lemert, Edwin M. "Is There a Natural History of Social Problems?" *American Sociological Review* 16 (April 1951), pp. 217–23.

An empirical test of Fuller's and Myers's three stages in the natural history of social problems—the stages of awareness, policy formation, and reform. Based on case histories of California trailer camps, interviews with public officials, and newspaper items and letters-to-the-editor regarding trailer camps, Lemert concludes that the Fuller-Myers formulation is inapplicable to trailer camps in California cities.

————. "Social Problems." In *International Encyclopedia of Social Sciences,* edited by David L. Sills, vol. 14, pp. 452–59. New York: Macmillan and Free Press, 1968.
A scholarly review of the various strands of thought that have been interwoven in the sociological analysis of social problems in America. Lemert concludes that analysis of such problems can be objective only if the analysts are aware of their values and make them explicit. Lemert also concludes that values are central to the development and resolution of problems.

Schur, Edwin M. "Recent Social Problems Texts: An Essay-Review." *Social Problems* 10 (Winter 1963), pp. 287–93.
With Mills's criticisms in mind, Schur examines eleven recent textbooks. He shows that a distinctively sociological approach to social problems has emerged since Mills's article. More general sociological theory has been applied to analyzing social problems; and most social problems textbooks combine theory and data in a sophisticated manner. Schur argues that sociologists should take a stand on social problems, drawing on their own discipline for factual support.

5. Deviant Behavior

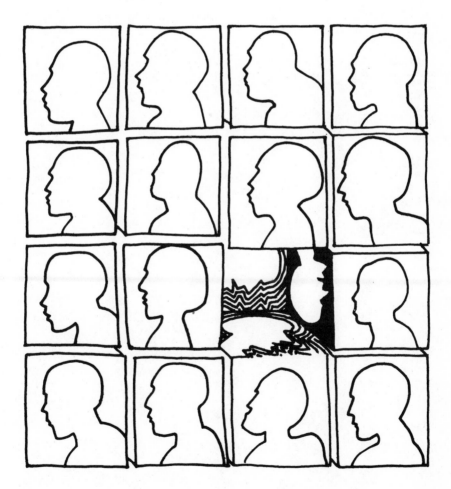

From World War I until 1954, the social disorganization perspective dominated sociological thought regarding social problems. And during these years, sociology, like the larger society, underwent a number of changes, becoming increasingly complex. Departments of sociology expanded, concepts multiplied, theoretical systems matured, and research became a prime objective. Yet despite overall conceptual developments, social disorganization remained the dominant perspective for the study of social problems. Competitors emerged only to be defeated or incorporated into the framework of social disorganization, and the disorganization perspective continued to dominate the textbooks on social problems.[1]

Why did the social disorganization perspective enjoy such

[1] Fuller argued in 1937 that textbooks on social problems usually took one of two approaches—to be conceptual or to be community-oriented. Conceptual textbooks either used a battery of sociological concepts or tried to fit all problems under just one concept. Community-oriented textbooks showed how different kinds of problems affected the community. Conceptual textbooks labored more on behalf of sociology, while community-oriented textbooks sought to perform a service for society. Yet, in both approaches, the disorganization perspective remained dominant. Thus, conceptual textbooks—whether eclectic or monistic—made social disorganization the key concept, usually explicitly. Disorganization was also the key concept in community-oriented textbooks, though this was more often implicit than explicit.

Perhaps the most influential textbook during these years was Mabel Elliott and Francis Merrill, *Social Disorganization* (New York: Harper, 1931). This book began as a single-concept book, but later editions were revised to include a developing battery of sociological concepts.

long-lived popularity? First, certain features of the perspective helped to sustain it. The perspective was systematic, it represented the best attempt at that time to determine a special subject matter for sociology, and it appeared to be faithful to the developing norms of science. Another reason is textbook lag. The textbook is one vehicle for the transmission of a discipline's ideas and findings. Sifting through and organizing them into a comprehensible and useful book is a lengthy process, especially in the early stages of a discipline's development. Then, once in print, a textbook and a perspective can have a long life.

Eventually, however, other factors undermined the popularity of the social disorganization perspective. As sociology became a channel of social mobility, its membership greatly increased.[2] And as the society became more affluent, it could afford more support for research. These factors were important in promoting an increase in social research that, in turn, was important in prompting a reformulation of the social disorganization perspective. This is discussed in more detail below.

The Refocusing of Sociological Thought

As more and more sociologists were trained, two schools of sociological thought developed. One school, centered at Harvard University, focused primarily on social structure. The other school, centered at the University of Chicago, emphasized social process. Both the Harvard and the Chicago sociologists recognized the importance of studying social problems in order to develop mature and systematic sociological theory. Controversy arose, however, over the correct approach to the study of social problems. The deviant behavior perspective has roots in both these sociological traditions. In order to understand how it developed, let us briefly review the character of sociology in each of these great universities.

Sociology at Harvard had a strongly theoretical bent. Classic

[2] In 1935, for example, the American Sociological Association began with a membership of 1,169. By 1945, membership had grown only slightly to 1,309. In the next decade, however, membership increased by 240%— reaching 4,454 in 1955. (Since then, the association has continued to grow, with 8,892 members in 1965 and 13,800 members in 1975.)

European sociologists such as Emile Durkheim, Max Weber, and Vilfredo Pareto were studied. In addition, Talcott Parsons and some of his students developed a broad theoretical perspective that later came to be known as structural-functionalism, a theoretical orientation that, according to many, dominated the next three decades of American sociology.[3]

At Chicago, by contrast, sociologists emphasized description rather than theory. Throughout the 1920s and early 1930s, Chicago faculty and students treated the city of Chicago as a natural laboratory for their studies.[4] Books on the hobo, the Gold Coast and the slum, the ghetto, the taxi dance hall, the hotel, mental disorders, and juvenile delinquency all appeared in quick sequence.

Although the Chicago sociologists were more concerned with describing the facts than with developing broader theories, this department did develop the concentric zone theory of urban development, a theory that predicted different rates of social disorganization in different sectors of the city.[5] Empirical studies found rates of juvenile delinquency and certain mental disorders to be consistent with this theory,[6] and numerous sociologists conducted other studies correlating various rates of deviance with census tracts or other ecological properties.

In 1950, however, a famous article pointed out that just because the rates of several characteristics are higher in some geographic areas than in others, one cannot conclude from this that the same people always manifest these various characteristics.[7] (For example, a census tract may have a large proportion of immigrants and a high rate of crime, but it does not

[3] For one important example, see Talcott Parsons, *The Social System* (Glencoe: The Free Press, 1951).

[4] For an informal history of the Chicago department, see Robert E. L. Faris, *Chicago Sociology 1920–1932* (San Francisco: Chandler, 1967).

[5] Robert E. Park, Ernest W. Burgess, and Roderick D. McKenzie, *The City* (Chicago: University of Chicago Press, 1925).

[6] Clifford Shaw, Henry McKay, et al., *Delinquency Areas: A Study of the Geographical Distribution of School Truants, Juvenile Delinquents, and Adult Offenders in Chicago* (Chicago: University of Chicago Press, 1929); Robert E. L. Faris and H. Warren Dunham, *Mental Disorders in Urban Areas: An Ecological Study of Schizophrenia and Other Psychoses* (Chicago: University of Chicago Press, 1939).

[7] The article first pointing out the "fallacy" of ecological correlations is: W. S. Robinson, "Ecological Correlations and the Behavior of Individuals," *American Sociological Review* 15 (June 1950), pp. 351–57.

necessarily follow that immigrants are more likely to be committing these crimes.) Recognition of the fact that individual correlations cannot be deduced from collective correlations helped to foster the deviant behavior perspective. Finding the conceptualizations of the disorganization perspective too broad for research on individuals, sociologists developed the deviant behavior perspective to discover why some people undertake a deviant line of conduct while others do not. As the deviant behavior perspective developed, the social disorganization approach became confined more to the discussion of social units than to the analysis of the behavior of individual persons.[8]

Roots in Classical Theory

Before examining the development of the deviant behavior perspective from these two traditions, a few words about its theoretical roots are in order. As numerous scholars in the history of science have pointed out, theory is often years ahead of its time. Theory must sometimes wait several decades before anyone develops the methodology and/or technology necessary to test its implications. Testing must sometimes await translation of the theory into another language, or the development of a scientific point of view with which later generations can grasp the essentials of the theory and formulate ways of testing, revising, extending, and generalizing it.

All this is true for the concept of anomie, which first appeared in Emile Durkheim's study of suicide, published in France in 1897. This classic work was not translated into English until 1951.[9] Thus, more than fifty years passed before several variations on this theory began to produce an impressive and growing list of empirical studies testing it in a number of problem areas.

Durkheim formulated a typology of suicide that concentrated on the nature of the social bond. He called one type of

[8] See, for example, Robert K. Merton and Robert Nisbet, *Contemporary Social Problems: An Introduction to the Sociology of Deviant Behavior and Social Disorganization*, 3rd ed. (New York: Harcourt Brace Jovanovich, 1971).

[9] Emile Durkheim, *Le Suicide: Étude de Sociologie* (Paris: Felix Alcan, 1897). The American edition is: Emile Durkheim, *Suicide: A Study in Sociology*, trans. John A. Spaulding and George Simpson (Glencoe: The Free Press, 1951).

suicide egoistic suicide. When people have weak social integration, there is little to deter them from taking their lives when stress arises. For example, responsibility to his family may deter a married man from committing suicide, while an unmarried man does not have this bond to restrain him. He called a second type of suicide altruistic suicide. When people have something positive to die for because of intense attachments to primary groups and strong social integration, they can be induced to sacrifice their lives—e.g., the Kamikaze pilot. Egoistic and altruistic suicides reflect the two poles of extremely weak social integration and attachment, and extremely strong social integration and attachment, respectively. A third type of suicide—anomic suicide—reflects something else. This type of suicide occurs in response to sudden changes—e.g., sudden wealth or sudden poverty. Others had noticed that suicide rates increase during times of economic hardship, but Durkheim found that suicide rates also increase during periods of increasing prosperity. Durkheim saw these suicides as a sign of anomie (i.e., normlessness). During sudden prosperity, Durkheim reasoned, the traditional rules that ordinarily limit people break down, and people find it hard to put limits on themselves. They do not know what limits to accept; they want more and more and are never satisfied. The result is frustration that may lead to suicide. During sudden poverty, on the other hand, people can feel demoralized if they do not accept such changes as just, and this may also lead to suicide.

The Development of Anomie Theory

In 1938, Robert Merton (a Harvard student of Parsons) published an extremely important paper entitled "Social Structure and Anomie." [10] Developing one line of Durkheim's theory, Merton argued that anomie could be the normal state of affairs for persons in certain segments of society when cultural goals (e.g., financial success) are overemphasized and legitimate opportunities to achieve those goals are blocked (e.g., among the lower class). Merton then theorized that this disjunction between legitimate means and cultural goals can pro-

[10] Robert K. Merton, "Social Structure and Anomie," *American Sociological Review* 3 (October 1938), pp. 672–82.

duce four types of deviance: *innovation,* where new, usually illicit means are adopted to achieve the goals; *ritualism,* where
people renounce the goals, only to overemphasize the means;
retreatism, where they renounce both cultural goals and institutionalized norms; and *rebellion,* where they wish to replace the
established system of goals and means with another system.

Several points are important here. First, this is a general
theory applicable to many different social problems. For instance, white-collar crime, organized rackets, vice, cheating on
exams, or doping horses or athletes, can reflect innovation;
psychosis, drug addiction, and Skid Row can reflect retreatism; etc.

Second, given Americans' emphasis on the success goal, anomie and some forms of deviant behavior may be construed as
normal responses to abnormal situations (rather than as abnormal or "sick" responses). As such, no assumptions about biological or psychological abnormalities are required to explain
the behavior.

Third, different segments of the population (America's
lower classes, Merton suggested) have higher rates of deviance
presumably because the goals of success are held out for all to
strive for while the legitimate means of attaining them are not
available to everyone. Thus, if people want things they cannot
afford, they may steal.

Merton's anomie theory has become one of the two most
powerful influences on the development of the deviant behavior perspective, and its influence grew as American sociologists
began cultivating specialties. Merton's paper inspired ten
pieces of empirical research between 1940 and 1944; and between 1955 and 1964, no fewer than sixty-four studies based
on Merton's theory appeared in the sociological literature.[11]

The Development of Differential Association Theory

The other profound influence on the development of the
deviant behavior perspective was provided by Edwin H. Sutherland, of the University of Chicago. Sutherland first published his deceptively simple theory of differential association

[11] See Robert K. Merton, "Anomie, Anomia, and Social Interaction," in Marshall B. Clinard, *Anomie and Deviant Behavior: A Discussion and Critique* (New
York: The Free Press, 1964), p. 216.

in 1939.[12] Following Thomas and Znaniecki, he thought social disorganization played an important role in the production of deviance. In his own work, however, Sutherland gave greater attention to the social process by which a person becomes deviant than to the social structural conditions that promote deviance. In his theory of differential association, Sutherland maintained that people learn to be deviant through association with "deviant" patterns. He identified four dimensions of such association (primacy, intensity, duration, and frequency), and he set forth seven propositions regarding such learning.

Later sociologists came to see that the differential association theory could be considered to be a complement to the anomie theory. Both theories extended Durkheim's axiom that deviant behavior is to be expected as a natural part of social life.[13] Merton's theory could explain why rates of deviant behavior are higher in some sectors of the society than in others; it could not, however, explain why some persons in these sectors engage in such acts while others do not. Sutherland's theory, because it is essentially a theory based on social interaction, is silent on the question of rates but can explain why some people, but not others, learn patterns of deviant behavior.

The first publication to synthesize anomie theory and differential association theory was by Albert Cohen in 1955.[14] In his theory of the delinquent subculture, Cohen maintained that working-class boys face a situation of anomie in middle-class school systems. As a result, they come together and devise a culture which is antithetical to middle-class values. Through the process of differential association, Cohen argued, they transmit a set of norms that requires the violation of legitimate codes, if only to achieve and maintain status in the gang.

In 1960, two sociologists made another attempt to synthesize anomie theory and differential association theory.[15] They

---

[12] Edwin H. Sutherland, *Principles of Criminology* (Philadelphia: J. B. Lippincott, 1939), pp. 4–9.
[13] For the contributions of both structural-functional theory and the Chicago school to naturalism in American sociology, see David Matza, *Becoming Deviant* (Englewood Cliffs, N.J.: Prentice-Hall, 1969).
[14] Albert K. Cohen, *Delinquent Boys: The Culture of the Gang* (Glencoe: The Free Press, 1955).
[15] Richard A. Cloward and Lloyd E. Ohlin, *Delinquency and Opportunity: A Theory of Delinquent Gangs* (New York: The Free Press, 1960).

suggested that *illegitimate* opportunity structures must also be considered, and that different types of delinquent subcultures arise in response to the presence or absence of illegitimate as well as legitimate opportunities. This formulation is exceedingly important for devising solutions to social problems. Opportunity theory was the basis for the War on Poverty and most of the community action programs that appeared in the 1960s.

The first textbook in deviant behavior appeared in 1957.[16] This book, *Sociology of Deviant Behavior* by Marshall Clinard, provided the first codification of the deviant behavior perspective. It called attention to the array of factors involved in the social production of deviant behavior, and while it drew heavily on Merton's and Sutherland's theories, other points of view were not neglected. Soon after this book appeared, social problems courses began to be redefined. Numerous courses, once called either Social Problems or Social Disorganization, were renamed Sociology of Deviant Behavior. This renaming presented a new question—does the term "deviant behavior" denote all social problems or only some of them? For example, Clinard's book includes chapters on family maladjustment, old age, minority groups, and discrimination and prejudice. Not everyone would agree that these problems fall under the rubric "deviant behavior."

Another question that arose was this: If deviant behavior does not include all social problems, then what *is* its relationship to other types of problems—e.g., problems of social disorganization? To Merton, Sutherland, and their followers, deviant behavior and social disorganization were separate and distinct; nonetheless, they tended to see each as causing the other.

Finally, since the deviant behavior perspective came into its own, sociologists have become aware of the difficulty of researching the causes of deviant behavior. As a result, this perspective has turned increasingly away from the study of etiology and toward the study of deviant behavior systems (which describe the characteristic social features of the particular deviant activity) and of social control (cf. the "Solutions" section below).

[16] Marshall B. Clinard, *Sociology of Deviant Behavior* (New York: Holt, Rinehart & Winston, 1957).

Characteristics of the Deviant Behavior Perspective

The key characteristics of the deviant behavior perspective are as follows:

Definition. Social problems reflect violations of normative expectations. Behavior or situations that depart from norms are deviant.

Causes. The cause of deviant behavior lies in inappropriate socialization—e.g., when the learning of deviant ways is not outweighed by the learning of nondeviant ways. This socialization is viewed as taking place within the context of primary group relations.

Conditions. Restricted opportunities for learning so-called conventional ways, increased opportunities for learning deviant ways, restricted opportunities for achieving legitimate goals, a feeling of stress, and access to a deviant mode of relief are all important background conditions for the evolution of deviant patterns of behavior.

Consequences. The deviant behavior perspective postulates a variety of consequences. Many kinds of deviant behavior are costly to society. One outcome, for example, is the firm establishment of illegitimate social worlds. In addition, however, some observable deviant behavior is useful, if only because it establishes negative role models showing what kinds of behavior will be punished.

Solutions. The principal solution for deviant behavior is resocialization, and the best way to resocialize is to increase meaningful primary group contact with legitimate patterns of behavior and reduce meaningful primary group contact with illegitimate patterns of behavior. At the same time, the opportunity structure must be opened in order to alleviate the strains that motivate people to behave in unacceptable ways. As legitimate opportunities increase, socially problematic behavior should decrease.

Summary

The social disorganization perspective dominated sociological thought on social problems during the second and third periods of American sociology—i.e., from the end of World War I until the mid-1950s. During the third period, however, more and more sociologists were trained in scientific analysis, more and more research was conducted, and sociologists became increasingly concerned with integrating theory and research.

Some sociologists focused on social structure while others concentrated on social process, and two traditions of sociological thought developed around this cleavage. The Harvard school centered on structure; the Chicago school, on process. From the former came Merton's anomie theory as a way of explaining rates of deviant behavior. From the latter came Sutherland's theory of differential association as a way of explaining how people learn deviant patterns. When these two conceptions were fused, the perspective of deviant behavior emerged.

The main postulate in this perspective is that deviant behavior is socially learned within the context of primary groups. Its cause, broadly speaking, is inappropriate socialization. Its conditions are blocked opportunities, stress, access to a deviant mode of relief, and deviant role models. Its consequences are sometimes beneficial to society. And its solutions lie in redistributed access to life chances, increased primary relations with legitimate role models, and reduction (if not complete elimination) of opportunities for contact with deviant role models.

Robert Merton: Anomie and Social Structure

Marshall B. Clinard

In this excerpt, Clinard reviews Merton's anomie theory and discusses how it links deviant behavior to social structure. Material success is a highly valued goal in America, but the legitimate avenues for

From Marshall B. Clinard, *Anomie and Deviant Behavior*, pp. 10–21. Copyright © 1964 by The Free Press of Glencoe, a division of The Macmillan Company. Reprinted by permission of the publisher.

attaining this goal are unavailable to lower-class people. This discrepancy places lower-class people in a frustrating position that may lead psychologically normal people to engage in deviant behavior. Clinard reviews the several ways in which Merton says people may adapt to this disjunction between cultural goals and social structural opportunities. These adaptations are innovation, ritualism, retreatism, and rebellion.

. . . In the essay "Social Structure and Anomie," which first appeared in 1938, was revised in 1949, and was further extended eight years later, Robert Merton set forth his now well known social and cultural explanation of deviant behavior in terms of anomie.[1] The significance for sociology of this formulation has been great, one writer stating: "Without any doubt, this body of ideas, which has come to be known as 'anomic' theory, has been the most influential single formulation in the sociology of deviance in the last 25 years, and Merton's paper, in its original and revised versions, is possibly the most frequently quoted single paper in modern sociology."[2]

While derived from Durkheim's concept of anomie, Merton's formulation was at the same time both broader in orientation and more specific in application. Durkheim's view that a situation of normlessness may arise from a clash of aspirations and a breakdown of regulatory norms was reformulated into a general principle that "social structures exert a definite pressure upon certain persons in the society to engage in nonconforming rather than conforming conduct."[3] Merton emphasized normative structures and, like Durkheim, viewed behavior such as crime as a "normal" response to given social situations; pressures toward deviation in a society could be such that forms of deviant behavior were psychologically as normal as conformist behavior.

While Durkheim confined his application of anomie chiefly

---

[1] See Robert K. Merton, "Social Structure and Anomie: Revisions and Extensions," in Ruth Nanda Anshen, *The Family: Its Function and Destiny* (New York: Harper & Row, 1949), 275–312; "Social Structure and Anomie," 131–60, and "Continuities in the Theory of Social Structure and Anomie," 161–94, in Robert K. Merton, *Social Theory and Social Structure,* [(Glencoe: The Free Press, 1957)]. The original essay was reprinted in the first edition (1949, rev. 1957) as "Social Structure and Anomie."

[2] Albert K. Cohen, "Towards a Theory of Deviant Behavior: Continuities Continued," paper presented to session on deviant behavior, American Sociological Association meeting, August 28, 1963.

[3] Merton, *Social Theory and Social Structure, op. cit.,* 132.

to suicide, Merton sought to explain not only suicide but crime, delinquency, mental disorder, alcoholism, drug addiction, and many other phenomena.[4]

Merton's definition of deviant behavior was never very clear in his two basic essays. In a later writing he said that it "refers to conduct that departs significantly from the norms set for people in their social statuses . . . [and] must be related to the norms that are socially defined as appropriate and morally binding for people occupying various statuses."[5]

Unlike Durkheim, Merton did not consider man's biological nature to be important in explaining deviation: what Durkheim considered the innate desires of man, such as ambition to achieve unattainable objectives, Merton felt were induced by the social structure. With an eye to the Freudians, he pointed out that man is not contending with society "in an unceasing war between biological impulse and social restraint. The image of man as an untamed bundle of impuses begins to look more like a caricature than a portrait."[6] Even if one were to grant some role to biological impulses, there still remained the question of "why it is that the frequency of deviant behavior varies within different social structures and how it happens that the deviations have different shapes and patterns in different social structures."[7]

In explaining anomie and deviant behavior, Merton therefore concentrated not on the individual but on the social order. He set what he admitted to be an arbitrary dichotomy between cultural goals and the institutional means to achieve these goals. For analytical purposes he first divided social reality into cultural structures, or culture, and social structure, or

[4] In this volume we are concentrating arbitrarily on behavior accompanied by a strong, negative societal reaction. Such deviant behavior includes delinquency and crime, mental disorder, alcoholism, and drug addiction. While Merton explained all as anomic adaptations, it should be emphasized that his analysis includes other behavior. It is, as he says, a theory "that distinguishes forms of deviant behavior which may be far removed from those which represent violations of law." To him deviant behavior includes, for example, the over-conformist with norms, the radical and the revolutionary, the "bureaucratic virtuosos," the person caught in the net of conformity, widows and aged persons who retreat into the past, and workers who develop passivity in response to anomic situations.

[5] Robert K. Merton, "Social Problems and Sociological Theory," in Robert K. Merton and Robert A. Nisbet, *Contemporary Social Problems* [(New York: Harcourt, Brace & World, 1961)], 723–24.

[6] Merton, *Social Theory and Social Structure, op. cit.,* 131.

[7] *Ibid.*

3. *Relative accessibility to the goal:* life chances in the opportunity structure.

4. *The degree of discrepancy* between the accepted goal and its accessibility.

5. *The degree of anomie.*

6. *The rates of deviant behavior* of the various types set out in the typology of modes of adaptation.[17]

In his writings, he confined his analysis of deviant behavior to those societies like the American, where certain goals tend to be stressed without a corresponding emphasis on institutional procedures to obtain them. American culture is characterized by great emphasis on the accumulation of wealth as a success symbol without a corresponding emphasis on using legitimate means to march toward this goal.[18] "The culture may be such as to lead individuals to center their emotional convictions upon the complex of culturally acclaimed ends, with far less emotional support for prescribed methods of reaching out for these ends. . . . In this context, the sole significant question becomes 'Which of the available procedures is most efficient in netting the culturally approved value?' " [19]

At the other extreme from American society on the continuum are those societies where the emphasis is on goals which have been largely subordinated to institutional means and lack their original meaning, and where conformity has become an end in itself. Other, more integrated societies fall between these two types of "malintegrated cultures" where goals and means to achieve them are in some sort of rough balance.

[17] *Ibid.*, adapted from 175.

[18] *Ibid.*, 135. This emphasis on wealth is not peculiar to an economic system. As Max Weber has pointed out, the impulse to gain money has nothing to do with capitalism. "This impulse exists and has existed among waiters, physicians, coachmen, artists, prostitutes, dishonest officials, soldiers, nobles, crusaders, gamblers, and beggars. One may say that it has been common to all sorts and conditions of men at all times and in all countries of the earth, wherever the objective possibility of it is or has been given." Max Weber, *The Protestant Ethic and the Spirit of Capitalism,* tr. Talcott Parsons (New York: Charles Scribner's Sons, 1930), 17.

[19] As a simple illustration of an anomic situation, Merton cites instances where winning the game may become the paramount goal. Rather than follow the rules of the game, universities may resort to illegitimate means, such as "surreptitiously slugging the star of the opposing team." The university alumni may "covertly subsidize 'students' whose talents are confined to the athletic field." Merton, *Social Theory and Social Structure, op. cit.,* 134–35.

It is important to recognize from Merton's analysis that the high frequency of deviant behavior among certain classes in American society cannot be explained by a lack of opportunity alone or by an exaggerated emphasis on a pecuniary value nexus. A more rigid class structure, such as a caste system, might restrict opportunities to achieve such goals even more, without resultant deviant behavior. It is the set of equalitarian beliefs in American society, stressing the opportunity for economic affluence and social ascent for all of its members, which makes for the difference.

As Merton points out, however, these are idealized goals: the same proportion of persons in all social classes does not internalize them. Since the number of persons in each of the social classes varies considerably, it is important to distinguish between absolute numbers and relative proportion. Only a substantial number or "a number sufficiently large to result in a more frequent *disjunction* between goals and opportunity among the lower-class strata than among the upper-class strata" need to be goal-oriented.[20] It is the restriction on the use of approved means for a considerable part of the population that is crucial to the discussion of adaptations which follows.

It is only when a system of cultural values extols, virtually above all else, certain *common* success-goals *for the population at large* while the social structure rigorously restricts or completely closes access to approved modes of reaching these goals *for a considerable part of the same population,* that deviant behavior ensues on a large scale.[21]

The discussion so far has dealt, in general, with anomie: it has not explained the origin of particular forms of deviant behavior. This brings us to one of the perhaps most important and certainly most intriguing parts of Merton's theory, the ways in which a person can adapt to a situation where *legitimate* means to reach a goal are not available to him.

Adaptations

There are five types of individual adaptations to achieve culturally prescribed goals of success open to those who occupy

[20] *Ibid.,* 174.
[21] *Ibid.,* 146.

different positions in the social structure. One is conformity; the others are the deviant adaptations of ritualism, rebellion, innovation, and retreatism. None of these adaptations, as Merton points out, is deliberately selected by the individual or is utilitarian, but rather, since all arise from strains in the social system, they can be assumed to have a degree of spontaneity behind them. The paradigm is the following.

A Typology of Modes of Individual Adaptation [22]

Modes of Adaptation	Cultural Goals	Institutionalized Means
I Conformity	+	+
II Innovation	+	−
III Ritualism	−	+
IV Retreatism	−	−
V Rebellion	±	±

+ = acceptance; − = rejection; ± = rejection of prevailing values and substitution of new values.

Conformity. Conformity to both cultural goals and institutional means is the most common adaptation, but can be passed in this discussion which deals with non-conformity, although Merton claims that all five forms of adaptation relate to deviant behavior. Conformity or commitment to goals and institutional norms on the part of a large proportion of people, however, makes human society possible. It is not in focusing on conforming or normal behavior that it is possible to find out about the basic stresses of a society but rather by directing attention to deviant behavior.

Ritualism. The abandoning or scaling down of the lofty goals of pecuniary success and rapid social mobility to the point where our aspirations can be satisfied is ritualism. "But though one rejects the cultural obligation to attempt 'to get ahead in the world,' though one draws in one's horizons, one continues to abide almost compulsively by institutional norms." [23] Actually this adaptation seems also to have little direct relationship

[22] *Ibid.,* 140.
[23] *Ibid.,* 150.

to deviation, except perhaps to some forms of compulsive neuroses, and Merton himself says that the behavior exhibited by the ritualist is not generally considered deviant. Still, he feels that those who "play it safe," who become "bureaucratic virtuosos," who avoid high ambitions and consequent frustration, clearly represent a departure from the cultural model in which men are obliged to strive actively, preferably through institutionalized procedures, to move onward and upward in the social hierarchy.

Rebellion. In this form of adaptation persons turn away from the conventional social structure and seek to establish a new or greatly modified social structure. This form of adaptation arises when "the institutional system is regarded as a barrier to the satisfaction of legitimized goals. . . ." [24] If it goes on to organized political action, the allegiance of persons such as the radical or revolutionary must be withdrawn from the existing social structure and transferred to new groups with new ideologies. The adaptation through rebellion requires little further discussion; in fact, the radical seldom is treated in conventional texts on deviant behavior.[25] In a sense Merton recognizes this for he points out that rebellion is an adaptation which is on a clearly different plane from the others. "It represents a transitional response seeking to *institutionalize* new goals and new procedures to be shared by other members of the society. It thus refers to efforts to *change* the existing cultural and social structure rather than to accommodate efforts *within* this structure." [26]

Merton, in a later paper, modified his view that rebellion was deviation in the same sense as were the other adaptations. Using different terms, he distinguished between rebellion, on the one hand, and innovation, ritualism, and retreatism, on the other.[27] In this paper he divided deviant behavior into two types, non-conforming and aberrant behavior, on the basis of

[24] *Ibid.,* 156.
[25] An exception is Edwin M. Lemert's *Social Pathology* (New York: McGraw-Hill Book Co., 1951), which contains the chapter "Radicalism and Radicals."
[26] Merton, *Social Theory and Social Structure, op. cit.,* 140.
[27] "The foregoing account of non-conforming behavior develops somewhat the pattern of behavior identified as 'rebellion' in the typology set forth in 'Social Structure and Anomie.' In that same typology, innovation, ritualism, and retreatism would comprise forms of aberrant behavior." Robert K. Merton, "Social Problems and Sociological Theory," *op. cit.,* 727.

social structure and consequences for the social system. Non-conformity is quite different from aberrant behavior such as crime and delinquency. The non-conformist announces his dissent publicly; the aberrant hides behind his departure from norms. The non-conformist challenges the legitimacy of social norms he rejects; the aberrant acknowledges the legitimacy of the norms he violates. The non-conformist tries to change the norms and may appeal to a higher morality; the aberrant merely wishes to escape the sanctioning force of present society. The non-conformist is often acknowledged by conventional society as departing from norms for disinterested purposes; the aberrant deviates to serve his own interests. Finally, the non-conformist draws upon the ultimate basic values of society for his goals, as distinguished from the aberrant whose interests are private, self-centered, and definitely antisocial.

Innovation. Societies where the culture emphasizes pecuniary success and the social structure places undue limitations on approved means provide numerous situations for the development of socially disapproved departures from institutional norms, in the form of innovative practices. The use of such illegitimate means as crime to achieve culturally prescribed goals of success, power, and wealth, therefore, has become common in our society. Such a form of adaptation presupposes that individuals have been inadequately socialized with respect to cultural goals emphasizing success-aspirations. As evidence Merton maintains that unlawful behavior such as delinquency and crime appears to be most common in the lower strata of our society and this is "a 'normal' response to a situation where the cultural emphasis upon pecuniary success has been absorbed, but where there is little access to conventional and legitimate means for becoming successful." [28] These pressures tend to result in the gradual reduction in efforts to use legitimate means and an increase in the use of more or less expedient illegitimate means. The opportunities of the lower class are largely restricted to manual labor, and this is often stigmatized. Consequently, "the status of unskilled labor and the consequent low income cannot readily compete *in terms of established standards of worth* with the promise of power and high income from organized vice, rackets and crime." [29]

[28] Merton, *Social Theory and Social Structure, op. cit.,* 145.
[29] *Ibid.*

Illegitimate innovations are not restricted to crime among the lower socioeconomic classes. Similar pressures for ever greater monetary status symbols are exerted on the upper socioeconomic groups and give rise to unethical business practices and what has been termed white collar crime. "On the top economic levels, the pressure toward innovation not infrequently erases the distinction between business-like strivings this side of the mores and sharp practices beyond the mores." [30] He points out, however, that "whatever the differential rates of deviant behavior in several social strata . . . the greatest pressures toward deviation are exerted on the lower social strata." [31]

In his second basic essay on anomie, Merton attempted to qualify his earlier all-embracing explanation of delinquency and crime as a form of anomie. He recognized that various types of behavior are included in the legal rubrics of delinquency and crime, and therefore that "the foregoing theory of anomie is designed to account for some, not all, forms of deviant behavior customarily described as criminal or delinquent." [32] Except, however, for specifically indicating that a theory of anomie does not account for much of the nonutilitarian character of behavior occurring in delinquent groups, he is vague as to which behavior is covered by his explanation and which is not.

The effect of innovative adaptation such as delinquency can be dynamic. Some individuals, because of their disadvantaged positions or personality patterns, are subjected more than others to the strains of the discrepancy between cultural goals and institutional means. They are, consequently, more vulnerable to deviant behavior. This "successful" adjustment tends to affect others and to lessen the legitimacy of the institutional norms for others. Others who did not respond to the original, rather slight anomie now do so. "This, in turn, creates a more acutely anomic situation for still other and initially less vulnerable individuals in the social system. In this way anomie and mounting rates of deviant behavior can be conceived as interacting in a process of social and cultural dynamics, with cumulatively disruptive consequences for the normative struc-

[30] *Ibid.*, 144.
[31] *Ibid.*, 141.
[32] *Ibid.*, 178.

ture, unless counteracting mechanisms of control are called into play." [33]

Not all deviations in the form of innovation are dysfunctional for society.[34] Some may form the basis for new institutions better equipped to function than older ones. In any event, innovation, even of a deviant nature, is likely to be dynamic. "Social dysfunction is not a latter-day terminological substitute for 'immorality' or 'unethical practice.' " [35] In some cases it may even be "the norms of the group which are at fault, and not the innovator who rejects them." Although the extent is unknown, some deviation from current norms is probably functional for the basic goals of a group.[36] As Merton has written later:

In the history of every society, one supposes, some of its culture heroes eventually come to be regarded as heroic in part because they are held to have had the courage and the vision to challenge the beliefs and routines of their society. The rebel, revolutionary, non-conformist, heretic or renegade of an earlier day is often the culture hero of today. Moreover, the accumulation of dysfunctions in a social system is often the prelude to concerted social change that may bring the system closer to the values that enjoy the respect of members of the society.[37]

Retreatism. The adaptation to disjunctive means and goals through retreatism is significant in understanding certain specific forms of deviant behavior. In a sense one might say this is not so much an adaptation but a rejection of both cultural goals and institutional means. "The retreatist pattern consists of substantial abandoning both of the once-esteemed cultural

---

[33] *Ibid.,* 180.

[34] There are a number of theoretical problems inherent in the terms "functional" and "dysfunctional," but since the terms are used by Merton and currently used extensively in sociological literature, we have employed them in this paper. See, for example, "Functionalism in Social Science," in Ernest Nagel, *The Structure of Science: Problems in the Logic of Scientific Explanation* (New York: Harcourt, Brace & World, 1961), 530–35, and Llewellyn Gross, Ed., *Symposium on Sociological Theory* (New York: Harper & Row, 1959).

[35] *Ibid.,* 182.

[36] The latent positive functions of deviance, such as innovation, have been developed by Lewis Coser, who has pointed out that the deviant helps to arouse the community to the consequences of the breach of norms, and that deviance from this point of view may have the aspects of "normalcy." Lewis A. Coser, "Some Functions of Deviant Behavior and Normative Flexibility," *Amer. J. Sociology,* 68 (September, 1962), 172–81.

[37] Merton, "Social Problems and Sociological Theory," *op. cit.,* 736.

goals and of institutionalized practices directed toward those
goals." [38] The individual has internalized fully the cultural
goals of success but finds inaccessible the institutionalized
means to obtain them. Under internalized pressure not to obtain the goal by illegitimate means such as innovation provides, the individual finds himself frustrated and handicapped. He does not renounce the success goal but instead
adopts escape mechanisms such as "defeatism, quietism and
retreatism."

Retreatism constitutes some of the adaptive activities of
"psychotics, autists, pariahs, outcasts, vagrants, tramps,
chronic drunkards and drug addicts." [39] Their mode of adaptation in many cases is derived from the social structure which,
in a sense, they have sought to repudiate. The retreatist form
of adaptation is particularly condemned by conventional society because it is nonproductive, nonstriving, attaches no value
to the success-goal of a society and does not use institutional
means. The conformist keeps the wheels of society running;
the innovator is at least "smart" and actively striving; the retreatist at least conforms to the mores. [40]

Retreatism is a private rather than a collectivized form of
adaptation. "Although people exhibiting this deviant behavior
may gravitate toward centers where they come into contact
with other deviants and although they may come to share in
the sub-culture of these deviant groups, their adaptations are
largely private and isolated rather than unified under the
aegis of a new cultural code." [41]

[38] Merton, *Social Theory and Social Structure, op. cit.,* 187.
[39] *Ibid.,* 153.
[40] *Ibid.,* 154. Merton later included in this adaptive response those whose
social relations and norms had become seriously disturbed. Examples of this
include widows and persons forced into retirement, and those experiencing
the anomie of prosperity and depression, where disruptions in status may
occur with great rapidity.
[41] *Ibid.,* 155.

Learning to Be Deviant

Edwin H. Sutherland and Donald R. Cressey

Although Durkheim had maintained that crime is normal in any society, many sociologists continued to regard deviant behavior as the result of individual pathology. Merton and Sutherland, however, helped to revive the Durkheimian notion of deviant behavior as a normal occurrence. On the level of social structure, Merton showed that deviant behavior could be seen as a normal response to an abnormal social situation. On the level of social interaction, Sutherland argued that people learn criminal behavior in the same way they learn law-abiding behavior. Thus, Sutherland concluded, deviant behavior is best explained by the principles of social learning rather than the principles of abnormal psychology.

If criminology is to be scientific, the heterogeneous collection of "multiple factors" known to be associated with crime and criminality should be organized and integrated by means of an explanatory theory which has the same characteristics as the scientific explanations in other fields of study. That is, the conditions which are said to cause crime should always be present when crime is present, and they should always be absent when crime is absent. Such a theory would stimulate, simplify, and give direction to criminological research, and it would provide a framework for understanding the significance of much of the knowledge acquired about crime and criminality in the past. Furthermore, it would be useful in control of crime, providing it could be "applied" in much the same way that the engineer "applies" the scientific theories of the physicist.

There are two complementary procedures which may be used to put order into criminological knowledge, to develop a causal theory of criminal behavior. The first is logical abstraction. Negroes, urban-dwellers, and young adults all have comparatively high crime rates. What do they have in common that results in these high crime rates? Research studies have shown that criminal behavior is associated in greater or less degree with the social and personal pathologies, such as poverty, bad housing, slum-residence, lack of recreational facilities, inadequate and demoralized families, feeble-mindedness, emotional instability, and other traits and conditions. What do these conditions have in common which apparently produces excessive criminality? Research studies have also demonstrated that many persons with those pathological traits and conditions do not commit crimes and that persons in the upper socio-economic class frequently violate the law, although they are not in poverty, do not lack recreational facilities, and are not feeble-minded or emotionally unstable. Obviously, it is not the conditions or traits themselves which cause crime, for the conditions are sometimes present when criminality does not occur, and they also are sometimes absent when criminality does occur. A causal explanation of criminal behavior can be reached by abstracting, logically, the mechanisms and processes which are common to the rich and the poor, Negroes and whites, urban and rural dwellers, young adults and old adults, and the emotionally stable and the emotionally unstable who commit crimes.

In arriving at these abstract mechanisms and processes, criminal behavior must be precisely defined and carefully distinguished from non-criminal behavior. The problem in criminology is to explain the criminality of behavior, not behavior, as such. The abstract mechanisms and processes common to the classes of criminals indicated above should not also be common to non-criminals. Criminal behavior is human behavior, has much in common with non-criminal behavior, and must be explained within the same general framework used to explain other human behavior. However, an explanation of criminal behavior should be a specific part of a general theory of behavior. Its specific task should be to differentiate criminal from non-criminal behavior. Many things which are necessary for behavior are not for that reason important to the criminality of behavior. Respiration, for instance, is necessary for any behavior, but the respiratory process cannot be used in an explanation of criminal behavior, for it does not differentiate criminal behavior from non-criminal behavior.

The second procedure for putting order into criminological knowledge is differentiation of levels of analysis. This means that the problem is limited to a particular part of the whole situation, largely in terms of chronology. The causal analysis must be held at a particular level. For example, when physicists stated the law of falling bodies they were not concerned with the reasons why a body began to fall except as this might affect the initial momentum. It made no difference to the physicist whether a body began to fall because it was dropped from the hand of an experimental physicist or rolled off the edge of a bridge because of vibration caused by a passing vehicle. Also, a round object would have rolled off the bridge more readily than a square object, but this fact was not significant for the law of falling bodies. Such facts were considered as existing on a different level of explanation and were irrelevant to the problem with which the physicists were concerned. Much of the confusion regarding criminal behavior is due to a failure to define and hold constant the level of explanation. By analogy, many criminologists would attribute some degree of causal power to the "roundness" of the object in the illustration above. However, consideration of time sequences among the factors associated with crime and criminality may lead to simplicity of statement. In the heterogeneous collection of factors associated with criminal behavior, one factor often occurs prior to another factor (in much the way that "roundness" occurs prior to "vibration," and "vibration" occurs prior to "rolling off a bridge"), but a theoretical statement about criminal behavior can be made without referring to those early factors. By holding the analysis at one level, the early factors are combined with or differentiated from later factors or conditions, thus reducing the number of variables which must be considered in a theory.

A motion picture several years ago showed two boys engaged in a minor theft; they ran when they were discovered; one boy had longer legs, escaped, and became a priest; the other had shorter legs, was caught, committed to a reformatory, and became a gangster. In this comparison, the boy who became a criminal was differentiated from the one who did not become a criminal by the length of his legs. But "length of legs" need not be considered in a criminological theory for, in general, no significant relationship has been found between criminality and length of legs and certainly many persons with short legs are law-abiding and many persons with long legs are criminals. The length of the legs does not determine criminality and has no necessary relation to criminality. In the illustration, the differential in the length of the boys' legs may be observed to be significant to subsequent criminality or non-criminality only to the degree that it determined the subsequent experiences and associations of the two boys. It is in these experiences and associations, then, that the mechanisms and processes which are important to criminality or non-criminality are to be found. A "one-level" theoretical explanation of crime would be concerned solely with these mechanisms and processes, not with the earlier factor "length of legs."

Two Types of Explanations of Criminal Behavior

Scientific explanations of criminal behavior may be stated either in terms of the processes which are operating at the moment of the occurrence of crime or in terms of the processes operating in the earlier history of the criminal. In the first case, the explanation may be called "mechanistic," "situational," or "dynamic"; in the second, "historical" or "genetic." Both types of explanation are desirable. The mechanistic type of explanation has been favored by physical and biological scientists, and it probably could be the more efficient type of explanation of criminal behavior. However, criminological explanations of the mechanistic type have thus far been notably unsuccessful, perhaps largely because they have been formulated in connection with the attempt to isolate personal and social pathologies among criminals. Work from this point of view has, at least, resulted in the conclusion that the immediate determinants of criminal behavior lie in the person-situation complex.

The objective situation is important to criminality largely to the extent that it provides an opportunity for a criminal act. A thief may steal from a fruit stand when the owner is not in sight but refrain when the owner is in sight; a bank burglar may attack a bank which is poorly protected but refrain from attacking a bank protected by watchmen and burglar alarms. A corporation which manufactures automobiles seldom or never violates the Pure Food and Drug Law, but a meat-packing corporation might violate this law with great frequency. But in another sense, a psychological or sociological sense, the situation is not exclusive of the person, for the situation which is important is the situation as defined by the person who is involved. That is, some persons define a situation in which a fruit-stand owner is out of sight as a "crime-committing" situation, while others do not so define it. Furthermore, the events in the person-situation complex at the time a crime occurs cannot be separated from the prior life experiences of the criminal. This means that the situation is defined by the person in terms of the inclinations and abilities which the person has acquired up to date. For example, while a person could define a situation in such a manner that criminal behavior would be the inevitable result, his past experiences would for the most part determine the way in which he defined the situation. An explanation of criminal behavior made in terms of these past experiences is an historical or genetic explanation.

The following paragraphs state such a genetic theory of criminal behavior on the assumption that a criminal act occurs when a situation appropriate for it, as defined by the person, is present. The theory should be regarded as tentative. . . .

Genetic Explanation of Criminal Behavior

The following statement refers to the process by which a particular person comes to engage in criminal behavior.

1. Criminal behavior is learned.   Negatively, this means that criminal behavior is not inherited, as such; also, the person who is not already trained in crime does not invent criminal behavior, just as a person does not make mechanical inventions unless he has had training in mechanics.

2. Criminal behavior is learned in interaction with other persons in a process of communication.   This communication is verbal in many respects but includes also "the communication of gestures."

3. The principal part of the learning of criminal behavior occurs within intimate personal groups.   Negatively, this means that the impersonal agencies of communication, such as movies and newspapers, play a relatively unimportant part in the genesis of criminal behavior.

4. When criminal behavior is learned, the learning includes (a) techniques of committing the crime, which are sometimes very complicated, sometimes very simple; (b) the specific direction of motives, drives, rationalizations, and attitudes.

5. The specific direction of motives and drives is learned from definitions of the legal codes as favorable or unfavorable.   In some societies an individual is surrounded by persons who invariably define the legal codes as rules to be observed, while in others he is surrounded by persons whose definitions are favorable to the violation of the legal codes. In our American society these definitions are almost always mixed, with the consequence that we have culture conflict in relation to the legal codes.

6. *A person becomes delinquent because of an excess of definitions favorable to violation of law over definitions unfavorable to violation of law.* This is the principle of differential association. It refers to both criminal and anti-criminal associations and has to do with counteracting forces. When persons become criminal, they do so because of contacts with criminal patterns and also because of isolation from anti-criminal patterns. Any person inevitably assimilates the surrounding culture unless other patterns are in conflict; a Southerner does not pronounce "r" because other Southerners do not pronounce "r." Negatively, this proposition of differential association means that associations which are neutral so far as crime is concerned have little or no effect on the genesis of criminal behavior. Much of the experience of a person is neutral in this sense, e.g., learning to brush one's teeth. This behavior has no negative or positive effect on criminal behavior except as it may be related to associations which are concerned with the legal codes. This neutral behavior is important especially as an occupier of the time of a child so that he is not in contact with criminal behavior during the time he is so engaged in the neutral behavior.

7. *Differential associations may vary in frequency, duration, priority, and intensity.* This means that associations with criminal behavior and also associations with anti-criminal behavior vary in those respects. "Frequency" and "duration" as modalities of associations are obvious and need no explanation. "Priority" is assumed to be important in the sense that lawful behavior developed in early childhood may persist throughout life, and also that delinquent behavior developed in early childhood may persist throughout life. This tendency, however, has not been adequately demonstrated, and priority seems to be important principally through its selective influence. "Intensity" is not precisely defined but it has to do with such things as the prestige of the source of a criminal or anti-criminal pattern and with emotional reactions related to the associations. In a precise description of the criminal behavior of a person these modalities would be stated in quantitative form and a mathe-

matical ratio be reached. A formula in this sense has not been developed, and the development of such a formula would be extremely difficult.

8. The process of learning criminal behavior by association with criminal and anti-criminal patterns involves all of the mechanisms that are involved in any other learning. Negatively, this means that the learning of criminal behavior is not restricted to the process of imitation. A person who is seduced, for instance, learns criminal behavior by association, but this process would not ordinarily be described as imitation.

9. While criminal behavior is an expression of general needs and values, it is not explained by those general needs and values since noncriminal behavior is an expression of the same needs and values. Thieves generally steal in order to secure money, but likewise honest laborers work in order to secure money. The attempts by many scholars to explain criminal behavior by general drives and values, such as the happiness principle, striving for social status, the money motive, or frustration, have been and must continue to be futile since they explain lawful behavior as completely as they explain criminal behavior. They are similar to respiration, which is necessary for any behavior but which does not differentiate criminal from noncriminal behavior.

It is not necessary, at this level of explanation, to explain why a person has the associations which he has; this certainly involves a complex of many things. In an area where the delinquency rate is high, a boy who is sociable, gregarious, active, and athletic is very likely to come in contact with the other boys in the neighborhood, learn delinquent behavior from them, and become a gangster; in the same neighborhood the psychopathic boy who is isolated, introverted, and inert may remain at home, not become acquainted with the other boys in the neighborhood, and not become delinquent. In another situation, the sociable, athletic, aggressive boy may become a member of a scout troop and not become involved in delinquent behavior. The person's associations are determined in a general context of social organization. A child is ordinarily reared in a family; the place of residence of the family is determined largely by family income; and the delinquency rate is in many respects related to the rental value of the houses. Many other aspects of social organization affect the kinds of associations a person has.

The preceding explanation of criminal behavior purports to explain the criminal and non-criminal behavior of individual persons. As indicated earlier, it is possible to state sociological theories of criminal behavior which explain the criminality of a community, nation, or other group. The problem, when thus stated, is to account for variations in crime rates and involves a comparison of the crime rates of various groups or the crime rates of a particular group at different times. The explanation of a crime rate must be consistent with the explanation of the criminal behavior of the person, since the crime rate is a summary statement of the number of persons in the group who commit crimes and the frequency with which they commit crimes. One of the best explanations of crime rates from this point of view is that a high crime rate is due to social disorganization. The term "social disorganization" is not entirely satisfactory and it seems preferable to substitute for it the term "differential social organization." The postulate on which this theory is based, regardless of the name, is that crime is rooted in the social organization and is an expression of that social organization. A group may be organized for criminal behavior or organized against criminal behavior. Most communities are organized both for criminal and anti-criminal behavior and in that sense the crime rate is an expression of the differential group organization. Differential group organization as an explanation of variations in crime rates is consistent with the differential association theory of the processes by which persons become criminals.

Anomie: Theory and Fact

Marshall B. Clinard

Most influential theories generate a good deal of criticism. Criticism usually focuses on the clarity and consistency of the concepts and on how well the theory fits the facts. In this excerpt, Clinard summarizes the criticisms of anomie theory that six sociologists made during a special symposium on the subject. The major criticisms are as follows:

From Marshall B. Clinard, *Anomie and Deviant Behavior,* pp. 40–47, 49–52. Copyright © 1964 by The Free Press of Glencoe, a division of The Macmillan Company. Reprinted by permission.

uniform values seem most unlikely in a complex society; there is no evidence of higher rates of deviant behavior among the lower classes; status discontent does not uniformly lead to deviant behavior; the so-called deviant's role in selecting a deviant style is much more complex than the theory allows for; and social control, as either cause or deterrent of deviant behavior, is completely overlooked by the theory.

The Uniformity of Cultural Values. Merton's theory of anomie tends to consider the social structure as consisting of more uniform values than an empirical examination of the diverse nature of most societies shows, according to Lemert. His main criticism of anomie is directed at the difficulty of identifying a set of values that could be considered universal in most societies today. There are not many societies, even pre-literate ones, in which "values learned in childhood, taught as a pattern, and reinforced by structured controls, serve to predict the bulk of the everyday behavior of members and to account for prevailing conformity to norms." [1] He adds also that to maintain that contemporary, urban, secular, and technologically based societies, such as the United States, "have a common value hierarchy, either culturally transmitted or structurally induced, strains credulity." [2] In societies where there is ethnic pluralism or newly migrant groups, or where a set of foreign values has been imposed, as on a colonial population, criminal behavior, for example, can be explained in the same way as conformity among members of the dominant group, i.e., by reference to traditionally patterned values and norms where there is *no* structural restriction of means. [3]

Rather than assuming "goals" to exist in American culture, as Merton does, Lemert believes that the "ends sought" grow out of the nature of associations in modern complex societies, the multi-value claims made on individuals, and the influence of modern technology. In this way it is possible to explain conformity as well as deviations without assuming "inherent" qualities or goals which apply to all members of a modern society. Individual members of a modern complex society may, as a result of interaction with diverse groups, modify their cultural values or change the order of their satisfaction. Con-

[1] Marshall B. Clinard, *Anomie and Deviant Behavior: A Discussion and Critique*, New York: The Free Press, 1964, p. 64.
[2] *Ibid.*, 66.
[3] *Ibid.*, 65.

sequently, it is doubtful whether study of the "ideal pattern"
or those values and norms presumably indoctrinated into individuals, will generally predict conformity in modern society.

*Evidence of Class Variations in the Distribution of Deviant Behav-
ior.* In his discussion, Lemert claims that Merton over-
emphasizes one aspect of social structure, class-limited access
to means, in explaining deviant behavior. He questions
whether we even have sufficient empiric evidence to support
the contention that deviant behavior is disproportionately
more common at lower class levels of society. A more discrimi-
nating concept or concepts than social class should, therefore,
be utilized in explaining how social structure influences deviation. Moreover, there is insufficient evidence to support the
view that deviation is the result of individual adaptations. . . .

*Pressures Toward Deviation Dependent on Position in the Social
Structure.* Several authors are critical of Merton's position that
limited access to the goals of society through legitimate means
by the lower socioeconomic groups is a principal source of
deviance. For example, while recognizing that social position
may play an important role in determining what means become available to reach certain ends, Lemert feels that other
factors are equally important, namely, group or collective adaptations, technology, psychic processes, and socio-biological
handicaps. All of these factors Merton largely neglects in his
emphasis on social class.

Lemert, moreover, maintains that "the discrete individual
remains for Merton the unit of analysis; the group as an arena
of interaction, influencing conformity and deviation, nowhere
comes to the fore in his treatment." [4] Many forms of deviant
behavior such as professional crime, prostitution, and opiate
addiction, are collective acts in which group-maintained values, as well as private values, are involved. Much of white
collar crime is of this order, as several studies have demonstrated. Likewise, much of what is termed conformity is a collective rather than an individual phenomenon or form of adaptation.

In their implementation of Merton's theory, Cohen, Cloward, and Ohlin made much of gang delinquency as a reflection of position or status discontent. In a test of this hypothesis, Short found this to be a chief component of those

---

[4] *Ibid.*, 76.

pressures toward deviant behavior, as measured by the magnitude of the mean discrepancy between the boys' occupational aspirations and occupational expectations; position discontent orders the boys in approximately the same manner as does their delinquency involvement, as measured by police records.[5] When position discontent was measured by a comparison of the occupational aspirations and expectations of the boys with the occupational achievements of their fathers, the Negro boys as a group had aspirations and expectations much higher than that of the white boys. On the other hand, there was an even higher degree of such position discontent among non-gang lower class boys, who had a lower rate of delinquency. A similar over-all picture was presented for perceiving educational opportunities as closed, but again, there were internal contradictions.

These contradictory findings suggest to Short the difficulty of conducting research on anomie theory. "High educational and occupational aspirations . . . seem clearly not to pressure the boys toward deviance, despite limitations, perceived and objective, in opportunities for achievement of these aspirations." [6] He offers a possible hypothesis that "high aspirations are indicative of identification with conventional values and institutions. The stake in conformity . . . serves to protect the boys from delinquency involvement." [7]

Again, contary to Cohen and Cloward and Ohlin, Short found that gang boys recognized the moral validity and legitimacy of middle class values. As opposed to Cohen, no rebellion against the social system nor evidence of reaction against middle class values was found. Short then advanced a significant point when he maintained that the conception of "social" which is basic to the anomie paradigm of opportunity structures and status deprivation must be "broadened to include situations which are more immediate to the boys, such as local community norms and opportunities, and normative and status considerations *within* the group." [8]

Short goes on to argue that while status considerations are important in explaining a gang boy's behavior, they do not have to be sought in middle class institutions and criteria of suc-

---

[5] *Ibid.*, 111–113.
[6] *Ibid.*, 115.
[7] *Ibid.*, 116.
[8] *Ibid.*, 115.

cess. Status deprivation can also be important in a more immediate context, such as the boy's status as a male or as a member
of a particular gang. As a tentative conclusion therefore, let us
take the position that the "behavior of gang boys may be understood as an attempt by these boys to seek and create alternative status systems in the form of the gang, and that delinquency arises sometimes as a by-product and sometimes as a
direct product of this attempt." [9] He enlarges the thesis that
while gang boys encounter status deprivation within "respectable society," the status situations which are of immediate concern are those which relate to ongoing processes which involve
their daily lives. Each boy then must adjust to a variety of statuses, a process which Short terms "status management."

This view is far removed from one which seeks to explain
delinquency by the economic, educational, and other depriva-
tions of the larger social structure, although Short says one
may consider his explanation as an extension of the larger
theory. He believes that the social structure operates to determine or to influence strongly economic and educational goals,
aspirations, and opportunities. The theory of anomie, however, fails to take into account the ongoing group processes of
interaction, from which delinquent behavior may develop. . . .

The Role of the Actor. Lemert has a major objection to Merton's view of choice and action by individuals in our type of society. He feels that Merton simplifies something that is actually
quite complex. The individual is not a free agent in his choice
of values, but rather is restricted by the claims of various
groups to which he belongs. The "pressures" on individuals
come from these conflicting claims rather than from cultural
emphasis on goals. Special interest groups in our society attempt to advance or protect their own sets of values. . . . As
Lemert says, . . . the "emphasis placed on normative means is
determined by their cost, that is, by the *particular* values that
must be sacrificed in order to adopt means." [10] . . .

In his paper on delinquency, Short states that anomie is too
mechanical a theory and that it disregards the actor. "What is
lacking in most models of gang behavior is precisely this type
of Meadian act, in which behavior is seen as a process of *con-
tinuous adjustment* of actors to one another, rather than as a

[9] *Ibid.*, 117.
[10] *Ibid.*, 70.

sort of mechanical reaction to some one factor or combination of factors in the situation, whether they be characteristics of actors, or subcultures, or other features. It is this conception, too, which is lacking in anomie theory." [11] What the theory of anomie refers to as "pressures toward deviance" needs both theoretical and empirical specification. . . .

Retreatism as an Adaptation of Means and Goals . . . Three characteristic types of retreatism are generally considered by anomie theory to be drug addiction, alcoholism, and mental disorder. Lindesmith and Gagnon maintain that drug addicts are not retreatists but rather claim that difficulties in securing the drug make the addict of necessity an "active" rather than retreatist person. Snyder, while recognizing the research difficulties in studying the phenomenon of alcoholism, which has a prolonged history and by definition is "retreatist," feels that there is evidence to support the contention that the alcoholic was anomic even before his addiction began. . . .

Lindesmith and Gagnon point out that while some of the characteristics ascribed to retreatism apply to some drug addicts, none is accurate as a general description. Addicts are not persons who have abandoned both goals and means and who are characterized, in Merton's terms, by "defeatism, quietism, and resignation." In actuality, there are substantial numbers of addicts to whom such a description does not apply; there are addicts who are "responsible and productive members of society, who share the common frame of values, who have not abandoned the quest for success and are not immune to the frustrations involved in seeking it." [12] They go on to point out that Merton's description of the retreatist, while it does not adequately describe the actual addict, "does provide a reasonably accurate portrait of the current popular stereotype of the addict."

The "double failure" hypothesis of drug addiction advanced by Cloward and Ohlin, and in part implicit by Merton, namely, that the addict cannot achieve success goals by either legitimate or illegitimate means, comes in for pointed criticism by Lindesmith and Gagnon. They state: (1) It is not clear whether there is an actual objective performance failure or whether the individual tends to feel simply frustrated by a

[11] *Ibid.,* 124.
[12] *Ibid.,* 178.

perceived block to success. (2) The hypothesis is not applicable to the doctor addict, among others. (3) The addicted person is not necessarily a failure in crime. (4) One cannot judge early adolescents, among whom such phenomena might occur, as double failures because of the age factor. . . . (5) While it may be conceded that there are many addicts who are failures in both the criminal and noncriminal world, it may be argued that addiction is probably more potent as a cause of failure than failure is a cause of addiction.[13]

For the addict in American society, the pursuit of drugs becomes a stimulus to action, not an escape from the requirements of society. One might describe the successful drug user as a "double success" rather than a double failure, the conventional rewards of accomplishment being an assured and adequate supply of drugs. In fact, one of the defects in the theory of anomie is the contention that the inner strain of anomie supposedly is reduced by the use of drugs, when actually, addiction ordinarily widens the "gap between aspirations and the means of achievement and to intensify, rather than resolve, inner anomie-generated conflict." [14]

The use of opiates by real addicts does not have the euphoric effect often described by those who assume that drugs are used for escape. As Lindesmith and Gagnon maintain, "The paradox anomie theory faces is that while opiates can be used for retreatist motives, they are used in this way primarily by those who are not addicted to them." [15] Addiction to opiates is not retreatism; rather, many persons are able to overcome retreatism through the use of drugs and to carry on their daily activities.

In an analytical paradigm they show that there is no invariant relationship between anomie, deviance, retreatism, and drug addiction. Not all drug addiction arises from anomie or is retreatist or deviant, and drug addiction may produce anomia. Addiction may, therefore, occur in any combination with the other three and also when all are absent. Likewise, anomie, deviance, and retreatism might also occur singly or in combination in the absence of addiction. Anomie as a theory does not, therefore, "specify the conditions under which the

[13] *Ibid.*, 177.
[14] *Ibid.*, 180.
[15] *Ibid.*, 183.

phenomenon being explained will occur and in the absence of which will not occur." [16]

Lindesmith and Gagnon disagree with the assumption that the use of drugs necessarily constitutes deviation, whether retreatist or otherwise, for like other forms of deviant behavior, the definition may shift according to time, place, the definer, and other considerations. They cite evidence that a substantial part of marihuana and opiate use today cannot be viewed as deviant behavior. Similarly, the nondeviant use of opiates can be illustrated by their wide use in Western society, in the past and today, either in therapy or to relieve pain. This may lead to addiction without the patient having voluntarily administered the drug. Their conclusion is: "Since the theory of anomie is proposed as a theory of deviance, and since some drug use is not deviant, the theory can hardly be relevant to the non-deviant portion. If the theory is applied to the non-deviant drug use, or if it is restricted to 'deviant drug use,' it meets substantial difficulties." [17]

Differential Association: Theory and Fact

Edwin H. Sutherland

> *As we have already noted, influential theories are likely to generate a great deal of criticism. Unsolicited self-criticism, however, is rare. In this excerpt, Sutherland examines his own theory of differential association, and his criticisms are almost as trenchant as the theory itself.*
>
> *Sutherland finds his original differential association theory deficient on three counts. Even with the kind of differential association most likely to eventuate in criminal behavior, he points out, the criminal behavior need not occur if (a) there are few opportunities to commit crime, (b) the need is relatively weak, and (c) there are alternative ways of solving the problem.*

[16] *Ibid.*, 188.
[17] *Ibid.*, 163.

The theory of differential association as the explanation of criminal behavior postulated criminal behavior as a closed system. Differential association was regarded as both the necessary and the sufficient cause of a person's entrance into the closed system of criminal behavior. Association with criminal patterns was defined as the necessary cause because it was felt that no person could enter the system of criminal behavior unless he had associated with criminal patterns. This was regarded as analogous to learning the English language: a person acquires the English language only by associating with it; he does not invent it, and he does not acquire it by associating with Republican politics or Presbyterian theology except as those cultural systems involve the English language. Also, differential association was regarded as the sufficient cause, in the sense that all persons who associate with criminal patterns participate in criminal behavior unless inhibited by associations with anti-criminal patterns. According to this hypothesis, whether a person enters or does not enter the closed system of criminal behavior is determined entirely by the ratio between associations with criminal patterns and associations with anti-criminal patterns, with their varying modalities of frequency, intensity, prestige of the source of the pattern, and other modalities. Variations in other social conditions and in personal characteristics were regarded as factors in the causation of criminal behavior only as they affected differential association with criminal and anti-criminal patterns.

While some questions have been raised regarding the necessity of association with criminal patterns, these questions are largely verbal and can be answered with approximate finality. The crucial questions and criticisms have been directed at the sufficiency of differential association as a cause of criminal behavior. Certain of the factors in the causation of crime which are extraneous to differential association will be considered in this analysis, which results in the conclusion that differential association is not a sufficient cause of criminal behavior. In the methodology which is used, with the explanation postulated as universal, the only thing needed to disprove an hypothesis is a single exception.

Opportunity

One factor in criminal behavior which is at least partially extraneous to differential association is opportunity. Criminal behavior is partially a function of opportunities to commit specific classes of crimes, such as embezzlement, bank burglary, or illicit heterosexual intercourse. Opportunities to commit crimes of these classes are partially a function of physical factors and of cultures which are neutral as to crime. Consequently criminal behavior is not caused entirely by association with criminal and anti-criminal patterns, and differential association is not a sufficient cause of criminal behavior.

This argument will be elaborated and illustrated. First, criminal behavior is partially a function of opportunity. Persons in prisons seldom commit illicit heterosexual intercourse because they are physically segregated from persons of the opposite sex and thus have little opportunity to commit this crime. Convictions of public intoxication in Germany during World War I decreased almost to zero because intoxicating beverages were not manufactured and were not available for consumption, and the Germans consequently had no opportunity to become intoxicated. Negroes are seldom convicted of embezzlement because they are seldom in positions of financial trust, in which alone embezzlement is possible. It is true, of course, that certain crimes, such as petty theft, may be committed by practically anyone in modern society and that opportunity is practically always present. The only thing necessary for the present purpose, however, is to indicate that criminal behavior is sometimes limited by lack of opportunity. It is axiomatic that persons who commit a specific crime must have the opportunity to commit that crime. On the other hand, opportunity is not a sufficient cause of crime, since some persons who have opportunities to embezzle, become intoxicated, engage in illicit heterosexual intercourse or to commit other crimes do not do so. Consequently opportunity does not differentiate all persons who commit a particular crime from all persons who do not commit that crime.[1]

Second, the opportunity to commit a specific crime is par-

[1] The complexity of the problem is increased, but the conclusion is not altered, by introducing the concepts of attempts or conspiracies to commit a particular crime. It is difficult to conceive of a situation in which a person may not attempt or conspire with others to commit a specific crime. While

tially a function of physical factors and of the non-criminal culture. The illustrations presented previously show that physical barriers, including physical space, interfere with crimes of certain types and also that occupational and general social positions are generally determined by cultural elements which are neutral so far as crime is concerned. For instance, the opportunity for a Negro to obtain a position of financial trust is limited by race prejudice, and consequently the low rate of embezzlement among Negroes is explained by race prejudice. While opportunity may be partially a function of association with criminal patterns and of the specialized techniques thus acquired, it is not determined entirely in that manner, and consequently differential association is not the sufficient cause of criminal behavior.

Intensity of Need

Another criticism of differential association as a sufficient cause of crime is that criminal behavior varies with the intensity of a particular need independently of variations in differential association with criminal and anti-criminal patterns. This criticism is illustrated by the following types of evidence. Thefts are most frequent in the lower socioeconomic class, which is in greater poverty than the upper socioeconomic class. The members of the Donner party, caught in the snow in the mountains during their trip to the Pacific Coast in the forties, with their food supply exhausted, generally resorted to cannibalism. Fathers who engage in incest with their daughters are concentrated in the age group between forty and sixty and in families in which the mothers have died, are sick, or are for other reasons not available for legitimate sex relations. Prisoners who are segregated from the other sex and unable to engage in legitimate heterosexual relations frequently resort to homosexual relations.

This evidence is not derived from careful studies of situations in which differential association is held constant, and it can to some extent be harmonized with the theory of differen-

---

the opportunities to attempt or conspire to commit a particular crime are much less limited than the opportunities to perform the primary tasks of a successfully consummated crime, the fact remains that variations in opportunities are associated with variations in crimes committed.

tial association. While thefts, as conventionally treated, are concentrated in the lower socioeconomic class, which is in the greatest poverty, more subtle forms of illegal appropriation of property flourish, perhaps with equal frequency, in the upper socioeconomic or white-collar class. Also, thefts do not increase appreciably in periods of depression, when poverty increases, presumably because a depression does not appreciably modify the associations of persons; this indicates that when associations are held constant, increased poverty does not result in increased thefts. Fathers whose wives are dead or sick often spend an increased portion of their time in low resorts where they may have more contact with various forms of illicit sex behavior, and this may include contact with the pattern of incest.

Furthermore, it is unnecessary to postulate an increase in the number of associations with criminal behavior in order to account for an increase in the crime rate. A person may learn, through association with a criminal pattern, a definition of the situation in which it is appropriate to commit a particular crime. He commits this crime, however, only when the situation defined as appropriate arises or can be located. Having learned through association with others that he should murder his wife if he catches her in an unfaithful relationship, he does so, in accordance with the learned definition, only when the situation arises. Even the general culture of the modern community includes a definition of theft as appropriate in conditions of great emergency. The statement has been frequently made by respectable persons: "If I could find no alternatives except starvation or theft, I would steal." Practically everyone in the modern community has come in contact with that definition of theft and may, without additional contact with thieves, engage in theft when he reaches that situation.

This rebuttal of the evidence that crimes vary with the intensity of needs, independently of differential association, is presumably to some extent justified. Neither the evidence for this criticism nor the evidence against it is conclusive. The conclusion may be reached, however, that the sufficiency of differential association as an explanation of crime is questionable.

Crime and Alternate Behaviors

In many situations, at least, criminal behavior is not absolutely determined but only in relation to other behaviors,
against which it may be balanced in the process of making
choices. The relativity of criminal behavior in this sense may
be illustrated in the following cases.

An isolated and unattractive girl was taken into an intimate
friendship by another girl and was being gradually inducted
into a homosexual relationship. In time the first girl became
vaguely aware that the relationship was progressing beyond
the conventional limits and became disturbed. She secured
books on homosexuality and discovered with horror that the
relationship was defined in the literature as the early stages of
sex perversion. She went to the other girl with a firm determination to sever the relationship. But as she talked with the
other girl and thought about it in more detail, she was con-
fronted with two alternatives: isolation and loneliness without
homosexuality, or a much desired intimate friendship that involved homosexuality. She chose the latter and became a confirmed homosexual not only because of her initial contacts
with that pattern but also because she could find no other way
of satisfying the need for intimacy and friendship. If she had
been an attractive and gregarious girl, she would presumably,
given the same contacts with the pattern of homosexuality,
have severed this initial relationship without hesitation.

McCracken, the owner of a new newspaper in a California
community, began a campaign of vilification of French, the
owner of an established newspaper in the same community.
For months McCracken used great ingenuity in ridiculing
French. French went to McCracken and remonstrated, but
this did no good. He consulted an attorney as to the possibility
of a suit against McCracken, and also consulted the postal
authorities as to the possibility of prosecuting under the postal
regulations; but these efforts were futile. He considered fis-
ticuffs, but McCracken weighed over two hundred pounds
and was over six feet tall, whereas French weighed one
hundred and thirty pounds and was five feet seven. The irrita-
tions continued, and French's anger accumulated. Finally he
secured a gun, killed McCracken, and then surrendered himself to the police.

French had tried several alternatives and had found them

futile. Presumably, if one of the legal methods had been successful, French would not have committed the murder. The case history gives no information as to French's contact with patterns of murder, and it is possible that some of his friends may have said repeatedly, "If he treated me that way, I would kill him." Even if this is true, the murder was caused not only by association with patterns of murder but by the failure of alternate ways of behavior.

The theory of differential association postulated the ratio between criminal patterns and anti-criminal patterns as the cause of criminal behavior. No organized effort has been made to develop that formula in a quantitative form, but the possibility of quantifying it is implicit in the abstract proposition. If a scoring method were developed, it might show, for instance, that association with a particular criminal pattern, such as murder or homosexuality, had a score of five, that association with the anti-criminal pattern also had a score of five, and that the differential association quotient was unity, which would be the ideal borderline between committing a particular crime and not committing that crime. Since associations with various patterns of crimes vary, the quotient would vary from one crime to another. A quotient in excess of unity would mean that the person would engage in crime, whereas a quotient of less than unity would mean that the person would not engage in crime.

The abstracts of case histories which have been presented demonstrate that a person does not engage in or refrain from a particular crime because of his criminal associations alone but because of those associations plus tendencies toward alternate ways of satisfying whatever needs happen to be involved in a particular situation. Consequently it is improper to view criminal behavior as a closed system, and participation in criminal behavior is not to be regarded as something that is determined exclusively by association with criminal patterns.

In the general area of juvenile delinquency it is probable that the most significant difference between juveniles who engage in delinquency and those who do not is that the latter are provided abundant opportunities of a conventional type for satisfying their recreational interests, while the former lack those opportunities or facilities. The ordinary child in the middle-class family presumably may have no more contacts with anti-delinquent patterns than the child in the slum areas, but his time is occupied more completely with activities which are neutral so far as the criminal code is concerned.

Methodologies

For the reasons that have been outlined and doubtless for additional reasons differential association as a sufficient explanation of criminal behavior is invalid. Consequently, questions arise as to the procedures that may be used in the future. Several possibilities may be considered.

First, the effort to state universal causes of criminal behavior might be abandoned and a retreat made to the "multiple-factor" approach (which should not be called a theory) to explanation. This method consists of the listing of all of the variables associated with criminal behavior, with a minimum of attention to the interrelations among these variables. For instance, needs and opportunities have been found to be associated with criminal behavior in ways which are not included in differential association. The multiple factor approach would merely add these two variables to differential association, regardless of the lack of discreteness in the factors and regardless of the fact that they overlap differential association in many respects. In many stages this approach may be the best that can be made, but it is regarded by some students as an interim condition, as a makeshift to be tolerated only until a more adequate approach can be developed. Knowledge which results from this approach has a limited utility either from the point of view of understanding or of control.

A second suggestion is that two approaches to the explanation of behavior supplement each other, one in terms of needs, wishes, values, goals, etc., which generally are oriented to the future, the other in terms of the genesis of those needs, wishes, etc., which are oriented to the past. According to this position, the first step in explanation is to analyze the overt behavior in terms of these needs, values, and goals, and the next step to trace the genesis of these factors, perhaps in terms of association with various patterns of behavior. This position has a certain plausibility, but analysis shows that it is fundamentally unsound.

In a study of a case history, such as those presented above for illustrative purposes, it is possible to analyze the alternate behaviors under consideration in terms of values and goals, and it is also possible to trace the genesis of each of these values. The difficulty arises when one attempts to go beyond an individual case and reach generalizations regarding a class of overt behaviors, such as all murders, or all thefts, or, outside the field of criminal behavior, all divorces or all church-goings. One person may go to church for the satisfaction of needs which another person satisfies by murder. Persons steal to satisfy hunger, to provide medical care for a sick child, to go to the movies, to secure flashy clothes, to make contributions to the USO, to acquire status in a certain group, to injure certain other persons. Also, they engage in lawful employment for all of the above reasons. These evaluations consequently do not differentiate one class of behaviors from another class of behaviors. The evaluations—needs, goals, etc.—are necessary in behavior of any kind, but they do not differentiate behavior of one kind from behavior of another kind if the behaviors are defined in terms such as crime, church-going, political action. The place of these needs and values in behavior is in this respect analogous to the place of muscular processes. Behavior would not occur without muscular processes, but the muscular processes do not differentiate stealing from lawful work. The study of muscular processes, of course, is desirable for certain purposes, but since the muscular processes in criminal behavior are not unique, their study contributes nothing to the understanding of criminal behavior. Similarly the needs, values, goals, etc., in criminal behavior are not unique, and explanations cannot be made in terms of them.

If the needs or goals are taken as specific, e.g., the need to dance, rather than the need to secure exercise, the procedure is tautological. The dancing behavior of a person may be "explained" by his "need to dance," but such an "explanation" contributes nothing to the understanding of the behavior. On the other hand, the dancing behavior cannot be explained by the need to secure exercise, since the need for exercise might be expressed in swimming, walking, playing golf, or sawing wood, as well as in dancing. If the psychological dynamism is stated as a specific drive, it explains nothing; and if it is stated as a general drive, it does not differentiate between one class of behaviors and another class of behaviors. The problem of criminal behavior is precisely the problem of differentiating one class of behaviors from another class.

The frustration-aggression hypothesis is a particular case of the attempt to explain behavior by a general psychological dynamism. Frustration is essentially another name for "need," and certain theorists postulate aggression as the universal reaction to frustration. In order to make this postulation they are compelled to define aggression in a manner which makes it include submission, ordinarily regarded as the opposite of aggression. Even if the concept, as defined, be accepted, the fact of frustration does not explain why lawful methods of aggression are used on some occasions and unlawful methods of aggression on others. That is, frustration does not differentiate between lawful and unlawful behavior and is therefore not an explanation of unlawful behavior. Many psychiatrists have been prone to conclude, when they find a maladjusted person to be frustrated, that the frustration is the explanation of the maladjustment. This procedure has no more logical justification than the explanation that someone sings well "because he is a Negro" or is guilty of sharp practices "because he is a Jew."

The conclusion is that a class of behaviors, such as all crimes, or all murders, cannot be explained by needs, goals, values, etc. If the analysis of behaviors in terms of needs and values is to be valid, the problems must be formulated in terms of needs and values rather than in terms of crimes, murders, or divorces. It is possible that if the problems are stated as value units, generalizations may be made in terms of values, but if they are stated in other terms (e.g., crimes, murders, or divorces) generalizations cannot be made in terms of values.

Another procedure is to regard differential association as one of the very important processes in the genesis of criminal behavior. In situations like those of the criminal tribes of India, where the differential association quotient may be presumed to be far above unity, differential association is essentially the total explanation; but the hypothesis becomes increasingly uncertain in its operation as the quotient approaches unity. This might then be regarded as a statement of a law which is valid only in ideal conditions, as the law of falling bodies is valid only in a vacuum, and efforts might be made to determine and perhaps measure the various extraneous factors which enter into the genesis of criminal behavior when the ideal conditions do not prevail. Perhaps this is not

different from the present stage in the explanation of tuberculosis, in which the tubercle bacilli are demonstrated to be
necessary factors but not sufficient factors, and in which the
other factors, which may be vaguely generalized as "susceptibility," have not been definitely formulated. Just as continued
work on these factors of "susceptibility" may be expected to
result in a generalization at some future time, so continued
work on the factors which interfere with the operation of the
hypothesis of differential association may result in a valid generalization regarding these other things. The two variables
which have been discussed previously are opportunities and
needs. It may be possible to describe in general the factor of
opportunities as Stouffer has, regarding mobility as a law of
intervening opportunities for crimes. Similarly, it may be possible to include with differential association those factors of
need which have to be included to provide a valid generalization regarding crime.

If these efforts do not succeed, and it is very probable that
they will not, the methodology must either remain at the multiple-factor stage of development, or else the attempt to explain criminal behavior must be abandoned and problems formulated in terms of value units. It is perhaps suggestive that
Lindesmith, who has been one of the foremost proponents of
this methodology, adopts substantially the latter procedure in
his study of drug addiction. In his explanations of the person
who ceases the use of narcotic drugs, perhaps for many years,
Lindesmith insists that this person is still an "addict" and is so
regarded by himself and by other addicts. This shows that his
unit, which he has attempted to explain, is a psychological or
value unit rather than a unit of overt behavior.

Questions for Discussion

1. Sutherland and Cressey discuss different levels of causal analysis. How
do Merton's anomie and Sutherland's differential association theories differ
in their levels?

2. How does Sutherland's theory integrate the multiple factors that may
help to explain criminal behavior?

3. Can Merton's and Sutherland's theories be integrated? In what way?

4. Consider Clinard's critique of Merton's anomie theory. Do you see it as
a plea for integration with differential association theory? How so, or why
not?

Selected References

Blake, Judith, and Kingsley Davis. "Norms, Values, and Sanctions." In *Handbook of Modern Sociology,* edited by Robert E. L. Faris, pp. 456–84. Chicago: Rand McNally & Co., 1964.
Focuses on the sources of unintentional deviance, the sources of deviant motivation, and the factors preventing deviant motives from erupting into deviant behavior. The answers are provided from existing sociological literature.

Clinard, Marshall B. *Sociology of Deviant Behavior.* 3rd ed. New York: Holt, Rinehart & Winston, 1968.
A textbook that led to the renaming of many courses. Clinard organizes this book around the adaptive response of the person to his special situation by means of cultural selection. Deviant behavior is regarded as one type of adaptive response.

————, ed. *Anomie and Deviant Behavior: A Discussion and Critique.* New York: The Free Press of Glencoe, 1964.
A useful dialogue regarding anomie theory. Clinard restates Merton's anomie theory and its implications. Six sociologists then criticize the application of anomie theory to particular types of deviant acts. Finally, Merton responds to these critics. A useful appendix inventories eighty-eight empirical and theoretical studies of anomie—itself a testimony to the tremendous influence of this theory.

Cohen, Albert K. "Deviant Behavior." In *International Encyclopedia of Social Sciences,* edited by David L. Sills, vol. 4, pp. 148–55. New York: Macmillan and Free Press, 1968.
A scholarly essay on the rise and development of the deviant behavior perspective.

————. *Delinquent Boys: The Culture of the Gang.* Glencoe: The Free Press, 1955.
A creative synthesis of the theories of anomie and differential association, in which Cohen develops an influential theory of delinquent subcultures. A landmark in the tradition of deviant behavior analysis.

Durkheim, Emile. *Suicide: A Study in Sociology.* Translated by John A. Spaulding and George Simpson. Glencoe: The Free Press, 1951.
The classic statement regarding anomie. Durkheim shows that rates of suicide are higher under certain types of social conditions. One such condition is anomie—i.e., normlessness.

6. Labeling

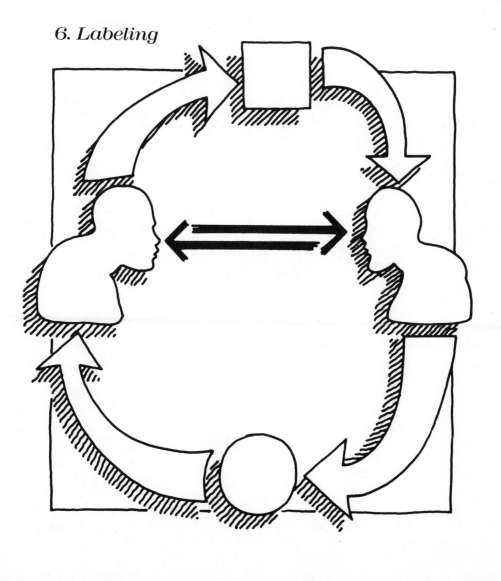

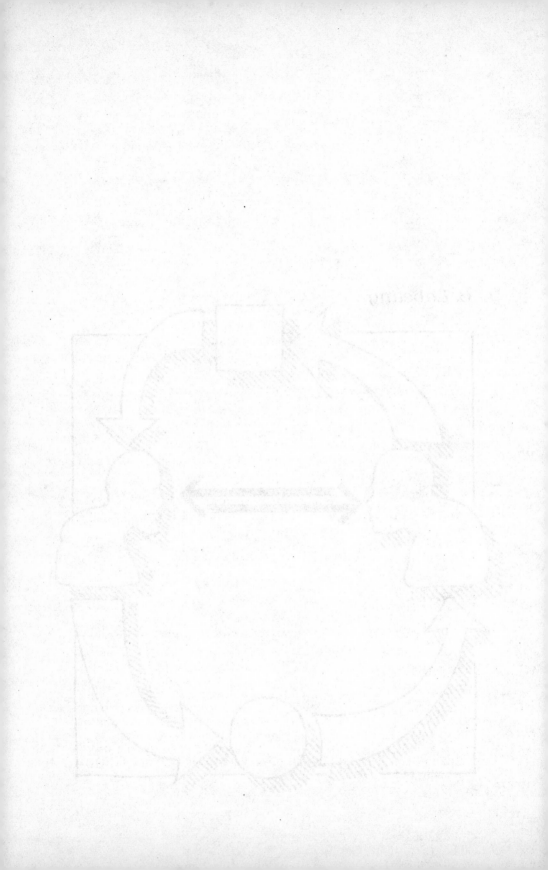

Perspectives differ in the questions they ask and the answers they yield. The sociology of deviant behavior, for example, initially asks *why people commit* crimes or other deviant acts. Sociologists in this tradition attempt to determine the necessary and sufficient conditions that produce deviant acts. The labeling perspective,[1] on the other hand, examines the social definition of deviance. Sociologists in this tradition want to know *how people define* situations, persons, processes, or events as problematic.

Inspired by Fuller, most sociologists agree that a social problem consists of a subjective definition and an objective condition. But, with few exceptions, sociologists have paid more attention to the objective condition than to the subjective definition. Students of labeling, however, have in recent years reversed the emphasis by taking a closer look at the process of subjective definition, and this has led to an entirely different line of sociological questioning.

This chapter discusses the people who developed the labeling perspective, the questions they raised, and the events in sociology that contributed to the development of this perspective.

[1] A growing number of sociologists now prefer to call this approach the "interactionist perspective" rather than "labeling theory." The newer name was first used by Earl Rubington and Martin S. Weinberg, eds., *Deviance: The Interactionist Perspective* (New York: Macmillan, 1968) to connote that the "labeling" perspective fits into the broader tradition of "symbolic interactionism." Becker now also prefers the term "interactionist."

Focus and Concerns of the Labeling
Perspective

Included in the labeling perspective is a set of assumptions about how people define situations. Perhaps the principal assumption is that people define all the recurrent situations in which they find themselves by means of interests and values. If so, then of course all definitions are related to people's positions in a given situation, the values they hold, and the interests they wish to further. A broad-gauged sociology, then, would have to study how all parties in a problematic situation define the situation and act in accordance with their own interests and values.

One line of attack of the labeling approach has been to look at the world from the vantage point of persons who have been socially defined by others as deviant, as well as from the vantage point of those who do the defining. Another has been to study the making of social rules (laws, organizational definitions, etc.) and the practices by which they are enforced. Both lines of attack have led to some very important research findings. They have also, however, led some sociologists to accuse the labeling approach of having a vested interest in the underdog, almost to the point of accepting a "distorted" view of social reality.[2] We turn now to some of the conditions that gave rise to the labeling perspective.

The Discipline and Its Problems

The labeling perspective arose relatively late in American sociology's fourth period (*the cultivating of specialties*: 1954 on). During this period, the study of crime, deviance, and social control became specialties. Thus, sociologists in both the deviant behavior and the labeling perspectives generally restricted themselves to the study of these social problems.

What transpired during this period to foster the labeling perspective? Three factors contributed—namely, extension of concepts, conflict between schools, and interest in questions left unanswered by the deviant behavior perspective.

[2] See, for example, David Bordua, "Deviant Behavior and Social Control," *The Annals* 369 (January 1967), pp. 149–63; and Alvin W. Gouldner, "The Sociologist as Partisan," *The American Sociologist* 3 (May 1968), pp. 103–16.

Extension of concepts. The drive to refine and extend concepts characterizes the history of most sciences, due to the efforts of scientists to explain a greater number of phenomena by a smaller number of concepts. During sociology's fourth period, theorists worked on refining concepts while researchers extended these concepts to new areas. This combination of labors contributed to the growing body of sociological knowledge. As a tradition called symbolic interactionism developed, researchers began to extend its concepts to the study of social problems, and the labeling perspective evolved out of this extension. (The role of the interactionist tradition in the development of the labeling perspective is dealt with more fully in the section on philosophical sources.)

Conflict between schools. Competition between Chicago sociology and Harvard sociology, noted in the preceding chapter, grew out of different conceptions of the sociological enterprise. Harvard emphasized structure, and many of its students developed, refined, and extended the concepts of structural-functionalism. Chicago, on the other hand, emphasized social process and developed, refined, and extended the concepts of symbolic interactionism. Of course, notions of the differences between these schools of thought were exaggerated and frequently bordered on caricature. Nonetheless, opposition between the two schools almost required that one segment of sociologists study the social processes involved in social problems while the others look for their sources in social structure. Thus, the politics of sociology, as it were, led sociologists congenial to the Chicago school to join the labeling camp and followers of the Harvard school to oppose it.

Unanswered questions. There are limitations in the deviant behavior perspective related to the specialized and complex nature of the society. In a multigroup society, conforming to the rules of one's own group sometimes requires violating another group's rules, whether legal, moral, or social. Similarly, not all violators are caught or punished, even though their offenses may be widely known. Finally, of those who are officially caught, not everyone is classified and treated in the same way.

These aspects of social problems seemed inexplicable from the deviant behavior perspective, leading some sociologists to ask different sorts of questions. Sociologists began to ask when violations are sanctioned, by whom, against whom, and with what social consequences. With these questions, the labeling perspective was born.

For those in the deviant behavior tradition, the labeling perspective stereotypes and oversimplifies the phenomenon of deviance. For those in the labeling tradition, it signifies a legitimate extension of interactionist concepts. Some differences between the interests of the two perspectives are summarized below.

Etiology. Whereas the underlying causes of deviant behavior (e.g., broken home, social class, anomie, psychiatric disorder) are of great interest in the deviant behavior perspective, they are of little interest in the labeling perspective.

Initiating factor. The initiating factor, or the last act in the etiological chain, is of considerable interest to those who use the deviant behavior perspective but of less interest to students of labeling.

Social reactions. Social reactions to alleged deviance are the central concern of labeling theory but not of the deviant behavior perspective.

The official record. The deviant behavior perspective takes official records for granted, using them as indicators of deviant behavior. Labeling finds official records interesting in and of themselves.[3] What acts are recorded, under what category, where, when, and with what consequences constitute a major focus of attention. The labeling perspective assumes that official records reflect primarily the processes of the organization compiling them. Thus, they are not assumed to present literal descriptions of the behaviors that they supposedly document.

In summary, the labeling perspective focuses on process rather than structure, on subjectivity rather than objectivity, and on reactions to deviance rather than initiations to deviance.

[3] A good example is John I. Kitsuse and Aaron V. Cicourel, "A Note on the Uses of Official Statistics," *Social Problems* 11 (Fall 1963), pp. 131–39.

Philosophical Sources of the Labeling Perspective

The labeling approach is an outgrowth of the social philosophies of George Herbert Mead [4] and Alfred Schutz.[5] Although both men were philosophers, each exerted tremendous influence on sociologists. Mead's influence has been felt for a longer period of time by a wider circle of sociologists, while Schutz's influence has been more recent and limited. Together, Mead and Schutz constitute the major background sources of the labeling perspective.

Mead. Mead taught philosphy at the University of Chicago. In his lectures, Mead presented a model of people and of social reality that, as it was adopted and developed by members of the Chicago department of sociology, came to be known as symbolic interactionism.

Mead held that the sense of self arises in the course of social interaction. People learn to take the "attitude of the other" toward themselves. In so doing, they come to see themselves as social objects, and they subsequently behave according to that self-conception.

Mead also conceived of social interaction as emergent and dynamic rather than static in character. By reading gestures and symbols, he stressed, people continually adjust their behavior to what others seem about to do. The labeling perspective highlights the relevance of this concept for the study of deviance.

Schutz. Schutz sought to explain social order by showing that people produce a set of typifications about the world.[6] These typifications include persons, places, things, and events; and insofar as people assume that other people are defining situations in much the same way, social order is produced. Schutz concerned himself with three important questions: What is the essence of any particular phenomenon in question? How do people make typifications? By what processes do typifications

[4] George Herbert Mead, *Mind, Self, and Society from the Standpoint of a Social Behaviorist* (Chicago: University of Chicago Press, 1934).
[5] Alfred Schutz, *Collected Papers I: The Problem of Social Reality,* Maurice Natanson, ed. (The Hague: Martinus Nijhoff, 1962).
[6] In his work, Schutz provides an important synthesis of the thought of Edmund Husserl, George Herbert Mead, and Max Weber.

come to be considered as shared? The labeling perspective picks up on these interests and asks related questions: What is the essence of deviance as a *sociological* phenomenon? What are the processes by which people typify others as deviant? How do people come to share these typifications?

Founders of the Labeling Perspective

The "grandfather" of labeling theory is Edwin Lemert. In 1951, Lemert published a book titled (or mistitled) *Social Pathology.*[7] In this book he set forth a systematic theory of deviant behavior based on the notion that deviance is defined by social reactions and that the frequency and character of deviation, together with the role of the deviant, are in large part shaped by the social reaction.

The labeling perspective was christened, however, in a book by Howard S. Becker, *Outsiders,* which appeared in 1963. The statement that helped to name the approach was:

Social groups create deviance by making the rules whose infraction constitute deviance, and by applying those rules to particular people and labeling them as outsiders. From this point of view, deviance is not a quality of the act the person commits, but rather a consequence of the application by others of rules and sanctions to an "offender." The deviant is one to whom that label has successfully been applied; deviant behavior is behavior that people so label.[8]

Though a change in thought on social problems was already under way, Becker's *Outsiders* crystallized it. Becker showed that becoming sociologically deviant is a dynamic interactive process, drawn out over time in sequences orderly enough to be called a career. He also observed that not everyone who breaks the rules gets labeled deviant, that ultimately the definition and the enforcement of moral rules are political acts, and that the meaning of a deviant act can change over time for the people involved.

In the years since Becker's book appeared in 1963, a number of other sociologists have contributed to the labeling

[7] Edwin M. Lemert, *Social Pathology: A Systematic Approach to the Theory of Sociopathic Behavior* (New York: McGraw-Hill, 1951).
[8] Howard S. Becker, *Outsiders: Studies in the Sociology of Deviance* (New York: The Free Press of Glencoe, 1963), p. 9.

perspective.[9] These sociologists have dealt primarily with the applications of rules to people who have apparently breached them, the conditions under which rules or labels are applied, and the consequences for the labeled person's self-image and future.[10]

Characteristics of the Labeling Perspective

Central to the labeling perspective is the notion that social problems and deviance exist in the eye of the beholder. The perspective seeks to study the processes of, and responses to, social differentiation. The principal elements in the labeling perspective are as follows:

Definition. A social problem or social deviant is defined by social reactions to an alleged violation of rules or expectations. This perspective focuses on the conditions under which behaviors or situations come to be defined as problematic or deviant.

Causes. The cause of a social problem is ultimately *the attention it receives* from the public or from social control agents, for social reactions cannot occur until the alleged behavior or situation is recognized.

Conditions. When a person or situation is labeled problematic or deviant, the labeler is usually in a position to gain by affixing such a label. The labeler must have a negative label to apply and the power to make it stick. Very often, the labeling is done by someone whose job it is to apply labels (e.g., social control agents, journalists), and assigning labels is often a mark of success in such jobs.[11] Occasionally, people may label themselves, and in doing so they may gain some advantages

[9] Other sociologists who have contributed to the development of this perspective include Aaron Cicourel, Kai Erikson, Erving Goffman, Harold Garfinkel, John Kitsuse, and Thomas Scheff.
[10] Despite their contributions, several of these writers disavow that they are proponents of labeling theory. For a useful discussion, see Erich Goode, "On Behalf of Labeling Theory," *Social Problems* 22 (June 1975), pp. 570–83.
[11] Examples are provided in Earl Rubington and Martin S. Weinberg, *Deviance.*

(e.g., people have reported that they are homosexual in order to be discharged from the military).[12]

Consequences. The definition of a person or situation as socially problematic or deviant may lead to a reordering of human relations in a way that promotes further "deviance." For example, after a person has been labeled "deviant," most people expect him/her to continue violating norms of conventional behavior. This may limit the labeled person's life chances and lead him/her to elaborate the deviant role—e.g., an ex-convict may be unable to obtain employment in a conventional job and may thus return to crime in order to make a living. This elaboration of deviant roles because of other people's reactions is called "secondary deviance." [13]

Solutions. The labeling perspective suggests two solutions: definitions can be changed, and the profit can be taken out of labeling. Changing definitions would mean becoming more tolerant, so that people stop labeling certain people and situations as problematic. Taking the profit out of labeling would presumably mean a consequent decrease both in people's labeling of themselves and others, and in the problems that result from such labeling.

Summary

The period since 1954 has been called *the cultivation of specialties.* Early in this period, the deviant behavior perspective became prominent. Nonetheless, certain problems remained unexplained by that perspective, and these unexplained problems generated the labeling perspective. The labeling point of view was rooted in symbolic interactionism, formulated by Mead and later elaborated by Schutz. As symbolic interactionism was extended to the study of the social processes surrounding deviance, the gap between structure and process views in sociology widened.

[12] For example, see Colin J. Williams and Martin S. Weinberg, *Homosexuals and the Military: A Study of Less than Honorable Discharge* (New York: Harper & Row, 1971).
[13] For an extended discussion of secondary deviance, see Edwin M. Lemert, *Human Deviance, Social Problems, and Social Control,* 2nd ed. (Englewood Cliffs, N.J.: Prentice-Hall, 1972), pp. 62–92.

The labeling perspective examines certain taken-for-granted aspects of social problems. Sociologists working within this perspective focus on the people who define problems, the conditions under which a person or situation is labeled problematic, and the consequences of this labeling. Thus, social problems and deviance are defined by social reactions to a presumed violation of rules or expectations. The cause is presumed knowledge of the violation, and the conditions affecting the labeling process are power relations and the gains to be made by labeling. The major consequences of successful labeling are an elaboration of deviance (secondary deviance) and expectations of continued violations. Solutions suggested by the labeling perspective are to change definitions and to eliminate labeling profits.

Outsiders

Howard S. Becker

Traditionally, sociologists studied deviance by examining the attributes of persons who violated rules, why they did so, what distinguished violators from nonviolators, and what could be done about it in a practical sense. Becker's excerpt exemplifies a more recent trend, in which deviance is studied in terms of the successful application of labels. With this reconceptualization, many sociologists have turned their attention from studying deviant behaviors to studying the social definition of deviance and the consequence of such definitions.

Deviance and the Responses of Others

[One sociological view] . . . defines deviance as the infraction of some agreed-upon rule. It then goes on to ask who breaks rules, and to search for the factors in their personalities and life situations that might account for the infractions. This assumes that those who have broken a rule constitute a homo-

From Howard S. Becker, *Outsiders: Studies in the Sociology of Deviance*, pp. 8–14, 31–33. Copyright © 1963 by The Free Press of Glencoe, a division of The Macmillan Company. Reprinted by permission.

geneous category, because they have committed the same deviant act.

Such an assumption seems to me to ignore the central fact
about deviance: it is created by society. I do not mean this in
the way it is ordinarily understood, in which the causes of
deviance are located in the social situation of the deviant or in
"social factors" which prompt his action. I mean, rather, that
*social groups create deviance by making the rules whose infraction
constitutes deviance,* and by applying those rules to particular
people and labeling them as outsiders. From this point of
view, deviance is *not* a quality of the act the person commits,
but rather a consequence of the application by others of rules
and sanctions to an "offender." The deviant is one to whom
that label has successfully been applied; deviant behavior is behavior that people so label.[1]

Since deviance is, among other things, a consequence of the
responses of others to a person's act, students of deviance cannot assume that they are dealing with a homogeneous category when they study people who have been labeled deviant.
That is, they cannot assume that these people have actually
committed a deviant act or broken some rule, because the process of labeling may not be infallible; some people may be
labeled deviant who in fact have not broken a rule. Furthermore, they cannot assume that the category of those labeled
deviant will contain all those who actually have broken a rule,
for many offenders may escape apprehension and thus fail to
be included in the population of "deviants" they study. Insofar
as the category lacks homogeneity and fails to include all the
cases that belong in it, one cannot reasonably expect to find
common factors of personality or life situation that will account for the supposed deviance.

What, then, do people who have been labeled deviant have
in common? At the least, they share the label and the experience of being labeled as outsiders. I will begin my analysis with
this basic similarity and view deviance as the product of a
transaction that takes place between some social group and

[1] The most important earlier statements of this view can be found in Frank
Tannenbaum, *Crime and the Community* (New York: McGraw-Hill Book Co.,
Inc., 1951), and E. M. Lemert, *Social Pathology* (New York: McGraw-Hill
Book Co., Inc., 1951). A recent article stating a position very similar to mine
is John Kitsuse, "Societal Reaction to Deviance: Problems of Theory and
Method," *Social Problems,* 9 (Winter, 1962), 247–256.

one who is viewed by that group as a rule-breaker. I will be less concerned with the personal and social characteristics of deviants than with the process by which they come to be thought of as outsiders and their reactions to that judgment.

Malinowski discovered the usefulness of this view for understanding the nature of deviance many years ago, in his study of the Trobriand Islands:

One day an outbreak of wailing and a great commotion told me that a death had occurred somewhere in the neighborhood. I was informed that Kima'i, a young lad of my acquaintance, of sixteen or so, had fallen from a coco-nut palm and killed himself. . . . I found that another youth had been severely wounded by some mysterious coincidence. And at the funeral there was obviously a general feeling of hostility between the village where the boy died and that into which his body was carried for burial.

Only much later was I able to discover the real meaning of these events. The boy had committed suicide. The truth was that he had broken the rules of exogamy, the partner in his crime being his maternal cousin, the daughter of his mother's sister. This had been known and generally disapproved of but nothing was done until the girl's discarded lover, who had wanted to marry her and who felt personally injured, took the initiative. This rival threatened first to use black magic against the guilty youth, but this had not much effect. Then one evening he insulted the culprit in public—accusing him in the hearing of the whole community of incest and hurling at him certain expressions intolerable to a native.

For this there was only one remedy; only one means of escape remained to the unfortunate youth. Next morning he put on festive attire and ornamentation, climbed a coco-nut palm and addressed the community, speaking from among the palm leaves and bidding them farewell. He explained the reasons for his desperate deed and also launched forth a veiled accusation against the man who had driven him to his death, upon which it became the duty of his clansmen to avenge him. Then he wailed aloud, as is the custom, jumped from a palm some sixty feet high and was killed on the spot. There followed a fight within the village in which the rival was wounded; and the quarrel was repeated during the funeral. . . .

If you were to inquire into the matter among the Trobrianders, you would find . . . that the natives show horror at the idea of violating the rules of exogamy and that they believe that sores, disease and even death might follow clan incest. This is the ideal of native law, and in moral matters it is easy and pleasant strictly to adhere to the ideal—when judging the conduct of others or expressing an opinion about conduct in general.

When it comes to the application of morality and ideals to real life, however, things take on a different complexion. In the case described it was obvious that the facts would not tally with the ideal of conduct. Public opinion was neither outraged by the knowledge of the crime to any extent, nor did it react directly—it had to be mobilized by a public statement of the crime and by insults being hurled at the culprit by an interested party. Even then he had to carry out the punishment himself. . . . Probing further into the mat-

ter and collecting concrete information, I found that the breach of exogamy—as regards intercourse and not marriage—is by no means a rare occurrence, and public opinion is lenient, though decidedly hypocritical. If
the affair is carried on *sub rosa* with a certain amount of decorum, and if no
one in particular stirs up trouble—"public opinion" will gossip, but not demand any harsh punishment. If, on the contrary, scandal breaks out—
everyone turns against the guilty pair and by ostracism and insults one or
the other may be driven to suicide.[2]

Whether an act is deviant . . . depends on how other people react to it. You can commit clan incest and suffer from no
more than gossip as long as no one makes a public accusation;
but you will be driven to your death if the accusation is made.
The point is that the response of other people has to be
regarded as problematic. Just because one has committed an
infraction of a rule does not mean that others will respond as
though this had happened. (Conversely, just because one has
not violated a rule does not mean that he may not be treated,
in some circumstances, as though he had.)

The degree to which other people will respond to a given
act as deviant varies greatly. Several kinds of variation seem
worth noting. First of all, there is variation over time. A person believed to have committed a given "deviant" act may at
one time be responded to much more leniently than he would
be at some other time. The occurrence of "drives" against
various kinds of deviance illustrates this clearly. At various
times, enforcement officials may decide to make an all-out attack on some particular kind of deviance, such as gambling,
drug addiction, or homosexuality. It is obviously much more
dangerous to engage in one of these activities when a drive is
on than at any other time. (In a very interesting study of crime
news in Colorado newspapers, Davis found that the amount of
crime reported in Colorado newspapers showed very little association with actual changes in the amount of crime taking
place in Colorado. And, further, that people's estimate of how
much increase there had been in crime in Colorado was associated with the increase in the amount of crime news but not
with any increase in the amount of crime.) [3]

The degree to which an act will be treated as deviant de-

[2] Bronislaw Malinowski, *Crime and Custom in Savage Society* (New York: Humanities Press, 1926), pp. 77–80. Reprinted by permission of Humanities
Press and Routledge & Kegan Paul, Ltd.
[3] F. James Davis, "Crime News in Colorado Newspapers," *American Journal of
Sociology*, LVII (January, 1952), 325–330.

pends also on who commits the act and who feels he has been harmed by it. Rules tend to be applied more to some persons than others. Studies of juvenile delinquency make the point clearly. Boys from middle-class areas do not get as far in the legal process when they are apprehended as do boys from slum areas. The middle-class boy is less likely, when picked up by the police, to be taken to the station; less likely when taken to the station to be booked; and it is extremely unlikely that he will be convicted and sentenced.[4] This variation occurs even though the original infraction of the rule is the same in the two cases. Similarly, the law is differentially applied to Negroes and whites. It is well known that a Negro believed to have attacked a white woman is much more likely to be punished than a white man who commits the same offense; it is only slightly less well known that a Negro who murders another Negro is much less likely to be punished than a white man who commits murder.[5] This, of course, is one of the main points of Sutherland's analysis of white-collar crime: crimes committed by corporations are almost always prosecuted as civil cases, but the same crime committed by an individual is ordinarily treated as a criminal offense.[6]

Some rules are enforced only when they result in certain consequences. The unmarried mother furnishes a clear example. Vincent [7] points out that illicit sexual relations seldom result in severe punishment or social censure for the offenders. If, however, a girl becomes pregnant as a result of such activities, the reaction of others is likely to be severe. (The illicit pregnancy is also an interesting example of the differential enforcement of rules on different categories of people. Vincent notes that unmarried fathers escape the severe censure visited on the mother.)

Why repeat these commonplace observations? Because, taken together, they support the proposition that deviance is not a simple quality, present in some kinds of behavior and

---

[4] See Albert K. Cohen and James F. Short, Jr., "Juvenile Delinquency," in Robert K. Merton and Robert A. Nisbet, editors, *Contemporary Social Problems* (New York: Harcourt, Brace and World, Inc., 1961), p. 87.

[5] See Harold Garfinkel, "Research Notes on Inter- and Intra-Racial Homicides," *Social Forces*, 27 (May, 1949), 369–381.

[6] Edwin H. Sutherland, "White Collar Criminality," *American Sociological Review*, V (February, 1940), 1–12.

[7] Clark Vincent, *Unmarried Mothers* (New York: The Free Press of Glencoe, 1961), pp. 3–5.

absent in others. Rather, it is the product of a process which involves responses of other people to the behavior. The same behavior may be an infraction of the rules at one time and not at another; may be an infraction when committed by one person, but not when committed by another; some rules are broken with impunity, others are not. In short, whether a given act is deviant or not depends in part on the nature of the act (that is, whether or not it violates some rule) and in part on what other people do about it.

Some people may object that this is merely a terminological quibble, that one can, after all, define terms any way he wants to and that if some people want to speak of rule-breaking behavior as deviant without reference to the reactions of others they are free to do so. This, of course, is true. Yet it might be worthwhile to refer to such behavior as *rule-breaking behavior* and reserve the term *deviant* for those labeled as deviant by some segment of society. I do not insist that this usage be followed. But it should be clear that insofar as a scientist uses "deviant" to refer to any rule-breaking behavior and takes as his subject of study only those who have been *labeled* deviant, he will be hampered by the disparities between the two categories.

If we take as the object of our attention behavior which comes to be labeled as deviant, we must recognize that we cannot know whether a given act will be categorized as deviant until the response of others has occurred. Deviance is not a quality that lies in behavior itself, but in the interaction between the person who commits an act and those who respond to it. . . .

In any case, being . . . branded as deviant has important consequences for one's further social participation and self-image. The most important consequence is a drastic change in the individual's public identity. Committing the improper act and being publicly caught at it place him in a new status. He has been revealed as a different kind of person from the kind he was supposed to be. He is labeled a "fairy," "dope fiend," "nut" or "lunatic," and treated accordingly.

In analyzing the consequences of assuming a deviant identity let us make use of Hughes' distinction between master and auxiliary status traits.[8] Hughes notes that most statuses have one key trait which serves to distinguish those who belong

[8] Everett C. Hughes, "Dilemmas and Contradictions of Status," *American Journal of Sociology*, L (March, 1945), 353–359.

from those who do not. Thus the doctor, whatever else he may be, is a person who has a certificate stating that he has fulfilled certain requirements and is licensed to practice medicine; this is the master trait. As Hughes points out, in our society a doctor is also informally expected to have a number of auxiliary traits: most people expect him to be upper middle class, white, male, and Protestant. When he is not there is a sense that he has in some way failed to fill the bill. Similarly, though skin color is the master status trait determining who is Negro and who is white, Negroes are informally expected to have certain status traits and not to have others; people are surprised and find it anomalous if a Negro turns out to be a doctor or a college professor. People often have the master status trait but lack some of the auxiliary, informally expected characteristics; for example, one may be a doctor but be female or Negro.

Hughes deals with this phenomenon in regard to statuses that are well thought of, desired and desirable (noting that one may have the formal qualifications for entry into a status but be denied full entry because of lack of the proper auxiliary traits), but the same process occurs in the case of deviant statuses. Possession of one deviant trait may have a generalized symbolic value, so that people automatically assume that its bearer possesses other undesirable traits allegedly associated with it.

To be labeled a criminal one need only commit a single criminal offense, and this is all the term formally refers to. Yet the word carries a number of connotations specifying auxiliary traits characteristic of anyone bearing the label. A man who has been convicted of housebreaking and thereby labeled criminal is presumed to be a person likely to break into other houses; the police, in rounding up known offenders for investigation after a crime has been committed, operate on this premise. Further, he is considered likely to commit other kinds of crimes as well, because he has shown himself to be a person without "respect for the law." Thus, apprehension for one deviant act exposes a person to the likelihood that he will be regarded as deviant or undesirable in other respects.

There is one other element in Hughes' analysis we can borrow with profit: the distinction between master and subordinate statuses.[9] Some statuses, in our society as in others, over-

---

[9] *Ibid.*

ride all other statuses and have a certain priority. Race is one of these. Membership in the Negro race, as socially defined, will override most other status considerations in most other situations; the fact that one is a physician or middle-class or female will not protect one from being treated as a Negro first and any of these other things second. The status of deviant (depending on the kind of deviance) is this kind of master status. One receives the status as a result of breaking a rule, and the identification proves to be more important than most others. One will be identified as a deviant first, before other identifications are made. . . .

Notes on the Sociology of Deviance

Kai T. Erikson

> *In this excerpt, Erikson shows that so-called deviant behavior is not inherently harmful to society and may in fact have the positive function of strengthening group identity. When a collectivity responds to "deviant" behavior, it draws attention to the boundaries that the "deviant" has allegedly overstepped. Thus, the societal response makes visible the limits of acceptable behavior and ideas, and thus it helps people to define their identity and their culture.*

It is common practice in sociology to picture deviant behavior as an alien element in society. Deviance is considered a vagrant form of human activity which has somehow broken away from the more orderly currents of social life and needs to be controlled. And since it is generally understood that this sort of aberration could only occur if something were wrong within the organization of society itself, deviant behavior is described almost as if it were leakage from machinery in poor condition: it is an incidental result of disorder and anomie, a symptom of internal breakdown.

The purpose of the following remarks will be to review this conventional outlook and to argue that it provides too narrow a framework for many kinds of sociological research. Devia-

From Kai T. Erikson, "Notes on the Sociology of Deviance," in Howard S. Becker (ed.), *The Other Side*, pp. 9–15, 1964, The Free Press of Glencoe. Reprinted by permission of the author.

tion, we will suggest, recalling Durkheim's classic statement on the subject, can often be understood as a normal product of stable institutions, an important resource which is guarded and preserved by forces found in all human organizations.[1]

I

According to current theory, deviant behavior is most likely to occur when the sanctions governing conduct in any given social setting seem to be contradictory [2]—as would be the case, for example, if the work rules posted by a company required one course of action from its employees and the longer-range policies of the company required quite another. Any situation marked by this kind of ambiguity, of course, can pose a serious dilemma for the individual: if he is careful to observe one set of demands imposed upon him, he runs the immediate risk of violating some other, and thus may find himself caught in a deviant stance no matter how earnestly he tries to avoid it. In this limited sense, deviance can be viewed as a "normal" social response to "abnormal" social circumstances, and we are therefore invited to assume that every act of deviation results from some imbalance within the social order—a condition of strain, anomie, or alienation.

This approach to the study of deviant behavior has generated a good deal of useful research, but it has at least one serious drawback for investigators who share an interest in what is known as "social problems." The "anomie" theory (if we may use that convenient label for a moment) is designed to account for all behavior which varies in some technical way from the norms of the community, whether or not that behavior is considered a problem by anyone else. For example, the bank teller who becomes a slave to routine and the armed bandit who relieves him of the day's receipts both register as deviants according to the logic of this scheme, since each is deviating in his own way from the ideal standards of the culture. Yet the most important difference between these men is one

---

[1] Emile Durkheim, *The Rules of Sociological Method* (translated by S. A. Solovay and J. H. Mueller), New York: The Free Press of Glencoe, 1958.
[2] The best-known statements of this general position, of course, are by Robert K. Merton and Talcott Parsons. Merton, *Social Theory and Social Structure*, Revised Edition, New York: The Free Press of Glencoe, 1957; and Parsons, *The Social System*, New York: The Free Press of Glencoe, 1951.

that the "anomie" theory cannot easily take into account: the bank teller, no matter how desperate his private needs, does not ordinarily create any concern in the rest of the community, while the bandit triggers the whole machinery of social control into vigorous action. In short, the "anomie" theory may help us appreciate the various ways in which people respond to conditions of strain, but it does not help us differentiate between those people who infringe the letter of the norm without attracting any notice and those who excite so much alarm that they earn a deviant reputation in society and are committed to special institutions like prisons and hospitals.

II

From a sociological standpoint, deviance can be defined as conduct which is generally thought to require the attention of social control agencies—that is, conduct about which "something should be done." Deviance is not a property *inherent in* certain forms of behavior; it is a property *conferred upon* these forms by the audiences which directly or indirectly witness them. The critical variable in the study of deviance, then, is the social audience rather than the individual actor, since it is the audience which eventually determines whether or not any episode of behavior or any class of episodes is labeled deviant.

This definition may seem a little indirect, but it has the advantage of bringing a neglected sociological issue into proper focus. When a community acts to control the behavior of one of its members, it is engaged in a very intricate process of selection. After all, even the worst miscreant in society conforms most of the time, if only in the sense that he uses the correct spoon at mealtime, takes good care of his mother, or in a thousand other ways respects the ordinary conventions of his group; and if the community elects to bring sanctions against him for the occasions when he does misbehave, it is responding to a few deviant details set within a vast array of entirely acceptable conduct. Thus it happens that a moment of deviation may become the measure of a person's position in society. He may be jailed or hospitalized, certified as a full-time deviant, despite the fact that only a fraction of his behavior was in any way unusual or dangerous. The community has taken note of a few scattered particles of behavior and has decided that they reflect what kind of person he "really" is.

The screening device which sifts these telling details out of the person's over-all performance, then, is a very important instrument of social control. We know very little about the properties of this screen, but we do know that it takes many factors into account which are not directly related to the deviant act itself: it is sensitive to the suspect's social class, his past record as an offender, the amount of remorse he manages to convey, and many similar concerns which take hold in the shifting moods of the community. This may not be so obvious when the screen is dealing with extreme forms of deviance like serious crimes, but in the day-by-day filtering processes which take place throughout the community this feature is easily observable. Some men who drink too much are called alcoholics and others are not, some men who act oddly are committed to hospitals and others are not, some men who have no visible means of support are hauled into court and others are not—and the difference between those who earn a deviant label and those who go their own way in peace depends almost entirely on the way in which the community sifts out and codes the many details of behavior to which it is witness. In this respect, the community screen may be a more relevant subject for sociological research than the actual behavior which is filtered through it.

Once the problem is phrased in this way we can ask: How does a community decide what forms of conduct should be singled out for this kind of attention? The conventional answer to this question, of course, is that society sets up the machinery of control in order to protect itself against the "harmful" effects of deviation, in much the same way that an organism mobilizes its resources to combat an invasion of germs. Yet this simple view of the matter has not always proven to be a very productive one. In the first place, as Durkheim and Mead pointed out some years ago, it is by no means clear that all acts considered deviant in a culture are in fact (or even in principle) harmful to group life.[3] In the second place, it is gradually becoming more evident to sociologists engaged in this area of research that deviant behavior can play an important part in keeping the social order intact.

[3] Emile Durkheim, *The Division of Labor in Society* (translated by George Simpson), New York: The Free Press of Glencoe, 1952; and George Herbert Mead, "The Psychology of Punitive Justice," *American Journal of Sociology*, 23 (1918), 577–602.

This raises a number of interesting questions for sociology.

III

In recent years, sociological theory has become more and more concerned with the concept "social system"—an organization of society's component parts into a form which sustains internal equilibrium, resists change, and is boundary maintaining. In its most abstract form, the "system" concept describes a highly complex network of relations, but the scheme is generally used by sociologists to draw attention to those forces in the social order which promote a high level of uniformity among human actors and a high degree of symmetry within human institutions. The main organizational drift of a system, then, is seen as centripetal: it acts to draw the behavior of actors toward those centers in social space where the core values of the group are figuratively located, bringing them within range of basic norms. Any conduct which is neither attracted toward this nerve center by the rewards of conformity nor compelled toward it by other social pressures is considered "out of control," which is to say, deviant.

This basic model has provided the theme for most contemporary thinking about deviation, and as a result little attention has been given to the notion that systems operate to maintain boundaries. To say that a system maintains boundaries is to say that it controls the fluctuation of its constituent parts so that the whole retains a defined range of activity, a unique pattern of constancy and stability, within the larger environment.[4] Because the range of human behavior is potentially so wide, social groups maintain boundaries in the sense that they try to limit the flow of behavior within their domain so that it circulates within a defined cultural territory. Boundaries, then, are an important point of reference for persons participating in any system. A people may define its boundaries by referring to a geographical location, a set of honored traditions, a particular religious or political viewpoint, an occupational specialty, a common language, or just some local way of doing things; but in any case, members of the group have some idea about the contours of the niche they occupy in

[4] Cf. Talcott Parsons, *The Social System, op. cit.*

social space. They know where the group begins and ends as a special entity; they know what kinds of experience "belong" within these precincts and what kinds do not.

For all its apparent abstractness, a social system is organized around the movements of persons joined together in regular social relations. The only material found in a system for marking boundaries, then, is the behavior of its participants; and the kinds of behavior which best perform this function are often deviant, since they represent the most extreme variety of conduct to be found within the experience of the group. In this sense, transactions taking place between deviant persons on the one side and agencies of control on the other are boundary maintaining mechanisms. They mark the outside limits of the area within which the norm has jurisdiction, and in this way assert how much diversity and variability can be contained within the system before it begins to lose its distinct structure, its cultural integrity.

A social norm is rarely expressed as a firm rule or official code. It is an abstract synthesis of the many separate times a community has stated its sentiments on a given kind of issue. Thus the norm has a history much like that of an article of common law: it is an accumulation of decisions made by the community over a long period of time which gradually gathers enough moral eminence to serve as a precedent for future decisions. And like an article of common law, the norm retains its validity only if it is regularly used as a basis for judgment. Each time the group censures some act of deviation, then, it sharpens the authority of the violated norm and declares again where the boundaries of the group are located.

It is important to notice that these transactions between deviant persons and agents of control have always attracted a good deal of attention in this and other cultures. In our own past, both the trial and punishment of deviant offenders took place in the public market and gave the crowd a chance to participate in a direct, active way. Today we no longer parade deviants in the town square or expose them to the carnival atmosphere of Tyburn, but it is interesting to note that the "reform" which brought about this change in penal policy coincided almost precisely with the development of newspapers as media of public information. Perhaps this is no more than an accident of history, but it is nevertheless true that newspapers (and now radio and television) offer their readers the same kind of entertainment once supplied by public hangings or the use of stocks and pillories. An enormous amount of modern "news" is devoted to reports about deviant behavior and its punishment: indeed the largest circulation newspaper in the United States prints very little else. Yet how do we explain what makes these items "newsworthy" or why they command the great attention they do? Perhaps they satisfy a number of psychological perversities among the mass audience, as commentators sometimes point out, but at the same time they constitute our main source of information about the normative contours of society. In a figurative sense, at least, morality and immorality meet at the public scaffold, and it is during this meeting that the community declares where the line between them should be drawn.

People who gather together into communities need to be able to describe and anticipate those areas of experience which lie outside the immediate compass of the group—the unseen dangers which in any culture and in any age seem to threaten its security. Traditional folklore depicting demons, devils, witches and evil spirits, may be one way to give form to these otherwise formless dangers, but the visible deviant is another kind of reminder. As a trespasser against the group norms, he represents those forces which lie outside the group's boundaries: he informs us, as it were, what evil looks like, what shapes the devil can assume. And in doing so, he shows us the difference between the inside of the group and the outside. It may well be that without this ongoing drama at the outer edges of group space, the community would have no inner sense of identity and cohesion, no sense of the contrasts which set it off as a special place in the larger world.

Thus deviance cannot be dismissed simply as behavior which *disrupts* stability in society, but may itself be, in controlled quantities, an important condition for *preserving* stability.

The "Wetback" as Deviant

Jorge A. Bustamante

Before 1924, thousands of Mexicans crossed into the American Southwest illegally. These illegal immigrants worked alongside legal immigrants from Mexico, and they were not accorded any special attention. After 1924, however, their status changed drastically. Strict immigration laws were passed, and a special agency was set up to enforce these laws. The illegal immigrants became known as "wetbacks," and their social position shifted downward.

Bustamante's article shows how the labeling process is related to power and to economic interests. The legal immigrants who have to compete with wetbacks for jobs, for example, favor stricter enforcement of immigration laws. The farmers who benefit from the cheap wetback labor, however, oppose strict enforcement, especially during the harvest season. Thus, the farmers, Bustamante suggests, are "antilaw entrepreneurs," using their power and influence to undermine the enforcement of immigration laws.

Introduction

Those who illegally stream across the Mexico-U.S. border are called "wetbacks" because they cross the Rio Grande without the benefit of a bridge. All other illegal migrants from Mexico are referred to by the same term. Thus, wetback characterizes anyone who enters illegally from Mexico. The term, then, carries an unavoidable connotation—one who has broken the law. This paper will deal with some of the questions that arise from that connotation. In the first part, we describe the historical emergence of the wetback, discussing the roles of the persons involved in the violation of the immigration law and some of the socioeconomic consequences of the wetback as a deviant. In the second part, we examine the wetback as a case of deviance through labeling theory. In this approach the deviant character of the wetback is analyzed as a process of interaction. Each role in this process will be discussed in terms of its interests, power, and consequences with respect to those

From Jorge A. Bustamante, "The 'Wetback' as Deviant: An Application of Labeling Theory," *American Journal of Sociology* 77:4 (January 1972), pp. 706–18. Copyright © 1972 by The University of Chicago Press. Reprinted by permission.

of the roles of the other participants. Finally, the concept of "antilaw entrepreneur" is introduced, and its explanatory potential is indicated.

Historical Background

In 1882, during President Arthur's administration, the first immigration law was passed following a strong nativist movement. The same year the first "Chinese exclusion act" established significant limits to what was considered an "invasion of Orientals" who had been a preferred source of cheap labor for West Coast employers (Wittke 1949, p. 13). The search for cheap labor turned to Japanese and Filipino immigrants, who then became the target of "exclusionists." Campaigns like the "swat the Jap" campaign in Los Angeles and those inspired by the writings of Madison Grant and Lothrop Stoddard led to further restrictions of immigration from the Orient. The "Asian barred zone" provisions excluded immigration from Oriental countries as a source for cheap labor (Daniels and Kitano 1970, p. 53).

In the first decade of the century, eastern and southern European immigration became the focus of nativist and exclusionist crusades. Pressure generated by those movements crystallized in the appointment of a commission by the U.S. Congress to study immigration; the result of that study is known as the Dillingham Commission Report (1907–10). Throughout this voluminous report a long-debated distinction between the "old" and "new" immigration was made. It was argued that the values and occupations of the "old immigrants" (Anglo-Saxons and Nordics) were threatened by the "newer immigrants," southern and eastern Europeans and Asians (Hourwich 1912, p. 19). The distinction between new and old immigration created a dichotomy about which many pages of "scientific" reports were written in support of the undesirability of the new immigration.

Campaigns demanding restriction of the new immigration finally crystallized in the immigration laws of 1921 and 1924, which established quotas restricting immigration from all countries except those in the western hemisphere.

In the meantime, social scientists conducted research on the immigration phenomenon; they found empirical evidence

showing that immigration to the United States has consistently
supplied cheap labor (Eckler and Zoltnick 1949, p. 16; Hourwich 1912, pp. 167–72).

All countries which provided cheap labor for the United
States were affected by the quota system established by the
Immigration Act of 1921. Thus, the search for cheap labor
turned to the western hemisphere, to which the quota system
did not apply (Marden and Meyer 1968, p. 104); Mexican immigrants were found to be the most suitable replacement (Samora and Bustamante 1971). The suitability of Mexican labor
rested on (1) geographical proximity; (2) the uninterrupted
tradition of immigration, which was internal when most of
the southwestern United States was still part of Mexico (McWilliams 1968, pp. 162–69); and (3) unemployment and unrest in
Mexico, created by several years of revolution (Bustamante, in
press).

A tremendous increase in Mexican immigration during the
first quarter of the century (Grebler 1966, p. 20) corre-
sponded to the increased demand for unskilled labor in the
economic expansion of the Southwest. Mexicans crossed 1,870
miles of an almost completely open border (Gamio 1930, p.
10) to reach the steel industry in East Chicago (Samora and
Lamanna 1970), railroad construction, and, most significantly,
agricultural expansion in the Southwest (Samora 1971).

In this period the Mexican who wanted to legally cross the
border had to go through a complicated procedure to be admitted into the United States. Those procedures included, in
particular, a literacy test, "a condition which many immigrants
cannot fulfill" (Gamio 1930, p. 11). Therefore, many took advantage of the "open" border policy toward Mexican laborers.

Moreover, the illegal immigrant could stay in the United
States untroubled as long as he avoided the authorities who
might disclose his status. Since no specific authorities were en-
trusted with apprehending illegal immigrants, the dangers of
being caught were further minimized (Jones 1965, p. 13).
Thus, the illegal immigrant's status was not visibly distinct
from the legal immigrant's. The illegal entrant was able to
maintain his violation in a state of "primary deviance" (Lemert
1951, pp. 70–78).

The appearance of the Border Patrol in 1924 altered the
primary deviance of the illegal entrant by crystallizing a new
social reaction to the violation of immigration laws. The new

police force was to reveal those primary deviants, violators of immigration laws. In this process, the term "wetback," previously purely descriptive, acquired a new meaning. It became the "label" or "stigma" by which the illegal immigrant was made visible. At the same time, the label "wetback" also became the symbol by which the illegal immigrant was able to identify a new "me" for himself (Mead 1918, pp. 577–602), and a new role which better equipped him to meet the social reaction to his behavior (illegal entrance) (Lemert 1967, pp. 42–51).

The establishment of the Border Patrol in 1924 not only made the wetback more visible as a law breaker; it also brought changes in the patterns of behavior of the illegal immigrants. The freedom of interaction the illegal immigrant had had before 1924 was considerably reduced. He now had to walk, to speak, and to bear any treatment with the fear of being caught by or "turned in" to the Border Patrol.

The interaction most significantly changed was between illegal migrant worker and employer. Before 1924 labor conditions resulted from differential access to mechanisms of power and from the interplay of labor-force supply and demand. The organization of the Border Patrol brought a new factor: the illegal migrant could always be caught and sent back to Mexico. To be "turned in" became a threat always present in the migrant's mind that interfered with his social contacts. Social contacts, except for those with an employer or prospective employer, could be avoided for self-protection. The explicit or implicit threat of being denounced by the employer became a new significant element in the settlement of work contracts. It could be used to impose oppressive salaries and working conditions. In his search for a job he could no longer freely accept or reject a given offer; he always had to consider the alternative of being denounced to the Border Patrol.[1]

The importance of the "wetback problem" gains further emphasis in its numerical proportions. Although no reliable

---

[1] Data from 493 interviews that I conducted with wetbacks in 1969 show that 8% of the interviewees were "turned in" by their employers without being paid for their work. A year later, similar situations were encountered by the author during a participant observation as a "wetback" conceived to validate previous findings (a report of these experiences and the larger research project appears in Samora 1971). Further evidence of these and other kinds of exploitation of the "wetback" are reported by Saunders and Leonard 1951, p. 72; Hadley 1956, p. 352; and Jones 1965, pp. 14–20.

statistics exist on the actual number of wetbacks who have entered the United States, an approximate idea can be inferred from the records of expatriated wetbacks. Records for the period 1930–69 indicate that 7,486,470 apprehensions of wetbacks were made by the U.S. Immigration Authority (U.S. Immigration and Naturalization Service 1966, 1967–68). The highest rates were concentrated in the decades 1941–60, during which 5,953,210 expulsions of wetbacks were made. The size of the population involved clearly defines the importance of the problem.

When we look at the sociocultural characteristics of the persons involved, we see that the problem is much larger. Most are poor peasants from central and northern states in Mexico who come to the United States only to find work to survive (Samora 1971, p. 102). They are willing to accept anything—good or bad treatment, illness, starvation, low wages, poor living conditions; all are taken philosophically and accepted without struggle. Their struggle is concentrated on pure survival (Saunders and Leonard 1951, p. 6).

The Network of Social Relations of Wetbacks

Various groups of people come in contact with the wetback in the United States. In this section we will review four major groups: (1) the employer who benefits from a cheap labor pool, (2) the southwestern Mexican-American farm worker who suffers from the competition of these low-paid workers, (3) the lawmaker who is in the ambiguous position of defender of the law and protector of the "illegal" interests of farm entrepreneurs, and (4) the law enforcer who is directly responsible for enforcing the laws.

The Employer. In all economic enterprises, and in particular agricultural enterprises, labor constitutes a major segment of production costs. Rational manipulation of all instruments of production in pure economic terms requires the minimization of costs in all areas to achieve the highest possible economic return. Workers willing to accept labor contracts below going wages clearly become a positive asset in that they assure higher returns for the entrepreneur. Moreover, other economic advantages besides low wages accrue from the employment of wetback labor. First, in some kinds of employment no strict accounting of working hours is kept, since work contracts based on daily labor may involve as many as twelve hours (Hadley 1956, p. 347). Second, little or no responsibility for disability occurs, since the wetback must assume responsibility for his own injuries and accidents. Third, the employer is under no obligation, legal or otherwise, to provide health and medical services, sanitary facilities, or even decent housing (American G.I. Forum of Texas and Texas State Federation of Labor 1953, pp. 17–27). As a result, what the wetback receives as wages and other standard "fringe benefits" is determined only by the employer's conscience and the current standards of neighbors and friends (Hadley 1956, p. 347). Even in pure economic terms, then, the position of the rural entrepreneur vis-à-vis the wetback is highly advantageous; by using wetbacks as workers, farmers can maximize possible economic gains in labor costs (Samora 1971, pp. 98–103).

The Mexican-American Farm Worker. Whereas the rural entrepreneur gains by the presence of wetbacks, the Mexican-American rural workers lose in competition for jobs. They feel that wetbacks push work contract conditions to the lowest possible level, a "charity" level out of step with living requirements in the United States. Their personal suffering from such competition is unjust, since, while being penalized by this competition, they have to pay the costs of citizenship (e.g., income and other taxes) and receive little or no benefit from such required contributions. Further, wetbacks break the possible cohesion of the rural labor force, and so they lose bargaining power with rural entrepreneurs. Finally, the manipulation of the mass media and urban lobbying groups by the rural entrepreneur creates an artificial shortage of labor which serves to ensure the permanence of wetbacks. At the same time, Mexican-American workers are prevented from speaking in the mass media to unmask the artificial labor shortage (Hadley 1956, p. 345).

The Lawmaker. The lawmaker should be the one to bridge the gap between the conflicting demands of the entrepreneur and the Mexican-American. Nevertheless, the most general pattern followed by lawmakers is to consider the wetback problem and the working situation on the border as something unavoidable or expected. Legal attempts to effectively prevent the wetback from crossing the border are stricken from proposed codes by the lawmakers on the rationale that the farmer along the border wants wetback labor (U.S. Congress, Senate 1953, p. 10). The "realistic" attitude of these lawmakers seems to be either that it is convenient to conform or worthless to struggle against the situation. Thus, the U.S. immigration law is broken in order to maintain a supply of wetbacks. For many southern, and in particular Texas, legislators, there is no evil in maintaining the influx of wetbacks.

Protection of the interests of wetback employers by lawmakers is best illustrated by a law (U.S. Congress, 8 U.S.C., section 1324, 1952) which makes it a felony to be a wetback but not to hire one.[2] This is a paradoxical situation which legitimizes the hiring of wetbacks in spite of the general recognition that it is the possibility of being hired that attracts Mexican workers to cross illegally to the United States. This situation was pointed out by Ruben Salazar (recently killed in the Chicago Moratorium in Los Angeles) in an article published in the *Los Angeles Times* (April 27, 1970): "There is no law against hiring wetbacks. There is only a law against being a wetback" (Samora 1971, p. 139).

The Law Enforcer. The Border Patrol is directly responsible for the prevention of wetback crossings and for the apprehension of wetbacks already in the United States. Theoretically, such a role would place the patrol in direct confrontation with the rural entrepreneurs using wetback labor, inasmuch as they enforce laws made in the interests of the total society. Their activities would, in part, protect the immediate interests of the legal rural workers.

Nevertheless, evidence suggests that such relationships of reciprocity are not realized (Saunders and Leonard 1951,

[2] That law provides that "any person who willfully or knowingly conceals, harbors, or shields from detection, in any place including any building or by any means of transportation, or who encourages or induces, or attempts to encourage or induce, either directly or indirectly, the entry into the United States of any alien shall be guilty of a felony. Upon conviction he shall be punished by a fine not exceeding $2,000 or by imprisonment for a term not exceeding five years, or both, for each alien in respect to whom the violation occurs. *Provided, however, that for the purposes of this section, employment, including the usual and normal practices incident to employment, shall not be deemed to constitute harboring*" (italics added; Samora 1971, p. 139).

p. 68); instead, the conflict between the Border Patrol and entrepreneurs is somehow transformed into covert cooperation
through a "pattern of evasion" of the law (see Williams 1951).
This transformation involves the following: first, the entrepreneurs offer little resistance to the apprehension of wetbacks,
in exchange for the patrol's overlooking the wetbacks when
work needs to be done. Second, wetbacks openly at work may
informally legitimate their status as workers and thus remain
unharassed. Third, complete enforcement of the law by state
and national authorities, and with minimum cooperation from
local people, is theoretically possible (Saunders and Leonard
1951, p. 68).

The Labeling Approach to Deviant Behavior

Theories which view deviance as a quality of the deviant act
or the actor cannot help us understand the wetback as deviant.
"Wetback" became the label for a deviant after the appearance
of the Border Patrol, and various social groups came to *react*
differently to the presence of wetbacks. It is singularly characteristic of this deviant type that it occurs in a cross-cultural
context; as a Mexican, the wetback breaks an American law
and receives negative legal sanction while, at the same time, he
positively fulfills the needs of specific American groups. This
context of deviance fits well into the framework of labeling
theory. According to Becker (1963, p. 91), deviance cannot be
viewed as homogeneous because it results from interaction
and consists of particular responses by various social groups to
a particular behavior of the prospective deviant or outsider.

In this context, we must analyze the wetback in interaction,
singling out the responses of the various groups making up
the network which labels his behavior as deviant. The deviant
character of the wetback, then, lies not in him nor in his behavior but in the superimposition of the deviant label on him.

Becker's use of labeling theory in deviance is of particular
interest to us because of his stress on the political dimensions
of the labeling processes. He emphasizes the fact that the legal
norms and the behavior classified as deviant must be viewed as
part of a political process in which group A, *in conflict* with
group B, defines the rules for group B. The degree of group
A's success in imposing such rules and in enforcing them de-

pends primarily upon the political and economic power of
group A. Furthermore, the will of group A is often an expression of a class interest rather than solely of individual
members of group A. In such a case, enforcement of the rules
becomes applicable to all members of that class, excluding
members of group B whose class interests are the same as
group A's.

Becker further indicates that labeling always begins with the
initiative of a "moral entrepreneur" (Becker 1963, pp. 147–
63), a leader (individual or group) who crusades for new
rules to stop something that he views as wrong. Moral entrepreneurs are interested in the content of rules and are very
often involved in what they view as humanitarian or moral
reformism. In their crusades, they typically say they want to
help those beneath them to achieve a better status, and in the
process "they add to the power they derive from the legitimacy of their moral position the power they derive from their
superior position in society" (Becker 1963, p. 149). The outcome of a successful moral crusade is the establishment of a
new set of rules (i.e., the immigration laws of 1921 and 1924)
and corresponding enforcement agencies and officials (i.e.,
the U.S. Border Patrol). The new law enforcers justify their
existence by attempting to fulfill the new activities, and, in
their performance, they try to win the respect of prominent
persons.

Once a law and its enforcers come into existence the process
of labeling becomes independent of the moral entrepreneur.
The enforcer becomes the most important actor, and while
enforcing the law he stigmatizes or labels certain individuals as
deviants. Thus, there is a process of interaction in which some
actors will enforce rules "in the service of their own interest,"
whereas others, also "in the service of their own interest,"
commit acts labeled as deviant (Becker 1963, p. 162).

The Wetback Labeling Process

The labeling process started with a moral crusade under the
leadership of moral entrepreneurs representing the moral
spirit of the American legal system. The results of the crusade
were new legal codes (the immigration laws of 1921 and 1924)
and the establishment of organizations and specialized person-

nel (e.g., the Border Patrol) to implement the new codes. The moral component of the legitimization of the new codes rests on the righteousness of the law, inasmuch as it protects the interests of nationals who otherwise would be defenseless against the threat of foreign competitors.

This organizational superstructure, whose purpose was to carry out the moral imperatives, resulted in a radical transformation of the previous interactions of foreign laborers. Of immediate concern was the reinforcement of the illegal status of immigrant workers under the deviant label of wetback. Nevertheless, moral imperatives, even those incorporated legally and implemented by specialized personnel, are not the only basis of motivation and rationalization of action. Others, especially political and economic interests, can be at variance with these new moral imperatives and influence behavior. When we examine such conflicting motivations we see that they may be selectively used, depending on the context of the action and the character of the actor—in particular his power. Thus, the rural entrepreneur in certain situations (e.g., harvest time) uses economic motivation to hire wetbacks with contracts calling for long hours of work and the lowest possible pay. In other situations (say, when he has unwanted workers) he uses the moral imperative to denounce wetbacks to the Border Patrol. A similar differential use of motivation occurs with other groups. It is necessary to specify the nature of motivations at play in the wetback case.

Looking at interests as a source of motivations, we shall focus on them at the juncture where they shape action; that is, at the point of interaction between wetbacks and the groups of actors discussed in this paper. A distinction will be made between group interests related to the presence of the wetback and group interests related only to each actor's role independent of the presence of the wetback. The latter would be those interests pertaining to the maintenance of the role played by actors of each group, that is, (1) the Mexican-American farm worker's role interest would be to maximize wages, (2) the farmer's (wetback employer's) role interest would be to maximize profit, (3) the lawmaker's role interest would be to provide legislation that meets the necessities of his constituencies and the country, (4) the law enforcer's (Border Patrol's) role interest would be to enforce immigration laws, (5) the moral entrepreneur's role interest would be to define good and evil for society. On the other hand, group interest related to the presence of the wetback seems to indicate a different dimension of each actor's role, as, respectively, (1) to stop the influx of wetbacks in order to avoid their competition for jobs and to increase bargaining power vis-à-vis the farmer, (2) to maximize profits by the use of the wetback cheap labor, (3) to gain political support from the farmers by protecting their interests, (4) to enforce immigration laws selectively, (5) to define protection of nationals against foreign competition as good and entrance to the United States without inspection as immoral.

This distinction of interests seems to promote understanding of some contradictions in the wetback phenomenon, such as (1) condemning the wetback by defining him as a deviant and, at the same time, maintaining a demand for his labor force which is reflected in a steadily increasing influx of wetbacks each year (Samora 1971, pp. 195–96); (2) penalizing a person for being a wetback, but not a farmer for hiring one (U.S. Congress, 8 U.S.C., section 1324, 1952); (3) maintaining an agency for the enforcement of immigration laws and at the same time exerting budget limitations and/or political pressures to prevent successful enforcement of the law (Hadley 1956, p. 348).

These are some of the contradictions that become apparent in the wetback case, but they are nothing less than reflections of contradictions in society at large. This is particularly obvious to us when we see the conflict of interests between the farmer and Mexican-American farm worker (each tries to maximize his economical gains at the expense of the other) and when we see the presence of the wetback kept undercover as a veil hiding deeper conflict. Indeed, when the role of the wetback is introduced in agricultural production, we see a different conflict of interests taking place—namely, that between the Mexican-American worker and the wetback. The former blames the latter for lowering working conditions and standards of living.

The nature of the two conflicts should be differentiated. Whereas the conflict of interests between the Mexican-American farm worker and the farmer is determined by the position each plays in a particular mode of agricultural production, the conflict between the Mexican-American worker and the wetback is determined primarily by a set of beliefs that are not necessarily grounded in reality, namely, that wages and working conditions are determined by external laws of supply and demand independent of the employers; that the wetback *causes* low wages and low standards of living for the farm worker, etc. It is important to note the point here that the conflicts "created" by the wetback would disappear with an unrestricted enforcement of immigration laws.

Another aspect of our discussion of group interest is the power that supports each specified interest and respective action. Since the groups themselves reflect status differentials, it is the differences in power (and possible collisions of power) that give form to the interaction. Furthermore, the power of legitimization of these actions sustains the existing form against any possible transformation.

Power differences among the various actors result from their ability to manipulate or influence interaction in the direction of their interests (see Gamson 1968). In this interpretation, the wetback employer is clearly the most powerful category, since he is able to influence all other actors. On the other extreme is the wetback. He clearly appears at a disadvantage. As an outsider he has no legitimacy. He is not eligible for public assistance or for the benefits of an eventual "moral entrepreneur," since he is not eligible to stay in the country, unless he is in jail. He is also not eligible for other benefits because of the stigma of having once broken the immigration laws. This might, technically, prevent him from acquiring legal residence or citizenship in the United States. The wetback only has the original motivation which made him cross the border (survival) and a new one resulting from the deviant label (not to be caught) which becomes another element of pure survival. As an outsider with such elemental interests he dares not complain—the only possible protest comes when his survival is in jeopardy and his only course of action is to return to Mexico.

A Conceptual Addendum to Becker's Schema. Labeling theory provides us with the concept of moral entrepreneur. Applying the elements of this type to the case under analysis, we find a new type in the role of the wetback employer. His crusade is directed toward the self-serving enforcement of existing laws. The source of his crusade is the threat of the loss of cheap labor that would occur if the laws were enforced. Evidently the characteristics of this second type are the polar opposites of those of the moral entrepreneur. The imperative he singles out as a banner is economic rather than moral. The crusade he leads is supported by power and economic interest rather than moral righteousness. This type can perhaps be characterized as an *antilaw entrepreneur*. In order to be successful he associates the law enforcer and the lawmaker in his enterprise and becomes able to manipulate the law in two ways: first, by preventing its enforcement whenever he needs cheap labor; second, by stimulating its enforcement when he needs to dispose of a complaining or useless wetback.

A view of the contradictions of society apparent in the wetback case has allowed us to introduce the antilaw entrepreneur. Such a concept is useful for the understanding of deviance because it shows that violation of a law can also become the goal of an enterprise in the same sense that the creation of a law may be the goal of an enterprise. Both crusades, to be successful, require leaders holding legitimate power, although in one case they have the added legitimization of answering to a moral imperative, whereas in the other they answer to the economic interests of a specialized group. The law enforcer, the lawmaker, and a powerful group of rural entrepreneurs can launch such a crusade against the law and yet not be "labeled" as deviants.

If a Border Patrol man states firmly that to enforce the law would "ruin the fields" (Saunders and Leonard 1951, p. 68), and a lawmaker refers to specific measures in the Senate to allow the influx of wetbacks (U.S. Congress, Senate 1953), and a former vice president of the United States (John Nance Garner) says, "If they [wetback employers] get the Mexican labor it enables them to make a profit" (Jones 1965, p. 17), then the essential objectives of the enterprise are spelled out. The continuing presence of wetbacks is in no little measure an indication of the success of the antilaw entrepreneur.

Conclusion

The preceding analysis leads us to see—

(1) the wetback as one who crosses the U.S.–Mexican border illegally, taking advantage of the limited enforcement of the U.S. immigration laws;

(2) the interaction process in which such a man is labeled as deviant, a label that will constitute a central element of a process of exploitation;

(3) the deviant label making the wetback more attractive as a worker than the Mexican-American (at the same time, paradoxically, such a label—an element of destitution— becomes what the wetback exchanges for an unstable taste of survival);

(4) the labeling process in which the wetback is "created," in which interests and power are arranged in an action that we have typified as an antilaw enterprise.

And finally, a human being with the alternatives of being exploited by a country forcing him to become a deviant or of facing misery in his own country by not doing so.

References

American G.I. Forum of Texas and Texas State Federation of Labor. 1953. *What Price Wetbacks?* Austin: American G.I. Forum of Texas and Texas State Federation of Labor (AFL).

Becker, Howard S. 1963. *Outsiders: Studies in the Sociology of Deviance.* New York: Free Press.

Bustamante, Jorge A. In press. *Don Chano: Autobiografía de un Emigrante Mexicano.* Mexico City: Instituto de Investigaciones Sociales of the National University of Mexico.

Daniels, Roger, and Harry H. L. Kitano. 1970. *American Racism: Exploration of the Nature of Prejudice.* Englewood Cliffs, N.J.: Prentice-Hall.

Eckler, Ross A., and Jack Zlotnick. 1949. "Immigration and Labor Force." In *The Annals,* edited by Thorsten Sellin. Philadelphia: American Academy of Political and Social Sciences.

Gamio, Manuel. 1930. *Mexican Immigration to the United States.* Chicago: University of Chicago Press.

Gamson, William. 1968. *Power and Discontent.* Homewood, Ill.: Dorsey.

Grebler, Leo. 1966. "Mexican Immigration to the United States." Mexican American Study Project, Advanced Report No. 2. Los Angeles: University of California.

Hadley, Eleanor M. 1956. "A Critical Analysis of the Wetback Problem." *Law and Contemporary Problems* 21 (Spring): 334–57.

Hourwich, Isaac A. 1912. *Immigration and Labor*. New York: Putnam.

Jones, Lamar B. 1965. "Mexican American Labor Problems in Texas." Ph.D. dissertation, University of Texas.

Lemert, Edwin M. 1951. *Social Pathology*. New York: McGraw-Hill.

―――. 1967. *Human Deviance, Social Problems, and Social Control*. Englewood Cliffs, N.J.: Prentice-Hall.

McWilliams, Carey. 1968. *North from Mexico*. Westport, Conn.: Greenwood.

Marden, Charles F., and Gladys Meyer. 1968. *Minorities in American Society*. New York: American Book Co.

Mead, George H. 1918. "The Psychology of Punitive Justice." *American Journal of Sociology* 23 (March): 577–602.

Samora, Julian, assisted by Jorge A. Bustamante and Gilbert Cardenas. 1971. *Los Mojados, the Wetback Story*. Notre Dame, Ind.: University of Notre Dame Press.

Samora, Julian, and Jorge A. Bustamante. 1971. "Mexican Immigration and American Labor Demands." In *Migrant and Seasonal Farmworker Powerlessness*. Pt. 7B. Hearings, U.S. Senate, Committee on Labor and Public Welfare. Washington, D.C.: Government Printing Office.

Samora, Julian, and Richard A. Lamanna. 1970. "Mexican American in a Midwest Metropolis: A Study of East Chicago." In *The Mexican American People: The Nation's Second Largest Minority*, edited by V. Webb. New York: Free Press.

Saunders, Lyle, and Olen F. Leonard. 1951. *The Wetback in the Lower Rio Grande Valley of Texas*. Inter-American Education Occasional Papers, No. 7. Austin: University of Texas.

U.S. Immigration and Naturalization Service. 1966. *Annual Report of the United States Immigration and Naturalization Service*. Washington, D.C.: Government Printing Office.

―――. 1967–68. *Report of Field Operations of the Immigration and Naturalization Service*. Washington, D.C.: Government Printing Office.

U.S. Congress, Senate 1953. Appropriation Hearings on S. 1917 before the Subcommittee of the Senate Committee of the Judiciary 83rd Cong., 1st sess., p. 123 (Senator McCarran).

Williams, Robin, Jr. 1951. *American Society: A Sociological Interpretation*. New York: Knopf.

Wittke, Carl. 1949. "Immigration Policy Prior to World War I." In *The Annals*, edited by Thorsten Sellin. Philadelphia: American Academy of Political and Social Science.

A Critique of Labeling

Gwynn Nettler

The labeling perspective is more interested in definitions of deviance than in deviant behaviors per se. Thus, it is less concerned with what so-called deviants actually do than with how others react. The advantage of the labeling perspective, Nettler says, is that it helps us see that in some cases people respond more to labels than to actual behaviors, and that by so doing they at times produce the very behaviors they condemn. In terms of explaining crime, however, Nettler does not think the labeling perspective is very useful. More specifically, it fails to predict or explain criminal behavior, it uses circular reasoning in treating the response to crime as the cause of crime, and it cannot tell us how to reduce criminal behavior.

The most popular new set of ideas employed by sociologists to explain crime is a bundle of assumptions known as the "labeling" hypothesis. This hypothesis depends heavily upon the belief that social relations are "constructed," that reality is defined and interpreted before it becomes meaningful. This is a way of saying that we act in terms of the *meanings* attributed to events rather than to objective events. Conditions, it is said, are *defined* before they are reacted to. How we respond to each other is a function of the way we have categorized each other and of the significance we have assigned to our interactions.

From this point of view, "crime" is a word, not an act. Crime is socially defined and criminals are socially "produced" in a process which allows majorities to apply labels to minorities and which, in many cases, permits majorities to enforce the consequences of this labeling. As a result, the "labeled" person—the stigmatized person—may be unable to act in any way different from the role ascribed to him.

The Transcendence of Roles over Behaviors. Labeling theory emphasizes the processes of human interaction that result in the attribution and acceptance of *roles*. The emphasis upon role construction calls attention to the way behavior may be shaped by the expectations of those with whom one is interacting and to the way our perceptions of each other are reinforced by the early assignment of labels to samples of our acts. Once roles are defined, clusters of attributes are inferred. Such inference stimulates a selective perception that permits a linking together of diverse acts under some meaningful label (Turner, 1972, p. 310).

The emphasis upon role formation means that less attention is paid to how people behave than to how they categorize each other on the basis of small segments of behavior. The tendency of the labeling theorist, then, is to deny or ignore differences in the ways in which people act and to stress the utility and the consequences of having the power to categorize. Throughout the literature, the prevailing sentiment is to deny differences and to cast doubt upon the validity and the justice of popular images of minorities.

Translating "Criminality" into "Deviance." Given this attitude toward difference, the labeling theorists find it more convenient to talk about "deviance" than about "criminality." This translation directs attention to the fact that majorities are reacting to minorities and that it is being different in the sense of being powerless because of small numbers that permits arrest, censure, and punishment to be attached to a difference.

Such a viewpoint is, obviously, sympathetic to minorities. The labeling school has, consequently, been termed an "underdog philosophy." Its spokesmen ask, "Whose side are we on?" (Becker, 1967).

The philosophy of the underdog turns the tables on conventional thought. Instead of assuming that it is the deviant's difference which needs explanation, it asks why the majority responds to *this* difference as it does. This shift of the question reverses the normal conception of causation; the labeling school suggests that the other person's peculiarity has not caused us to regard him as different so much as our labeling has caused his peculiarity. This reversal, among other characteristics of the labeling hypothesis, has made the theory interesting and has contributed to its popularity (Davis, 1971).

Proponents of the labeling hypothesis distinguish between "primary deviance," that is, some offensive act, and "secondary deviance" (Lemert, 1951), that is, the process by which the reaction of society to an initial difference may confirm the deviant in the stigmatized behavior. Being cast out means being an outcast and makes it comfortable for stigmatized persons to band together in defense of their egos and in justification of their "peculiar" interests.

The labeling theorist deemphasizes the difference in the deviant. He holds that "initially" everyone deviates somewhat from some standards some of the time. What confirms the difference is some official attachment of a label to the apprehended deviant. The labeling theorist is concerned, then, to study how much deviance is produced by the very correctional agencies that are supposed to reduce difference. How much delinquency do reform schools manufacture? How much crime do prisons create? How much psychosis is perpetuated by mental hospitals?

What is to be explained is not so much the deviant as the people who have the power to attach the scarlet letter and thus to confirm the deviation. The labeling theorist sees the judicial response to crime as "the dramatization of evil" (Tannenbaum, 1938).

Implications for Methodology. The research method advocated by the labeling theorist is intensive observation of labelers and their victims. Field work is preferred to the collection of statistics. The result of such study is a description of how the labeler comes to recognize and define the deviant and of how the deviant reacts to and interprets his own world. The test of the adequacy of such a description is understanding and insight rather than prediction and control.

As compared with statistical and experimental studies, the reportorial field work recommended by the labeling theorist is more fun for students. It is good sport to engage in "participant observation," particularly among people who are "different." To this element of pleasure, labeling theory has added the advocacy of the "rights" of minorities. Its appreciative methodology and its political stance have combined to make it a fashionable way of thinking about undesirable behaviors and "social problems." The fashion has spread from its application to crime and has been extended, with variations, to attempts to understand blindness (Scott, 1969), stuttering (Lemert, 1967), illness (Lorber, 1967), civil disturbances (Turner, 1969), "welfarism" (Beck, 1967), paranoia (Lemert, 1962), death and dying (Sudnow, 1966), mental retardation (Mercer, 1965), and neurosis and psychosis (Braginsky et al., 1969; Plog and Edgerton, 1969; Scheff, 1966). An evaluation of this popular mode of explanation must recognize both its advantages and its liabilities.

The Advantages of the Labeling Hypothesis. The value of the labeling hypothesis lies in its attention to the possibilities that (1) people may respond more to their definitions of others than to the behaviors of others and (2) stigmatizing definitions may produce the bad behaviors they condemn.

1. The labeling hypothesis asks "society" whether it is reacting to the deviant's behavior or to its own definition of the deviance   The idea that deviance is produced in some process of interaction that results in our pinning tags on each other calls attention to the possible inaccuracy of the names we apply. To say that "deviance" is created by labeling is to suggest that the labels may be inappropriate, and to raise the question whether we are responding more to what the other person did or more to the image of the other person that is called up by the name we have given him.

This is a valuable question, and it deserves a scientific answer. Thus far, the answer has been assumed by the labeling theorists rather than tested. This assumption partakes of a tradition in social psychology that has itself applied a label to the common-sense categories which most of us use to order our social worlds. The label applied by social psychologists to such popular concepts is "stereotype." Calling a popular image a "stereotype" assumes, without adequate evidence, that the ordinary citizen's notions about the "different" kinds of people around him are mostly wrong. However, the sociopsychological assumption itself seems more false than true. The few studies that have attempted to test the accuracy of popular images have shown that "stereotypes" are more accurate than inaccurate. This has been found true of popular perceptions of occupations (Rice, 1928) and of ethnic groups (Mackie, 1971, 1973). No adequate research has yet been completed on the validity of popular images of various kinds of criminals, although one such study is under way (Solhaug, 1972). Until some research on this matter has been completed, we can appreciate the point made by the labeling theorists without subscribing to it.

2. The labeling hypothesis alerts us to the possibility that official reactions to some disapproved behaviors may do more harm than good   The chief value of the labeling hypothesis has been to call attention to the possibility that official reactions to some kinds of disapproved behaviors may confirm the actors in their deviant ways. It is suggested, for example, that some "sick behaviors" improve more rapidly when they are untreated and that some cures are worse than the diseases they treat.

The labeling theorist emphasizes how minor events in the stream of life may become major events through official reaction. The careers of some different kinds of people are made even more different by the fact that some portion of their lives must be spent in dodging the consequences of the official response to their deviance. The model here is that of the marijuana user, [1] whose life may be changed by the criminalization of his preference.

Labeling theory gains credence as it develops biographies showing that being "officially handled" increases the chances of future official attention. There is evidence that some part of this risk is incurred by the discrimination associated with a criminal label. *There is no way of knowing, however, how much of repeated offense is so caused.*

The labeling hypothesis could prove more useful if its ideas were associated with a taxonomy of offenders in such a way that we might know who could be best "saved" from future criminality by ignoring his present offense. This is not an easy question.[2] It is, however, part of what probation is about.

The labeling hypothesis is politically important because it challenges the *status quo*. This is congenial to revolutionaries, of course, whose ideology translates the label "convict" as "political prisoner." Less radically, the labeling hypothesis stimulates thinking about the costs of applying the criminal law to certain categories of disapproved behaviors. It suggests that there may be limits to the efficacy of the legal sanction (Packer, 1968) and urges assessment of the relative costs and benefits of the criminalization or decriminalization of immoral, peculiar, or unhealthful conduct.

[1] The labeling theorist's point can be made by substituting for marijuana the criminalization of any other chemical, like tobacco or alcohol, that many people habitually use.
[2] The answer to this question is made difficult by the possible antagonism among the various goals of justice. The antagonism is the desire to rehabilitate some apprehended offenders, the need to deter others, and the need to express, through the symbolism of punishment, society's rejection of criminal conduct.

The Liabilities of the Labeling Perspective. (1) Labeling theory has been criticized for ignoring the differences in behavior described by labels. The labeling schema draws attention from deeds to the public definitions of those deeds. Such diversion means that (2) labeling theory does not increase, and may well decrease, our ability to predict individual behavior. Its low predictive power is a result not only of its neglect of individual differences but also of the fact that (3) it contains a defective model of causation. This in turn means that (4) its relevance to social policy is lessened. Each of these points will be amplified.

1. Labeling theory does not explain the behaviors that lead to the application of labels   The labeling theorists argue as if popular and legal categories were devoid of content, as if they were never "well earned." The labeling explanation pays little or no attention to the fact that people do *not* behave similarly. It slights the possibility that a label may *correctly* identify consistent differences in conduct, and it pays little attention to the reasons why "society" continues to apply a label once it has been used.

Labeling theory denies, therefore, the causal importance and explanatory value of personality variables. In fact, labeling theorists regard as futile the search for personality differences that might distinguish categories of more or less criminal persons. The labeling hypothesis prefers a political interpretation to such a psychological one. It prefers to believe that deviants are minorities lacking power to challenge the rules by which a majority has labeled them. The theory denies, then, that a label may be properly applied to describe personality differences which may underlie real behavioral differences. This denial has unfortunate consequences for the prediction of individual behavior.

It has unfortuante consequences, too, for the development of public policy. The prescription that follows from the labeling hypothesis is to change the attitudes of majorities toward misbehaving minorities. In reply, majorities tell us that they are not yet convinced that a more compassionate attitude toward the robber or the burglar will change the offender's behavior and reduce the pain he gives.

2. When applied to the understanding of individual behavior, the labeling hypothesis has low predictive power   The low predictive power of labeling theory results from its denial of personality

differences. The interactional bias of the labeling theorist encourages such optimistic but risky beliefs as these:

> He will be honest if I trust him.
> She will be reasonable if you are.
> He will be pacific if we are.
> Her psychosis is not "in her," but "in her situation." When
the mirrors in which she sees herself are changed, she will
change.

On the contrary, there *are* personality differences that are
reliably associated with behavioral differences and that are re-
markably persistent. These persistent ways of feeling and
acting are not readily changeable with changes in the labels
attached to them. Regardless of what we have been called,
most of us continue to be what we have been a long time be-
coming.

The research literature on this subject is vast. It may be
sampled in the works of Honzik (1966), Kelly (1963), Mischel
(1969), Robins and O'Neal (1958), Roff (1961), Schaefer and
Bayley (1960), Thomas et al. (1970), Witkin (1965), and Zax et
al. (1968). The point is made in the autobiography of the play-
wright S. N. Behrman (1972) who, after years of failure and
impoverished struggle, wrote a play that was a hit. Behrman
comments, "With the production of a successful play, . . . you
acquire overnight a new identity—a public label. But this label
is pasted on you. It doesn't obliterate what you are and have
always been—doesn't erase the stigmata of temperament" (p.
37).

The statement that there are persistent temperamental and
cognitive differences underlying our behaviors can be quali-
fied by adding that such personality variables have more of an
impact upon behavior as circumstances are equalized. Nevertheless, most of us can tell the difference between behavior—
our own and others'—that is only situationally reactive and behavior that is characteristic. All of us operate, implicitly or explicitly, with the idea of *character*—the idea that there *are* enduring personal predispositions relevant to moral behavior.
This means that, unless there are tremendous changes in envi-
ronments, people are likely to continue to behave as they have
behaved. Against the optimistic recommendations of the interactionist, it seems more sensible to believe that:

The embezzler may need to be arrested, and stigmatized, before he "turns honest."

Being reasonable with a fanatic is futile.

A soft answer turns away the wrath of some men, but not of others, and there is no point in pleading for your life with a Charles Manson.

The cures of psychoses are exceptional. Most people who are "peculiar" are not disordered in all ways, all the time. Misbehavior may be episodic; but ordinarily, safety lies in the assumption of behavioral continuity.

3. The model of causation implicit in the labeling hypothesis is questionable Every explanation of human behavior makes assumptions about its causes. The labeling theory locates the causes of adult behavior in an unusual place—in the people who respond to it. It shifts the "responsibility" for my action from me to you. It stresses how much of what I do is a result of what you have done to me, and for me. My "self," it is said, is reflected to me by the social mirrors available to me. My "self" is the presumed agent of my actions, but my "self" is itself largely constructed by the responses of "significant others" to my initial efforts.

This is a shorthand statement of the hypothesis of "socialization." In its general formulation, there is no quarrel with such a hypothesis. All theories that would explain human behavior, including popular theories, assume that our behavior has been shaped by the actions of others. The sociopsychological hypotheses of the "control" variety pay particular attention to the "how" of this socialization process.

It is not denied, then, that how people respond to us when we misbehave may affect our subsequent conduct. The lively questions are, however, at what periods of our development, and to what degree, others mould us. What is at issue is *how much* of the adult behavior to be explained varies with the response of others to it.

It is our ignorance that permits the continuing quarrel, for no one knows which kinds of behaviors, in which kinds of personalities, at which "stage" of life, are affected how much, by which kinds of response, from which others, in which situations. Some generalization about this is part of our popular wisdom, but much of that is truistic. We expect more than truisms from criminological theories.

The valuable contributions of the labeling hypothesis have tended to obscure its deficiencies. It is one thing to study the way in which a defining process affects our response to the behavior of others. It is another matter to study the causes of the events we are defining. Studying how we respond to deviant others may suggest to us a more economical (more rational) mode of reacting. This suggestion should not be confused, however, with information about the causes of the crimes that concern us.

Such confusion is created when spokesmen of the labeling theory tell us, for example, that *"social groups create deviance by making the rules whose infraction constitutes deviance,* and by applying those rules to particular people and labeling them as outsiders" (Becker, 1963, p. 9). Some readers will translate statements like this as saying that "social groups create crime by making the laws whose infraction constitutes crime." This translation is slippery: it slides between the truth that social groups create the *definition* of "crime" and the falsehood that the *injuries* condemned by these definitions would disappear (or would not have been "created") if the definition had not been formulated. To the layman, it sounds as though the labeling theorist believed that people would not wish to defend themselves against burglary or murder if they had not learned a rule defining these acts as crimes. It sounds, also, as though the labeling theorist believed that there would be less "burglary" if we did not use that term. The nonprofessional consumer of criminological explanations recognizes this for the semantic trick that it is—the trick of saying, "If a crime is a breach of a rule, you won't have the crime if you don't have the rule." The ordinary reaction to this semantic sleight of hand is to say, "A mugging by any other name hurts just as much."

Applied to "real life," the labeling hypothesis functions as another of the "power of positive thinking" philosophies: "If disease is an error of thought, positive thinking will cure it." "If crime resides in our definitions of deviance, redefining it will change it."

Our question has to do with the location of causation. When the causation implied by the labeling hypothesis is tested, it fails. The causes specified by this schema do not account for the production of the behaviors that disturb us. "Mental hospitals" do not cause "mental illness" (Gove, 1970), nor do the agencies of social control, or the labels they apply, account for crime (Ward, 1971).

The assumption of labeling theory is that those who become "criminal" are mostly those who, while behaving much like everyone else, just happened to get tagged, or that those labeled "criminals" were more liable to the tagging because they fit some public's prejudiced stereotype of the criminal. Contrary to these assumptions, however, studies of the operation of the system of justice show that it works like a sieve: as we have seen, the people who end up caught in the sieve tend to be the more serious and persistent lawbreakers (Black and Reiss, 1970; Bordua, 1967; Terry, 1967).

In summary, the labeling theorist does not think about causes and effects, about antecedents and consequents; he prefers to think about interactions. This preference does not eliminate the idea of causation; it only obscures it by shifting the locus of causes from actors to their judges. This shift has some moral and political value in the fight between outsiders and insiders. It justifies a challenge of the police and the courts, or any other mechanism of social control, that would condemn the conduct of minorities. When the labeling hypothesis is applied to the explanation of the serious crimes, however, its model of causation reduces its value for public policy.

4. On the level of social concerns, the labeling hypothesis does not answer the perennial questions about crime   We are reminded that explanatory theories are only as good as the questions they answer. The answers provided by the labeling theorists are not addressed to the questions about crime that are asked by most people. These questions are, again, "What causes crime?" "What accounts for increases or decreases in crime rates?" "How can crime be reduced?"

To these questions, the labeling theorists give no good reply. The policy recommendation of the labeling hypothesis comes down to "Avoid unnecessary labeling" (Schur, 1971, p. 171). This may be helpful in decriminalizing some activities. It is a recommendation that is already being followed in some areas, as in the euphemistic use of language that substitutes kind words for harsh ones—"sanitary engineer" for "garbage collector" and "special child" for "imbecile." Such translations bespeak a change in attitude, yet the categories persist. Categorizing is an inevitable part of our response to the world.

We should wish our categories to be clean, accurate, and useful, as social psychologists have urged. It is doubtful, however, whether attention to our vocabularies will tell citizens and public officials how better to reduce robbery and rape.

Bibliography

Beck, B. 1967. "Welfare as a moral category." *Social Problems* 14 (Winter):258–277.

Becker, H. S. 1963. *Outsiders: Studies in the Sociology of Deviance*. Glencoe, Ill.: The Free Press.

———. 1967. "Whose side are we on?" *Social Problems* 14 (Winter):239–247.

Behrman, S. N. 1972. "People in a diary, I." *The New Yorker* 48 (13 May):36–94.

Black, D. J., and A. J. Reiss, Jr. 1970. "Police control of juveniles." *American Sociological Review* 35 (February):63–77.

Bordua, D. J. 1967. "Recent trends: Deviant behavior and social control." *The Annals of the American Academy of Political and Social Science* 369 (January):149–163.

Braginsky, B. M., et al. 1969. *Methods of Madness: The Mental Hospital as a Last Resort*. New York: Holt, Rinehart, and Winston, Inc.

Davis, M. S. 1971. "That's interesting!" *Philosophy of the Social Sciences* 1 (December):309–344.

Gove, W. R. 1970. "Societal reaction as an explanation of mental illness: An evaluation." *American Sociological Review* 35 (October):873–884.

Honzik, M. P. 1966. "Prediction of behavior from birth to maturity." In J. Rosenblith and W. Allinsmith (Eds.), *The Causes of Behavior*. Second Edition. Boston: Allyn and Bacon.

Kelly, E. L. 1963. "Consistency of the adult personality." *American Psychologist* 10 (November):659–681.

Lemert, E. M. 1951. *Social Pathology*. New York: McGraw-Hill Book Company.

———. 1962. "Paranoia and the dynamics of exclusion." *Sociometry* 25 (March):2–20.

———. 1967. *Human Deviance, Social Problems and Social Control*. Englewood Cliffs, N. J.: Prentice-Hall.

Lorber, J. 1967. "Deviance as performance: The case of illness." *Social Problems* 14 (Winter):302–310.

Mackie, M. M. 1971. *The Accuracy of Folk Knowledge Concerning Alberta Indians, Hutterites and Ukrainians: An Available Data Stereotype Validation Technique.* Edmonton: The University of Alberta, Department of Sociology, Ph.D. dissertation.

———. 1973. "Arriving at 'truth' by definition: The case of stereotype inaccuracy." *Social Problems* 20 (Spring):431–447.

Mercer, J. R. 1965. "Social system perspective and clinical perspective: Frames of reference for understanding career patterns of persons labelled as mentally retarded." *Social Problems* 13 (Summer):18–34.

Mischel, W. 1969. "Continuity and change in personality." *American Psychologist* 24 (November):1012–1018.

Packer, H. L. 1968. *The Limits of the Criminal Sanction.* Stanford: Stanford University Press.

Plog, S. C., and R. B. Edgerton (Eds.) 1969. *Changing Perspectives in Mental Illness.* New York: Holt, Rinehart, and Winston, Inc.

Rice, S. A. 1928. *Quantitative Methods in Politics.* New York: Alfred A. Knopf, Inc.

Robins, L. N., and P. O'Neal. 1958. "Mortality, mobility, and crime." *American Sociological Review* 23 (April):162–171.

Roff, M. 1961. "Childhood social interaction and young adult bad conduct." *Journal of Abnormal and Social Psychology* 63 (September):333–337.

Schaefer, E. S., and N. Bayley. 1960. "Consistency of maternal behavior from infancy to preadolescence." *Journal of Abnormal and Social Psychology* 61 (July):1–6.

Scheff, T. J. 1966. *Being Mentally Ill.* Chicago: Aldine.

Schur, E. M. 1971. *Labeling Deviant Behavior: Its Sociological Implications.* New York: Harper and Row, Publishers.

Scott, R. A. 1969. *The Making of Blind Men.* New York: Russell Sage.

Solhaug, M. L. 1972. "Accuracy of 'bad men' stereotypes: A comparison of autostereotyping by lawbreakers with stereotyping by more lawful others." Edmonton: The University of Alberta, Department of Sociology. M. A. thesis prospectus.

Sudnow, D. 1966. *Passing On.* Englewood Cliffs, N. J.: Prentice-Hall.

Tannenbaum, F. 1938. *Crime and the Community.* Boston: Ginn and Company.

Terry, R. M. 1967. "Discrimination in the handling of juvenile offenders by social-control agencies." *Journal of Research in Crime and Delinquency* 4 (July):218–230.

Thomas, A., et al. 1970. "The origin of personality." *Scientific American* 223 (August):102–109.

Turner, R. H. 1969. "The public perception of protest." *American Sociological Review* 34 (December):815–831.

––––––. 1972. "Deviance avowal as neutralization of commitment." *Social Problems* 19 (Winter):308–321.

Ward, R. H. 1971. "The labeling theory: A critical analysis." *Criminology* 9 (August–November):268–290.

Witkin, H. 1965. "Psychological differentiation and forms of pathology." *Journal of Abnormal Psychology* 70 (October):317–336.

Zax, M., et al. 1968. "Follow-up study of children identified early as emotionally disturbed." *Journal of Consulting and Clinical Psychology* 32 (August):369–374.

Questions for Discussion

1. What is the difference between master and subordinate statuses, on the one hand, and master and auxiliary status traits on the other? How do these apply to "deviants"?
2. Describe Erikson's views of deviance and boundary maintenance. Along similar lines, it has been suggested that the more stress a collectivity puts on a particular value, the more likely it is to have deviants with respect to that value. Do you agree? Why or why not?
3. Are Erikson's remarks about community boundaries relevant to an understanding of political backlash? If yes, in what ways? If no, why not?
4. Do you agree with Nettler's evaluation of the labeling perspective? Why or why not? How applicable are Nettler's criticisms to Bustamante's article?

Selected References

Becker, Howard S. *Outsiders: Studies in the Sociology of Deviance.* New York: The Free Press of Glencoe, 1963.
A succinct statement of the labeling perspective, together with some empirical studies of jazz musicians, marijuana use, and social controls on marijuana.

Lemert, Edwin M. *Social Pathology: A Systematic Approach to the Theory of Sociopathic Behavior.* New York: McGraw-Hill, 1951.
An early, influential, and systematic theory that centers its attention on the social reactions to rule-breaking behavior. Clearly a book that was ahead of its time.

Roby, Pamela A. "Politics and Criminal Law: Revision of the New York State Penal Law on Prostitution." *Social Problems* 17 (Summer 1969), pp. 83–109.

An empirical study of the controversy surrounding the revision of New York's prostitution laws. Combining the value conflict and the labeling perspectives, Roby shows how definitions of prostitution change with shifts in the power of specific groups, the values they seek to protect, and the interests they seek to realize.

Rubington, Earl, and Martin S. Weinberg, eds. *Deviance: The Interactionist Perspective.* 2nd ed. New York: Macmillan, 1973.
Coined the term "interactionist perspective." The editors have amassed some fifty-five articles and organized them according to their relevance for the labeling perspective.

Scheff, Thomas J. *Being Mentally Ill: A Sociological Theory.* Chicago: Aldine, 1966.
A theoretical statement and an empirical test of labeling theory with regard to mental illness.

Schur, Edwin M. "Reactions to Deviance: A Critical Assessment." *American Journal of Sociology* 75 (November 1969), pp. 309–22.
Reviewing theories, applications, and critiques, Schur concludes that the labeling perspective, not yet a theory, has made a great contribution to the understanding of deviance and social control.

Spector, Malcolm, and John I. Kitsuse. "Social Problems: A Re-Formulation." *Social Problems* 21 (Fall 1973), pp. 145–59.
A most useful synthesis of the value conflict and the labeling perspectives, which contends that a social problem is a phenomenon in its own right, and that it has to be approached on its own terms. Spector and Kitsuse present a new model of the stages by which something comes to be defined as a social problem.

Weinberg, Martin S., and Colin J. Williams. *Male Homosexuals: Their Problems and Adaptations.* New York: Penguin Books, 1975.
Discusses the problems and adaptations of homosexual males. A total of 2,437 homosexual men in the United States, the Netherlands, and Denmark were studied from the interactionist perspective.

Williams, Colin J., and Martin S. Weinberg. *Homosexuals and the Military: A Study of Less than Honorable Discharge.* New York: Harper & Row, 1971.
Examines how homosexuals are discovered and labeled by the military, and the effects of receiving a less than honorable discharge.

III. the prospects

7. A Sociological Review
of the Perspectives

The purpose of this book has been to show the different ways in which American sociologists have viewed social problems from the early 1900s until the present. In this chapter, we would like to review briefly the central themes of the perspectives, their relative strengths and weaknesses, and how they represent different ways of resolving the dual mandate. (The "dual mandate," it will be recalled, refers to sociology's dual goals of solving social problems and of developing sociology as a discipline.)

The Five Perspectives: A Rapid Review

The study of social problems is entangled as much with changes in American society as with the development of American sociology. A rapid review of the perspectives illustrates the point. (See also Figure 1.)

1. *Social pathology.* In the early years of American sociology, an optimistic spirit gripped its founders. Committed to a broad social philosophy, they saw their task as the demonstration of how society could grow to fulfill a scheme of natural law and progress. These sociologists became social reformers, and as they focused on the social problems of the day, their work was infused with moral indignation. They formulated this indignation in terms of a medical model, regarding one set of social

Figure 1. *Prime Periods of the Five Perspectives*

	Period 2: Forming a	Period 3: Integrating	
Period 1: Establishing a Base (1905 to 1918)	Scientific Policy (1918 to 1935)	Theory, Research and Application (1935 to 1954)	Period 4: Cultivating Specialties (1954 on)
Social Pathology	Social Disorga- nization	Value Conflict	Deviant Behavior
			Labeling

problems as the work of persons who were "sick"—i.e., "defective, delinquent, or dependent." At the same time, these early sociologists were also morally indignant with those who occupied command posts in business, industry, and government, attributing many of their actions to vice, greed, corruption, and power.

Today, a revised version of the pathology perspective shows even more concern with institutional arrangements. The moral indignation remains, but now it is the society and its institutions, rather than nonconformity, that modern social pathologists regard as "sick." At the same time, they continue to advocate the moral education of the individuals involved as the solution to such problems.

2. Social disorganization. In the second phase of American sociology, reformism began to give way to a conception of the sociologist as a scientist building a new academic discipline. Sociologists in this period directed their efforts toward devising concepts, developing theories, and producing empirical research rather than moral, philosophical, or critical pronouncements. Thomas and Znaniecki, for example, argued that sociology must follow in the footsteps of other, more developed sciences, by staking out a special subject matter. In an effort to develop sociology along these lines, sociologists of this period focused on social rules rather than persons in their study of social problems. In so doing, they fashioned the social disorganization perspective, attributing a large variety of problems to a breakdown in tradition, a conflict between rules, or an absence or inadequacy of rules.

3. *Value conflict.* During the third period of American sociology, most sociologists continued to argue for the development of sociological theory. Nonetheless, a relatively small band of sociologists began to argue against pursuing the development of sociology as a value-free science. Instead, they advocated working for the benefit of society. As this critical band examined social problems, most of them came to feel that such problems are inevitable because people cannot agree on social policies. And usually the reason people disagree is not because they do not know the rules, but rather because they hold different values or pursue their own interests. Given the turmoil of the Great Depression and World War II, the value conflict perspective made sense. And whereas the social disorganization perspective encouraged sociologists to remain aloof from struggles within the society, the value conflict position encouraged them to integrate theory, research, and application, and to espouse values and take sides on social issues.

4. *Deviant behavior.* Early in the fourth period of American sociology, the deviant behavior perspective came into being. Building on the social disorganization perspective, it continued the orientation that sociology is, first and foremost, a science. It assumed the sociologist's job to be one of testing the implications of theory, rather than solving society's numerous problems. Although people have since drawn on the deviant behavior perspective in efforts to solve problems of crime and delinquency, sociologists in this tradition studied social problems primarily because they had relevance for sociological theory. In the process of specialization, however, these sociologists restricted their attention almost exclusively to the study of deviant behavior, defined as a violation of normative expectations. Thus, this influential perspective on social problems concentrated attention on the causes of deviance, on deviant behavior systems, and on social control.

5. *Labeling.* Late in the fourth period of American sociology the labeling perspective arose, in large part from questions left unanswered by the deviant behavior perspective. For example: How do people and situations come to be defined as problematic or deviant? With what effects? And how are some people able to avoid being so labeled even though they may have done something "deviant"? Thus, while the deviant be-

havior perspective defines social problems as objective violations of normative expectations, the labeling perspective sees
social problems as being whatever people say they are (i.e., as
subjectively constructed). Like the deviant behavior perspective, the labeling perspective is also specialized, focusing primarily on social definitions of and reactions to deviance, with
little interest in other facets and types of social problems.

Thus, each of the five perspectives has its own emphasis.
The social pathology perspective focuses on *persons;* the social
disorganization perspective stresses *rules;* the value conflict
perspective looks at *values and interests;* the deviant behavior
perspective emphasizes *roles;* and the labeling perspective examines *social reactions.*

In addition, each perspective implies its own causal chain by
which these elements (persons, rules, values, roles, and social
reactions) are linked. For example, the deviant behavior and
the labeling perspectives both deal with deviant roles and social reactions. In the deviant behavior perspective, however,
the deviant role is seen as *precipitating* the social reaction, while
in the labeling perspective it is seen as *following* the social reaction.

Applicability

Each perspective has been more powerful in dealing with
some types of problems than with others, and each seems
more likely to be employed in some cases than in others. In
this section, we briefly consider the relative strengths and
weaknesses of the five perspectives.

When notions about the person as an immoral or dehuman-
ized entity are strongly held, the pathology perspective finds
fertile ground. Instances of destructiveness to self or others
are examples.[1] Unless there are clearcut and unambiguous indicators of the "pathological" elements, however, such an analysis is likely to embody merely the analyst's personal prejudice.

The social disorganization approach works best when it is

---

[1] See, for example, Viola W. Bernard, Perry Ottenberg, and Fritz Redl,
"Dehumanization: A Composite Psychological Defense in Relation to Mod-
ern War," in Milton Schwebel, ed. *Behavioral Sciences and Human Survival*
(Palo Alto, Calif.: Science and Behavior Books, 1965), pp. 64–82.

restricted to studying the organization of specific social units, and the effects of rapid change on such units.[2] For example, it is a powerful idea for understanding the disorganizing effects of advancing technology on particular towns (e.g., "Hilltown"). The social disorganization approach has been faulted, however, for its failure to provide objective indicators of social disorganization and, in the absence of such indicators, for using abstract concepts to conceal implicit value judgments.

The value conflict approach has proven particularly useful where issues are sharply defined by polarization and conflict between groups. The history of Prohibition is a good example.[3] Where the conflicting values or interests of opposing groups cannot be clearly identified, however, this perspective is not as applicable.

Deviant behavior analysis has had and can be expected to have continued popularity in the study of deviance. Interestingly enough, the strengths of the labeling perspective are precisely the weaknesses of the deviant behavior approach, and vice versa. Where clearly defined and uniformly supported norms are involved, the deviant behavior perspective is relatively straightforward and useful. On the other hand, where agreement on norms is lacking, and where norms do not have strong social support, the labeling perspective makes a special contribution by focusing on the situational contingencies and consequences of labeling.[4] Thus, while the social processes surrounding such crimes as armed robbery and burglary are likely to be studied more from the perspective of deviant behavior, the social processes surrounding "crimes without victims," such as marijuana use and abortion, are more likely to be studied from the labeling perspective.

The type of social problem, however, is not the only factor that influences which perspective a sociologist will employ. In the next section, we speculate about some of the other factors involved in the selection of perspectives.

[2] See, for example, Robert K. Merton and Robert Nisbet, *Contemporary Social Problems: An Introduction to the Sociology of Deviant Behavior and Social Disorganization*, 3rd ed. (New York: Harcourt Brace Jovanovich), 1971.
[3] See Joseph R. Gusfield, *Symbolic Crusade: Status Politics and the American Temperance Movement* (Urbana, Ill.: University of Illinois Press, 1969).
[4] The affinity of labeling theorists for socially ambiguous subject matter is not theoretically necessary. This focus does, however, dramatize the perceptibility of the imputational process. See Prudence Rains, "Imputations of Deviance: A Retrospective Essay on the Labeling Perspective," Social Problems 23 (October 1975), pp. 1–11.

The Dual Mandate and Sociological Perspectives

As we see it, the major point of tension for sociologists studying social problems lies in the dual mandate—i.e., to solve social problems as well as to develop sociology as a discipline. In responding to this dual mandate, there are four predominant roles that sociologists adopt. Although sociologists may switch roles during the course of their careers or combine all four roles at once, one of the four roles is usually dominant in the work of any particular sociologist. And along with that dominant role goes a preference for one perspective on social problems rather than another.

The four roles are theorist, researcher, applier, and critic. Both theorists and researchers focus on developing sociology as a discipline. Theorists develop a network of interrelated propositions that they hope will ultimately explain a vast array of seemingly unrelated events. The social disorganization perspective, for example, contains the nucleus of a theory advanced to explain a broad assortment of social problems. And the labeling perspective has elaborated the theoretical framework of symbolic interactionism.[5]

Researchers, on the other hand, seek empirical data. They may derive a set of testable hypotheses from a given sociological theory in order to support or disprove it by means of empirical research. The growing body of studies based on the deviant behavior and labeling perspectives reflects the work of researchers.

For appliers and critics, sociology should work primarily on behalf of society. Appliers draw on the implications of a given sociological theory in order to propose solutions for specific social problems. The deviant behavior perspective has been particularly popular among appliers, and numerous rehabilitation programs have been fashioned along these lines—e.g., for juvenile delinquents or drug addicts.[6] The labeling per-

---

[5] See, for example, Earl Rubington and Martin S. Weinberg, eds., *Deviance: The Interactionist Perspective*, 2nd ed. (New York: Macmillan, 1973).

[6] Opportunity theory was applied in President Lyndon Johnson's War on Poverty and in the New York community action agency called Mobilization for Youth. For the source of these programs, see Richard A. Cloward and Lloyd E. Ohlin, *Delinquency and Opportunity: A Theory of Delinquent Gangs* (New York: The Free Press, 1960). For an application of sociological theory to the rehabilitation of juvenile delinquents, see Lamar T. Empey and Jerome Rabow, "The Provo Experiment in Delinquency Rehabilitation,"

spective has also proved to be useful in this regard. More and more people have become aware of the negative consequences of labeling various "crimes without victims," and with this increased awareness there has been a trend toward decriminalization.[7] Abortion has been legalized, some states have changed their laws regarding marijuana use, etc.[8]

Critics tend to protest against the status quo and to seek broader changes in the structure of society (the most extreme being revolution). Critics draw on one or more broad sociological theories, one of their major theoretical inspirations being Karl Marx.[9] Critics tend to draw on the value conflict perspective, the reviving social pathology perspective, or a combination of the two.[10]

In responding to the dual mandate, sociologists also adopt different stances in teaching social problems courses. In the late 1960s and early 1970s, for example, students clamored for greater "relevance" in their college courses, and they pressured sociologists to make social problems courses more substantive and less theoretical. Thus, many sociologists began in their teaching to give more attention to the concrete problems of society than they had in the past and to assume the role of applier or critic in their teaching. This demand has been short-lived, however, and today most sociologists have returned in their teaching to a study of the work of theorists and researchers and to the development of knowledge in the discipline.

Lastly, it is impossible to predict what the future holds. Nonetheless, the interaction between sociology and society promises to continue. As such, it will probably influence sociological perspectives on social problems for some time to come.

American Sociological Review 26 (October 1961), pp. 679–95. For an application to the rehabilitation of drug addicts, see Rita Volkman Johnson and Donald R. Cressey, "Differential Association and the Rehabilitation of Drug Addicts," *American Journal of Sociology* 69 (September 1963), pp. 129–12.

[7] See, for example, Rubington's study of responses to the repeal of the public drunkenness statute in Massachusetts: Earl Rubington, "Top and Bottom: How Police Administrators and Public Inebriates View Decriminalization," *Journal of Drug Issues* 5 (Fall 1975), pp. 412–25.

[8] For an example of this approach to juvenile delinquency, see Edwin M. Schur, *Radical Nonintervention: Rethinking the Delinquency Problem* (Englewood Cliffs, N.J.: Prentice-Hall, 1973).

[9] Perhaps the best example to date of a call for a "radical sociology" is Alvin W. Gouldner's *The Coming Crisis of Western Sociology* (New York: Basic Books, 1970).

[10] For example, "critical theory" (see p. 100n, above).

Questions for Discussion

1. Now that you are familiar with all five perspectives, which one(s) do you prefer for analyzing social problems? Why? Does the usefulness of each perspective depend on which particular social problem you are trying to analyze? If so, how? If not, why not?

2. Consider some social problem currently discussed in the mass media or among your acquaintances. Which of the five perspectives is reflected in the way the problem is conceptualized by each of the following: you, your parents, experts on the subject, newsmen, legislators, the people directly involved in the problem, churches, people of different ages, people of different classes? What might account for differences in the perspectives of these different groups?

3. To what extent do the five perspectives overlap? Can any of the perspectives be seen as to some degree subsuming any of the others? Why or why not?

4. Using some social problem that interests you, analyze the problem from each of the five perspectives. What are the major differences between your five analyses? Now provide an *eclectic* analysis, using elements from a number of the perspectives.

Selected References

Blumer, Herbert. "Social Problems as Collective Behavior." *Social Problems* 18 (Winter 1971), pp. 298–306.
A useful theoretical article that combines the value conflict and labeling perspectives and treats social problems as aspects of social movements.

Denzin, Norman K. "Who Leads: Sociology or Society?" *The American Sociologist* 5 (May 1970), pp. 125–27.
A concise argument that sociology should itself lead the society, rather than being led by it, in formulating problems for study.

Horton, Paul B., and Gerald R. Leslie. *The Sociology of Social Problems.* 5th ed. Englewood Cliffs, N.J.: Prentice-Hall, 1974.
A very successful college textbook on social problems. Horton and Leslie examine a series of problems from three perspectives: deviant behavior, value conflict, and social disorganization.

Lazarsfeld, Paul F., William H. Sewell, and Harold L. Wilensky, eds. *The Uses of Sociology.* New York: Basic Books, 1967.
A collection of essays on the general topic of applied sociology. Part Four contains seven papers on the application of sociology for the solution of social problems.

Levine, Donald N. "Sociology Confronts Student Protest." *School Review* 78 (August 1970), pp. 529–41.
A concise discussion of the different roles sociologists can play with regard to societal problems and student protests.

Lowry, Ritchie P. *Social Problems: A Critical Analysis of Theories and Public Policy.* Lexington, Mass.: D. C. Heath, 1974.
An important study tracing the development of three sociological perspectives on social problems—"deviance," "disorganization," and "functionalism." Lowry relates each perspective to certain popular myths about social problems and concludes that new perspectives will probably arise out of a synthesis of these three perspectives.

Lynd, Robert S. *Knowledge for What? The Place of Social Science in American Culture.* Princeton, N.J.: Princeton University Press, 1939.
Perhaps the best argument to date for using scientific knowledge to help society.

Mauss, Armand L. *Social Problems as Social Movements.* Philadelphia: J. B. Lippincott, 1975.
A textbook with a genuinely new approach to social problems. Blending the value conflict perspective with the labeling perspective, Mauss analyzes social problems as a special kind of social movement.

Merton, Robert K., and Robert Nisbet. *Contemporary Social Problems.* 3rd ed. New York: Harcourt Brace Jovanovich, 1971.
A highly influential textbook that examines social problems from both the deviant behavior and the social disorganization perspectives.

Rose, Arnold M. "Theory for the Study of Social Problems." *Social Problems* 4 (January 1957), pp. 189–99.
A stimulating attempt to reconcile conflict and disorganization theories as a means of both studying and solving social problems.

Rubington, Earl, and Martin S. Weinberg, eds. *The Solution of Social Problems: Five Perspectives.* New York: Oxford University Press, 1973.
A text-reader on the application of the five sociological perspectives to the solution of social problems.

DATE DUE